EDITED BY **HENRY EHLERS**

Associate Professor of Philosophy, Duluth Branch
University of Minnesota

CRUCIAL ISSUES
IN EDUCATION

AN ANTHOLOGY

HENRY HOLT AND COMPANY · NEW YORK

370.82
E33C

22222—0115

PREFACE

"Experimentation there may be in many things of deep concern, but not in setting boundaries to thought; for thought freely communicated is the indispensable condition of intelligent experimentation, the one test of its validity." [1] These words of the late Justice Cardozo represent the basic assumption of this anthology.

But this general assumption is no philosopher's stone for the solution of specific issues. Consider three examples: Does "intelligent experimentation" mean that *all* truths should be subject to test by scientific method—or does it assume that there are certain realms of truth to which experimentation does not apply? Are moral standards to be derived from social relationships—or are such standards to be based on an absolute creed? Is liberty basically a matter of protecting the individual against government regulation—or should government regulation be greatly extended in order that the individual may enjoy *real* liberty? Granted the general thesis that thought shall be free, different thinkers will come to widely different interpretations of most specific problems.

This book deals with several such problems: Loyalty, Censorship, Religious Education, Racial Segregation, and Progressive Education. These may be studied in any order.

Each problem is highly controversial, and it is the editor's hope that opposing viewpoints are fairly represented. If some selections seem dogmatic and intolerant, let the reader recognize the limitations of language and of human nature. Actually, all statements should be considered as hypotheses, i.e., as suggestions or proposals to be examined. Were it not for the clumsy style involved, would it not be well if all our assertions could be made in the form of questions? Should not the reader be encouraged to subject every paragraph, every sentence, to critical examination? Should he not constantly inquire: "Is this true? Is this sound? Is this adequate? Is this practical?" Even if the reader holds a non-democratic out-

[1] Benjamin Cardozo, *Paradoxes of Legal Science,* New York: Columbia University Press, 1928, p. 105.

look (according to the criteria set forth in some selections), is not this one of his "rights" in a liberal society? If democracy means shared thinking, is not the person who *fails* to think, rather than the one who *differs* from the majority, the least democratic in his basic attitude?

Study of the pros and cons of these issues—mostly from writings of the past ten years—should help develop the type of citizens on which a democratic society depends. For "It is one thing to educate people to the end that control *of* them may be developed; it is quite another thing to educate to the end that control *by* the people may be increased and perfected." [2] True education should open many channels of inquiry; it should consider many types of belief. Lest education be reduced to propaganda, teachers must not only be informed about the many partisan groups and interests around them, but must also be courteous and considerate toward various conflicting viewpoints. Parents have entrusted their most precious possession to the school, and it behooves every teacher to be alert lest, perhaps unconsciously, he serve as a partisan for one particular viewpoint.

This anthology does not provide clear-cut answers to any of the problems raised. Rather, each chapter presents claims and counterclaims, assertions and denials, proofs and disproofs, conflicting values and rival hypotheses. Such an approach may tend to unsettle the young mind—sometimes to the point of confusion and bewilderment—but it also unsettles the habit of dismissing great issues in terms of verbal generalities or catchword stereotypes. And we should always remember that the human mind is like a parachute—useless until open.

This anthology would not be possible were it not for the generous permissions to reprint selections of many authors and publishers. Acknowledgments of these are made in the accompanying footnotes. Many colleagues, librarians, students and friends have contributed to one of its several revisions. Of these, I am particularly indebted to Professors R. Freeman Butts and Robert Beck (Education), Albert Tezla and William Rosenthal (English), Wilfrid Sellars and Melvin Rader (Philosophy), Gerhard von Glahn, Ben Lippincott and Mulford Q. Sibley (Political Science), Robert C. McClure (Law); and to my wife (Domestic Relations!).

H. E.

Duluth, Minnesota
January 1955

---

[2] A. V. Sayers, *A First Course in the Philosophy of Education*, New York: Henry Holt, 1952, p. 3-4. A similar viewpoint is found in the popular booklet, *Man's Right to Knowledge and the Free Use Thereof*, by Mark Van Doren and others, New York: Columbia University Press, 1954.

CONTENTS

C. FREEDOM OF ASSEMBLY AND THE RIGHT TO PUBLIC EMPLOYMENT

D. QUESTIONS AND READINGS FOR STUDY AND DISCUSSION

II. FREEDOM FOR LEARNERS

A. THE CASE FOR CENSORSHIP

B. THE CASE AGAINST CENSORSHIP

C. SOME SPECIFIC EXAMPLES

D. QUESTIONS AND READINGS FOR STUDY AND DISCUSSION

III. RELIGION AND PUBLIC EDUCATION

A. RELIGION IN A PLURALISTIC SOCIETY

IV. RACIAL SEGREGATION IN EDUCATION

A. THE SOCIOLOGICAL BACKGROUNDS

B. THE PRESENT SITUATION

C. QUESTIONS AND READINGS FOR STUDY AND DISCUSSION

V. CLASSROOM METHODS AND MATERIALS

A. CONTEMPORARY EDUCATION UNDER CRITICISM

1. FREEDOM FOR TEACHERS

Section A: Dangers of Irresponsibility

1.1. INTRODUCTION: THE NEED FOR INTELLECTUAL INTEGRITY

Thirty years ago, democratic liberals could point with pride to a hundred years of solid achievement, and to a resounding victory over Kaiser Bill. Democracy had steadily advanced over large areas of the world, monarchy and authoritarianism were on the decline. Scientific discoveries and technological developments astonished each new generation. The spread of education and a rising standard of living were bringing these benefits to ever-increasing numbers. The continued success of democracy seemed assured.

Then, within a single generation, came three major catastrophes: a world-wide depression, World War II, and the rise of Russian totalitarianism. In large areas of the world fanaticism replaced moderation; extremism replaced compromise; and hate, tolerance. Religion often assumed its most vicious form—an ideological "front" for power politics. Education was turned into propaganda, free inquiry into fawning servility. And the scientific vehicles of humanitarian progress were retooled into weapons destructive of civilization, until even the words "progress" and "science" became for many people symbols of fear and despair rather than ideals of confidence and hope.

The tragedy of a depression, the horrors of a world war, and the ruthlessness of a totalitarian purge are obvious. What is not so

1

obvious is why "liberalism," "democracy" and "science" are so frequently blamed for these tragedies. In the following selections we shall find at least a partial answer. "Science" once meant a body of organized knowledge based on open communication between thinkers of all races and nations. Today "scientific materialism" implies the iron curtain; and well-meaning thinkers (untrained in scientific method) have sometimes been duped into accepting Marxism as "scientific sociology." "Liberalism" and "democracy" once symbolized the freedom of the common man to discuss problems in a frank and open manner; but today the Russian "dictatorship of the proletariat" is called the "people's democracy." [1] Even in America many organizations—conservative as well as liberal—have been taken over by masters of double talk and the calculated lie, whose basic thinking is in complete opposition to the traditions of science, liberalism and democracy. [2]

From the educator's viewpoint, one disturbing feature about Fascism was the fact that the governments of Hitler and Tojo boasted extremely high rates of literacy; [3] and an incredible feature about Communism has been its persistent attraction for many so-called "intellectuals." [4] We recall that in the declining period of the middle ages some scholastics believed that God could do nothing contrary to the logic of Aristotle. So today many Communists be-

---

[1] Read J. C. Talmon, *The Rise of Totalitarian Democracy*, Beacon Press, 1952; also "Fastest-Spreading Revolution: Communism: 80,000 in 1917—A Fourth of the World Now," *U. S. News and World Report* 35: 35-37, Nov. 13, 1953.

[2] Such extremism occurs at both ends of the political spectrum. Read J. Edgar Hoover, FBI Director, "The Disloyalty of Communists and Fellow Travellers," testimony before the Committee on Un-American Activities, House of Representatives, 80th Congress, 1st Session, on H.R. 1884 and H.R. 2122, March 26, 1947; Summary from the *Providence Journal*, "McCarthy, Hunt, and *Facts Forum*," *Reporter* 10: 19-26, Feb. 16, 1954.

[3] Read Howard R. Huse, *The Illiteracy of the Literate*, New York: Appleton-Century, 1933.

[4] John Dewey has shown why so-called "intellectuals," untrained in the methods of science, sometimes mistake Marxian pseudo-science for "science." Read Dewey's *Freedom and Culture*, New York: Putnams, 1939, pp. 83-96; also James B. Conant, *Science and Common Sense*, New Haven, Conn.: Yale University Press, 1951.

For an example of the type of "science" (i.e., "scientific sociology") which these authors criticize, read Alexander Miller, *The Christian Significance of Karl Marx*, New York: Macmillan, 1947, pp. 9-51.

lieve that Nature can do nothing contrary to the dialectic of Marx. Believing that this dialectic is not a personal or cultural belief, but is Nature's Grand Strategy, Communists indulge in extreme measures to hasten the "inevitable" revolution from capitalism to communism. Such fanaticism is patently opposed to the open-mindedness and tolerance of science and democracy.

Man is not fully free unless he can explore the unknown, unless he has full scope to exercise the limitless possibilities of his mind. The man on the street may say "I think" when he means "I feel" (i.e., "I am attached to these prejudices"). But for a scholar, "I think" is intellectually meaningless unless that thinking has included an impartial study of competing points of view. No pattern of ideas is so sacred that the thinker's mind should be closed to other alternatives. "You have been told to prove you are right," said Louis Pasteur, "but I say, try to prove you are *wrong*." The scientist, like the inventor, believes that if we all worked on the assumption that what is accepted as true is really true, there would be little hope for advance. Hence the heritage of knowledge is always slightly tentative and subject to reconstruction in the light of new discovery. But through the cooperative endeavors of many investigators, "the great community" [5] gradually accumulates a body of knowledge which progressively acquires "the virtues characteristic of science: clarity and consistency, testability and adequacy, precision and objectivity." [6] In the words of Nobel prize-winner P. W. Bridgman:

> . . . the most vital feature of the scientist's procedure has been merely to do his utmost with his mind, *no holds barred*. This means in particular that no special privileges are accorded to authority or to tradition, that personal prejudices and predilections are carefully guarded against, that one makes continued check to assure oneself that one is not making mistakes, and that

[5] For an elaboration of the significance of "the great community," read Max Fisch, ed., *Classic American Philosophers*, New York: Appleton-Century-Crofts, 1951, pp. 32-39. Compare Sir Walter Moberly, *The Crisis in the University*, London: Student Christian Movement Press, 1949, p. 125 f; Paul Tillich, *The Protestant Era*, Chicago: University of Chicago Press, 1948, p. 292 f.

[6] Wilfrid Sellars and Herbert Feigl, eds., *Readings in Philosophical Analysis*, New York: Crofts, 1949, "Introduction," p. 5.

any line of inquiry will be followed that appears at all promising.[7]

Unfortunately, fascist and communist ideologies involve severe restriction of the invaluable freedom to think, and expect adherents to toe the line of conformity laid down by some prior authority no matter how irrational or intolerant it becomes. But any theory or belief that ceases to be subject to criticism, examination and reconstruction has no place in a community of free scientists and scholars. Such theory is anti-intellectual, even anti-intelligent, for by edict it holds some components of intellectual activity forever closed to scrutiny.

The selections which follow would disqualify Communists as teachers because Communist dogma denies the application of intelligence in many areas of life. In judging the rights of Communists in our society, say the writers of the following articles, it is important to ask the right questions. Do Communists have legal *rights* in a free society? Of course they do.[8] But do these legal rights give them the *privilege* of holding positions of influence in our schools? They do not. For by joining the Communist Party they have relinquished their intellectual integrity. Persons whose basic assumptions are determined for them by the organization to which they belong are no longer free to think for themselves. And this freedom is basic for all who prepare American youth for the arduous duties of citizenship in a free society.

1.2. AMERICAN vs. EUROPEAN POLICIES REGARDING COMMUNISM AND EDUCATION [9]

William F. Russell

When we try to make a generalization as to how Americans or Europeans look upon Communism it is impossible to draw upon

---

[7] P. W. Bridgman, *Reflections of a Physicist,* New York: Philosophical Library, 1950, p. 370.

[8] The legal rights of members of the American Communist Party were curtailed in 1954. Read: "Outlawing the Communist Party," *New Republic* 131: 7-8, Aug. 30, 1954; "No Place for Communists to Hide?" *U.S. News* 37: 42-43, Sept. 3, 1954.

scientific studies. There are no polls, censuses, or objective researches to consult. Nevertheless it is proposed here to give one person's idea of how he thinks many Europeans and Americans look upon Communism and its educational implications, and why they take this point of view. Obviously it is not intended to include the point of view of everyone (naturally in Europe and America there are persons of all shades of opinion), but rather to come to an estimate of the preponderance of American in contrast with European beliefs. He who makes such judgments cannot protect his readers or listeners from his prejudices or errors. However, he speaks from a fairly wide acquaintance.

With all the limitations just stated in mind, the European view of Communism can be described in the following three assumptions:

1. That Communism is merely a political movement.

2. That Communism does not threaten the liberty of the free peoples, and its inroads are greatly exaggerated and based upon untrustworthy evidence.

3. That Communism has little appeal for the mass of the people.

Assumption 1: That Communism is merely politics

In Britain and in most of the countries of Free Europe, there is an officially recognized Communist party which announces party policies, nominates candidates for office, takes part in elections, and in some cases shares in a coalition government. Teachers may join the Communist party (and do in some countries in substantial numbers), and not infrequently they have considerable power in teachers' organizations. The Communist party is treated just like any other political party.

The principle "No Politics in the School" is so generally accepted and so widely followed in Europe that it may be taken as universal. Schools should present the facts, produce the results of accepted

---

[9] From William F. Russell, "American *vs.* European Policies Regarding Communism and Education," *Teachers College Record* 54: 175-183, January 1953. By permission. At the time this article was written, Mr. Russell was president of Teachers College, Columbia University.

Compare: "How Britain Handles Communists"; interview, D. M. Fyfe, *U.S. News* 37: 86-90, Oct. 15, 1954.

scholarship and research, consider and discuss various theories, philosophies, and practices objectively; but when it comes to "politics" they must take no sides. . . .

Under this principle, European schools exclude attacks against Communism in the schools, permit Communists to teach, admit them to their associations, and treat them as if they were members of any other political party. Any other course would seem to them to be dangerous in the extreme.

Assumption 2:   That Communism is not a threat

Many teachers and other intellectuals, both in Britain and on the Continent, do not accept the idea that the USSR is aggressive; that there is any danger of its attacking Europe; that it will be so foolish as to bring on a third World War. They explain the present apparent attitude of Russia by the fact that the capitalist countries have never been friendly, in fact invaded Russia after World War I, and have remained hostile ever since. All the free people need to do is to hold out a friendly hand.

Furthermore, many believe that the Communists in the free countries are not real Communists at all, "not like Russian Communists." I have heard such statements repeatedly. In one town in the Pyrenees I asked a friend why a certain man was a Communist. The answer was: "Oh! He isn't a real Communist at all. He is only going along with his old comrades who fought together in the *maquis* during the war." Of another man he said, "He is not a real Communist at all. He just votes that way because he doesn't like the local priest." Many of us remember the frequent occasions on which we were told that the Chinese Communists were not real Communists at all, merely "agrarians."

The Europeans do not seem to know very much about the revelations of Douglas Hyde, Whittaker Chambers, or Elizabeth Bentley; and those who know about them refuse to believe them. What European comment I have heard on the Hiss case or the trial of the eleven Communist leaders makes me think that they consider them miscarriages of justice and intimidation of the courts by mass hysteria. When you bring up the case of Fuchs, they shrug their shoulders. What did these traitors give away that intelligent people would not have found out anyway?

Assumption 3:   That Communism has no appeal to the mass of the people

Whatever threat Communism may hold, European teachers seem to minimize it because they believe that it has no appeal to "people like you and me." The Communists are few in number, and those who join the Party are the "seedy," the "envious," the "haters," those who would be against everything anyway, even if Marx, Lenin, and Stalin had never existed.

It is hard for them to think that Douglas Hyde ever was a "real Communist"; and certainly in their opinion Chambers, Bentley, and Massing were either liars, immoral, or insane. These teachers cannot bring themselves to believe that a nice man like Hiss ever could have been a Communist.

Thus, if Communism appeals to only a few, it cannot be considered as an important threat from within.

To summarize, many British and Continental teachers and intellectuals view Communism as a social theory that need not cause alarm. It is a matter of politics; its threat has been greatly exaggerated; and since it has only limited appeal, it will not gain many adherents. The schools should remain neutral. Communists should be permitted to teach. Restrictive measures would have dangerous consequences. . . .

In America

In contrast with Europe, Americans are coming to take quite contrary views with regard to the three assumptions regarding Communism discussed above. Communism is not a political party, we think, but rather a philosophy, a religion, a way of life not only different but actively hostile. We believe that Communism in the USSR is a threat to free institutions. Among the ranks of Communists we find not only the seedy, the envious, and the haters but also "people like you and me"—people more idealistic and more willing to sacrifice.

1. The American regards American Capitalism *vs.* USSR Communism as a struggle between Good and Evil, and the tactics employed by the Communists are not those of a political party so much as those of conspiracy and the seizure of power.

Many Americans have read Marx, Lenin, and Stalin. The tactics of the *coup d'état,* revolutions, seizure of power are plainly stated. USSR actions indicate no deviation whatever from basic doctrines announced thirty-five years ago. Even our information about the Soviet educational system plainly reveals the aggressive nature of Soviet policy. Not only did Chambers, Bentley, and Massing plainly testify that these are the Soviet tactics, but their testimony was specifically corroborated by Philbrick and other witnesses under oath before our courts. Either there is a powerful, dangerous conspiracy within our ranks or there is the unthinkable alternative that great numbers of people have banded together for fame or fortune to make a gang of liars, bluffers, or practical jokers. The American has come to know that the Communist party is only camouflage for a movement which repeatedly and publicly has stated that it contemplates seizure of power by direct action in some future time of crisis.

2. Americans believe that Soviet Communism has penetrated deeply into American life and that reports of informers have not exaggerated this menace.

American teachers and intellectuals seem to know a great deal more about the various trials (Hiss, the eleven Communist leaders, etc.) and the reports of the informers than do the British or Continentals.

Americans (and here I remind you again of the qualifications with which I introduced this discussion: not *all* Americans, but the general trend of American opinion) are inclined to accept as generally true the reports of the informers. We read the testimony of a series of witnesses who had worked underground for the FBI at great personal sacrifice, indeed at their peril; and those who studied the Communist movement from the inside certainly support the revelations of Bentley, Chambers, and Massing. Chambers, they think, is telling the truth. . . .

3. Americans have learned that not all Communists are "queer," and that Communism may have appeal for even the most able and idealistic of our young people.

The revelations of the informers have given the Americans a new idea of what a Communist is like. For over a third of a century—

ever since I first came to know Communists and Communism in Siberia in 1918—I have stated now and then in public addresses that the fight against Communism would be easier if we could recognize our enemy. If only every Communist wore a tall fur cap, a black beard, a smock, a sheepskin coat, carried a gun in each hand, hand grenades in his belt, and a knife in his teeth, then you would know whom you had to fight. But the Communists I met in Siberia were mostly quiet people, scholarly, with strong sympathy for the underdog and a resolve to do something about him. . . .

Chambers and Bentley joined the Communist movement precisely because its purpose was one to which each believed he could wholly subscribe, and because its program seemed practical and called for their full participation—even more, for their complete dedication. They seemed to go into it for the same reasons that one would enter the ministry or teaching or the missionary field.

The Chambers and Bentley stories should be interesting to professors and administrators hereabouts and should cause them furiously to think; for after all they were our students or pupils not so long ago.

Judging upon the basis of sheer native ability alone, it is obvious that Chambers and Bentley were students of great promise. Chambers, without influence, rose to the top of the editorial ladder. Bentley later revealed great administrative ability in her operation of an intricate Communist apparatus. Yet despite their ability, both made great mistakes when they were students; and it is a great tragedy that their educational experience did not help them at that time to foresee their errors and that they were not attracted to a life of devotion to American ideals. Obviously, so far as these two were concerned, Communism offered a more attractive and practical program for social betterment.

Our schools and colleges and universities will be recreant to their duty, will fail to play the part in the defense of freedom that the American people demand, if young people of great ability continue to be so easily seduced; if we fail to attract them and command their consecration to the defense and furtherance of our ideals. That is why I think our Citizenship Education Project and similar projects are so important and deserve our fullest support.

Conclusions

The analysis we have just made, in general, supports the American side of this controversy.

The Communist threat is too dangerous to be ignored. We at Teachers College well remember two occasions just after World War II when we consulted with Jan Masaryk and heard a lecture by the then Ambassador from Czechoslovakia to Washington. Each expressed no fear of Communism, stated that his country could live happily between the two great powers and could well interpret the one to the other. Czech liberty, they thought, was in no danger of extinction. Yet it was only a short time until the crushed body of Jan Masaryk lay beneath his window and the Ambassador languished in exile, far from the country which had been betrayed by enemies within.

Europeans run grave risks when they underestimate the Communist threat. They run even greater risks when they permit their schools to remain neutral regarding a question of life and death.

The above analysis also supports the American decision that schools must take definite action with regard to Communism. Schools cannot remain neutral when it comes to the question of liberty *vs.* tyranny, any more than they can refuse to take sides on questions of right and wrong. The American school administrator, the college president will fail in his duty if he ignores education for citizenship and refuses to give it every encouragement and support. No future student should be condemned to attend a school or a college which makes no conscious effort to capture the enthusiasm and idealism of the young and offers no program capable of enlisting his willingness to serve. This analysis puts education for American citizenship at the top of the list in our program of studies.

When American schools and colleges have strong programs of citizenship education; when the teachers have developed high skill in presenting such instruction and in guiding such activities; when materials of instruction have been well prepared and made widely available; when pupils take advantage of such opportunities; then the negative side of anti-Communist activities may assume lesser importance. There will obviously be far less need for teachers' oaths, Communist banning, and textbook inquiries when pupils and teachers are engaged in powerful programs of Americanism. The more positive the teaching, the less need for restrictive measures.

We Americans know that we are .... in a cold war that may continue for a long time. In modern war we cannot leave the fighting to hired mercenaries or to professional warriors. In total war, every person, every institution must do its part. Education cannot remain aloof.

Oliver Cromwell once gave a definition of his ideal soldier. He said, "I had rather have a plain russet-coated Captain that knows what he fights for and loves what he knows, than that which you call a gentleman and nothing else." That is what the free people of the world need in this modern, total war in which we are all engaged: *Citizens who know what they fight for and love what they know*. What they fight for they learn in school. What they love they gain in school. Clad in such shining armor, neither they nor we need fear any foe.

1.3.   THE PRESENT DANGER: A REPORT FROM THE UNIVERSITY PRESIDENTS [10]

Association of American Universities, A. Whitney Griswold, Committee Chairman

The Nature of a University

A university is the institutional embodiment of an urge for knowledge that is basic in human nature and as old as the human race.

[10] "The Rights and Responsibilities of Universities and their Faculties," a report prepared by a committee of five university heads: A. Whitney Griswold (Yale), chairman, Arthur H. Compton (Washington University), Franklin D. Murphy (University of Kansas), John E. W. Sterling (Stanford) and Harry W. Wriston (Brown). This report was unanimously approved by the thirty-seven college heads who comprise the Association of American Universities. Harold W. Dodds, president of Princeton University, was head of the A.A.U. at the time this statement was issued, and has allowed the report to be reprinted here. The present version appeared in the *Atlantic* 191: 44-46, June 1953.

See also: Association of Land-Grant Colleges and Universities, Russell I. Thackrey, Exec. Sec. Bulletin J56, "The Land-Grant Colleges and Universities and the Principles of Freedom," Washington, D. C., November 1953.

It is inherent in every individual. The search that it inspires is an individual affair. Men vary in the intensity of their passion for the search for knowledge as well as in their competence to pursue it. History therefore presents us with a series of scholarly pioneers who advanced our knowledge from age to age and increased our ability to discover new knowledge. Great scholars and teachers drew students to them, and in the Middle Ages a few such groups organized themselves into the first universities.

Like its medieval prototype, the modern American university is an association of individual scholars. Their effectiveness, both as scholars and as teachers, requires the capitalizing of their individual passion for knowledge and their individual competence to pursue it and communicate it to others. They are united in loyalty to the ideal of learning, to the moral code, to the country, and to its form of government. They represent diversified fields of knowledge, they express many points of view. Even within the same department of instruction there are not only specialists in various phases of the subject, but men with widely differing interests and outlook.

Free enterprise is as essential to intellectual as to economic progress. A university must therefore be hospitable to an infinite variety of skills and viewpoints, relying upon open competition among them as the surest safeguard of truth. Its whole spirit requires investigation, criticism, and presentation of ideas in an atmosphere of freedom and mutual confidence. This is the real meaning of "academic" freedom. It is essential to the achievement of its ends that the faculty of a university be guaranteed this freedom by its governing board, and that the reasons for the guarantee be understood by the public. To enjoin uniformity of outlook upon a university faculty would put a stop to learning at the source. To censor individual faculty members would put a stop to learning at its outlet.

For these reasons a university does not take an official position of its own either on disputed questions of scholarship or on political questions or on matters of public policy. It refrains from so doing not only in its own but in the public interest, to capitalize the search for knowledge for the benefit of society, to give the individuals pursuing that search the freest possible scope and the greatest possible encouragement in their efforts to preserve the learning of the past and advance learning in the present. The scholar who pursues the search on these terms does so at maximum advantage to society. So does the student. To the scholar lie open new discoveries in the whole field of knowledge, to the student the opportunity of sharing in those discoveries and at the same time developing his powers of rational thought, intelligent judgment, and an understanding use of acquired knowledge. Thus essential qualities of learning are combined with essential qualities of citizenship in a free society.

To fulfill their function the members of university faculties must continue to analyze, test, criticize, and reassess existing institutions and beliefs, approving when the evidence supports them and disapproving when the weight of evidence is on the other side. Such investigations cannot be confined to the physical world. The acknowledged fact that moral, social, and political progress have not kept pace with mastery of the physical world shows the need for more intensified research, fresh insights, vigorous criticism, and inventiveness. The scholar's mission requires the study and examination of unpopular ideas, of ideas considered abhorrent and even dangerous. For, just as in the case of deadly disease or the military potential of an enemy, it is only by intense study and research that the nature and extent of the danger can be understood and defenses against it perfected.

Timidity must not lead the scholar to stand silent when he ought to speak, particularly in the field of his competence. In matters of conscience and when he has truth to proclaim, the scholar has no obligation to be silent in the face of popular disapproval. Some of the great passages in the history of truth have involved the open challenge of popular prejudice in times of tension such as those in which we live.

What applies to research applies equally to teaching. So long as an instructor's observations are scholarly and germane to his subject, his freedom of expression in his classroom should not be curbed. The university student should be exposed to competing opinions and beliefs in every field, so that he may learn to weigh them and gain maturity of judgment. Honest and skillful exposition of such opinions and beliefs is the duty of every instructor, and it is equally his privilege to express his own critical opinion and the reasons for holding it. In teaching, as in research, he is limited by the requirements of citizenship, of professional competence and good taste. Having met those standards, he is entitled to all the protection the full resources of the university can provide.

Whatever criticism is occasioned by these practices, the universities are committed to them by their very nature. To curb them, in the hope of avoiding criticism, would mean distorting the true process of learning and depriving society of its benefits. It would invite the fate of the German and Italian universities under Fascism and the Russian universities under Communism. It would deny our society one of its most fruitful sources of strength and welfare and represent a sinister change in our ideal of government.

The Obligations and Responsibilities of University Faculties

We must recognize the fact that honest men hold differing opinions. This fundamental truth underlies the assertion and definition of individual rights and freedom in our Bill of Rights. How does it apply to universities? In the eyes of the law, the university scholar has no more and no less freedom than his fellow citizens outside a university. Nonetheless, because of the vital importance of the university to civilization, membership in its society of scholars enhances the prestige of persons admitted to its fellowship after probation and upon the basis of achievement in research and teaching. The university supplies a distinctive forum and, in so doing, strengthens the scholar's voice. When his opinions challenge existing orthodox points of view, his freedom may be more in need of defense than that of men in other professions. The guarantee of tenure to professors of mature and proven scholarship is one such defense. As in the case of judges, tenure protects the scholar against undue economic or political pressures and ensures the continuity of the scholarly process.

There is a line at which "freedom" or "privilege" begins to be qualified by legal "duty" and "obligation." The determination of the line is the function of the legislature and the courts. The ultimate interpretation and application of the First and Fourteenth Amendments are the function of the United States Supreme Court; but every public official is bound by his oath of office to respect and preserve the liberties guaranteed therein. These are not to be determined arbitrarily or by public outcry. The line thus drawn can be changed by legislative and judicial action; it has varied in the past because of prevailing anxieties as well as by reason of "clear and present" danger. Its location is subject to, and should receive, criticism both popular and judicial. However much the location of the line may be criticized, it cannot be disregarded with impunity. Any member of a university who crosses the duly established line is not excused by the fact that he believes the line ill-drawn. When the speech, writing, or other actions of a member of a faculty exceed lawful limits, he is subject to the same penalties as other persons. In addition, he may lose his university status.

Historically the word "university" is a guarantee of standards. It implies endorsement not of its members' views but of their capability and integrity. Every scholar has an obligation to maintain this reputation. By ill-advised, though not illegal, public acts or utterances he may do serious harm to his profession, his university, to education, and to the general welfare. He bears a heavy responsibility to weigh the soundness of his opinions and the manner in which they are expressed. His effectiveness, both as scholar and teacher, is not reduced but enhanced if he has the humility and the wisdom to recognize the fallibility of his own judgment. He should remember that he is as much a layman as anyone else in all fields except those in which he has special competence. Others, both within and without the university, are as free to criticize his opinions as he is free to express them; "academic freedom" does not include freedom from criticism.

As in all acts of association, the professor accepts conventions which become morally binding. Above all, he owes his colleagues in the university complete candor and perfect integrity, precluding any kind of clandestine or conspiratorial activities. He owes equal candor to the public. If he is called upon to answer for his convictions it is his duty as a citizen to speak out. It is even more definitely his duty as a professor. Refusal to do so, on whatever legal grounds, cannot fail to reflect upon a profession that claims for itself the fullest freedom to speak and the maximum protection of that freedom available in our society. In this respect, invocation of the Fifth Amendment places upon a professor a heavy burden of proof of his fitness to hold a teaching position and lays upon his university an obligation to re-examine his qualifications for membership in its society.

In all universities, faculties exercise wide authority in internal affairs. The greater their autonomy, the greater their share of responsibility to the public. They must maintain the highest standards and exercise the utmost wisdom in appointments and promotions. They must accept their share of responsibility for the discipline of those who fall short in the discharge of their academic trust.

The universities owe their existence to legislative acts and public charters. A state university exists by constitutional and legislative acts, an endowed university enjoys its independence by franchise from the state and by custom. The state university is supported by public funds. The endowed university is benefited by tax exemptions. Such benefits are conferred upon the universities not as favors but in furtherance of the public interest. They carry with them public obligation of direct concern to the faculties of the universities as well as to the governing boards.

Legislative bodies from time to time may scrutinize these benefits and privileges. It is clearly the duty of universities and their members to cooperate in official inquiries directed to those ends. When the powers of legislative inquiry are abused, the remedy does not lie in noncooperation or defiance; it is to be sought through the normal channels of informed public opinion.

The Present Danger

We have set forth the nature and function of the university. We have outlined its rights and responsibilities and those of its faculties. What are the implications for current anxiety over Russian Communism and the subversive activities connected with it?

We condemn Russian Communism as we condemn every form of totalitarianism. We share the profound concern of the American people at the existence of an international conspiracy whose goal is the destruction of our cherished institutions. The police state would be the death of our universities, as of our government. Three of its principles in particular are abhorrent to us; the fomenting of world-wide revolution as a step to seizing power; the use of false-hood and deceit as normal means of persuasion; thought control—the dictation of doctrines which must be accepted and taught by all party members. Under these principles, no scholar could adequately disseminate knowledge or pursue investigations in the effort to make further progress toward truth.

Appointment to a university position and retention after appointment require not only professional competence but involve the affirmative obligation of being diligent and loyal in citizenship. Above all, a scholar must have integrity and independence. This renders impossible adherence to such a regime as that of Russia and its satellites. No person who accepts or advocates such principles and methods has any place in a university. Since present membership in the Communist Party requires the acceptance of these principles and methods, such membership extinguishes the right to a university position. Moreover, if an instructor follows communistic practice by becoming a propagandist for one opinion, adopting a "party line," silencing criticism or impairing freedom of thought and expression in his classroom, he forfeits not only all university support but his right to membership in the university.

"Academic freedom" is not a shield for those who break the law. Universities must cooperate fully with law-enforcement officers whose duty requires them to prosecute those charged with offenses. Under a well-established American principle their innocence is to be assumed until they have been convicted, under due process, in a court of proper jurisdiction.

Unless a faculty member violates a law, however, his discipline or discharge is a university responsibility and should not be assumed by political authority. Discipline on the basis of irresponsible accusations or suspicion can never be condoned. It is as damaging to the public welfare as it is to academic integrity. The university is competent to establish a tribunal to determine the facts and fairly judge the nature and degree of any trespass upon academic integrity, as well as to determine the penalty such trespass merits.

As the professor is entitled to no special privileges in law, so also he should be subject to no special discrimination. Universities are bound to deprecate special loyalty tests which are applied to their faculties but to which others are not subjected. Such discrimination does harm to the individual and even greater harm to his university and the whole cause of education by destroying faith in the ideals of university scholarship.

Conclusion

Finally, we assert that freedom of thought and speech is vital to the maintenance of the American system and is essential to the general welfare. Condemnation of Communism and its protagonists is not to be interpreted as readiness to curb social, political, or economic investigation and research. To insist upon complete conformity to current beliefs and practices would do infinite harm to the principle of freedom, which is the greatest, the central, American doctrine. Fidelity to that principle has made it possible for the universities of America to confer great benefits upon our society and our country. Adherence to that principle is the only guarantee that the nation may continue to enjoy those benefits.

1.4.   MEETING THE THREAT OF TOTALITARIANISM[11]

Educational Policies Commission

With the prospect of continuing ideological conflict before us, the main lines of strategy for American education seem clear.

(1) *Young citizens should have an opportunity to learn about the principles and practices of totalitarianism, including those represented by the Soviet Union and by the Communist Party in the United States.*

Study of such topics should be accurate and objective, and should make use of basic official documents. (Many important Communist

---

[11] Educational Policies Commission, *American Education and International Tensions*, Washington: National Education Association, 1949, pp. 37-40. By permission. For a somewhat contrary view, endorsed by a dozen leading educational organizations, read "The Public School and the American Heritage," *Harvard Educational Review* 21: 137, Summer 1951 (with an analysis by David K. Berninghauser, *ibid.*, pp. 128-154). See also Sidney Hook, "Should Our Schools Study Communism?" *New York Times Magazine*, p. 7 f, August 29, 1954; reply by Howard Selsam, *ibid.*, p. 6, September 26, 1954; counter-reply by Sidney Hook, *ibid.*, p. 6, October 10, 1954.

documents are contained in *The Tactics and Strategy of World Communism,* Document 619, Committee on Foreign Affairs, House of Representatives, 80th Congress.) These studies should increase civic intelligence with reference to such specific questions as these: How did fascistic and other tyrannical governments come to power? Why do some people in all parts of the world embrace communist ideology? How do dictators manage to gain and hold political power in other countries? How does the Communist Party of the United States operate?

(2) *Teaching about Communism or any other form of dictatorship does not mean advocacy of these doctrines. Such advocacy should not be permitted in American schools.*

Rejection of all forms of totalitarianism by American youth is more likely to result from the objective exposure of facts in the classroom than from a situation in which youth, denied an opportunity to learn about them at school, are left to be the prey of propaganda through out-of-school channels—often possessing the enhanced appeal of forbidden fruit. While we expose and combat subversive activities in this country and abroad, great vigilance and wisdom will be required to avoid the use of undemocratic measures. We must, at the same time, curb reactionary forces which would use "anti-communist" sentiment as a club to threaten every effort to improve society through education.

(3) *The schools should continue with vigor their programs for giving young citizens a clear understanding of the principles of the American way of life and a desire to make these principles prevail in their own lives and in the life of their country.*

Recent history has demonstrated again that from such understanding and such attitudes there arises a deep loyalty to the ideals that have been developed and applied in our country. We must develop a greater measure of intelligent loyalty to democratic ideals. We must make those ideals more fully operative in American society—in economic life and intergroup relations and education, no less than in politics and government. There is no better way to prevent the spread of communism and other forms of dictatorship than to show the people that they can achieve a maximum of freedom, justice, and well-being by actively supporting and improving

American democracy. Amelioration of economic injustice, psychological insecurity, racial discrimination, substandard housing, and other evils that beset us will help to produce a soil in which the seeds of communism cannot thrive.

The existence of unusual tensions is quite certain to continue to produce violent attacks by some sections of the public on the schools and the teaching staff. Most common is the charge that the schools and teachers are "subversive" or "leftist." Less loud, but still clearly audible, are other voices who call the school system "reactionary" or "a tool of capitalism." Educators are accustomed to this attack from all sides and recognize that a certain amount of it is a necessary hazard of their occupation. However, if such charges, with their usual accompaniment of "investigations," book-banning, and efforts at intimidation, become too violent, frequent, and widespread, they can seriously impair the efficiency of the school system in discharging its essential functions in American life. The educational profession will need, in the time of growing and sometimes irrational public apprehensions, to explain and defend the true role of education in American life.

(4) *Members of the Communist Party of the United States should not be employed as teachers.*

Such membership, in the opinion of the Educational Policies Commission, involves adherence to doctrines and discipline completely inconsistent with the principles of freedom on which American education depends. Such membership, and the accompanying surrender of intellectual integrity, render an individual unfit to discharge the duties of a teacher in this country.

At the same time we condemn the careless, incorrect, and unjust use of such words as "Red" and "Communist" to attack teachers and other persons who in point of fact are not Communists, but who merely have views different from those of their accusers. The whole spirit of free American education will be subverted unless teachers are free to think for themselves. It is because members of the Communist Party are required to surrender this right, as a consequence of becoming part of a movement characterized by conspiracy and calculated deceit, that they should be excluded from employment as teachers.

Section B: Dangers of Intellectual Restriction

1.5. INTRODUCTION: THE EDUCATOR'S RESPONSIBILITY FOR FREEDOM [12]

The age-old mission of universities is ". . . the transmission of our cultural heritage, its reappraisal and reinterpretation in a changing time, and the discovery of new knowledge and ideas bound in themselves to bring new change for the enrichment of the future." [13] In the scholar's world there are no ideas or associations around which magic circles may be drawn. A university not only tolerates, but needs the representation of conflicting ideas in order that thinking may be real and that education be more than indoctrination. In his search for a type of knowledge which rises above preconceived notions and popular prejudices, the scholar disciplines himself to question common assumptions, to be rigorous in deductive thinking, and to appraise beliefs on the basis of factual evidence.

In order for reason to operate effectively, it must be able to appraise facts and situations with some degree of objectivity. Reason cannot operate where extreme emotional tensions exist, or where thinking is dominated by overpowering aggressive drives. The questions arise: Can a mind dedicated to Communism be free to think objectively? Can Americans become violent in their hatred of Communism without themselves reverting to authoritarian, nonscientific

[12] Portions of the introductions to sections B and C of this chapter are from a Report to the President of the University of Minnesota by the Faculty Consultative Committee, June 1954. For help in preparing this report, the editor is indebted to the following other committee members: Professors William Anderson, E. H. Heilman, O. B. Jesness, Robert C. McClure, Lloyd M. Short, Maurice B. Visscher and John H. Williams.

[13] James Lewis Morrill, Address at Stillwater, Minnesota, March 13, 1953, *The Minnesotan* 6: 15, April 1953. Compare Grayson L. Kirk, "Janus, the Modern University," *School and Society* 77: 321-324, May 23, 1953; Samuel P. Capen, *The Management of Universities,* Buffalo, N. Y.: Stewart, 1953, pp. 272-287.

attitudes? Is adherence to authoritarianism in some sphere absolutely incompatible with academic usefulness to society?

A community of scholars, we believe, should normally exclude anyone who would argue: "All pigs are animals; therefore, all animals are pigs." We certainly ought to be suspicious, then, of anyone who falls for the Communist line: "All Fascists are anti-Communists. Therefore, all anti-Communists are Fascists." But must we not then also judge as mentally incompetent any who fall for the analogous argument: "All McCarthyites are anti-Communists. Therefore, all anti-Communists are McCarthyites"? If the argument against aggressive drives is valid, it cuts both ways. Extreme anti-Communism is as irrational as extreme Communism.

Before reason can operate, emotional slogans and question-begging epithets must be replaced by hypotheses which admit of reasonable answers. Consider the currently popular phrase "Fifth Amendment Communist." By association, if these three words are repeated together often enough, American citizens will come to hate the Fifth Amendment as they now hate Communists. All the force of hatred now directed against Communism may soon be directed against one of the pillars of our own society. Every scholar knows that the Fifth Amendment is a device by which the Founding Fathers hoped to prevent American democracy from degenerating into mob tyranny. No scholar is morally obligated to defend the Fifth Amendment; he is perfectly free to advocate its repeal.[14] But everyone has a positive moral obligation to see to it that his own thinking, and that of his fellow citizens, does not degenerate to the level of Pavlov's dog. The primary obligation of a university is to help raise problems to a rational level.

---

[14] Concerning the privilege of teachers to invoke the Fifth or First Amendments in their own behalf, read: B. D. Metzler *vs.* Harry Kalven, Jr., "Invoking the Fifth Amendment—Some Legal and Practical Considerations," *Bulletin of the Atomic Scientists* 9: 176-184, June 1953: Sidney Hook, "The Fifth Amendment—A Moral Issue," *New York Times Magazine,* p. 9 f, Nov. 1, 1953; Francis W. Coker, "Academic Freedom and the Congressional Investigations: Free Speech and the Silent Professor," *Journal of Politics* 16: 491-508, August 1954 (bibliography) ; Thomas E. Joyner, "Self-Incrimination and the Duty to Testify: Changing Concepts," *Journal of Politics* 16: 509-538, August 1954 (bibliography) ; Milton R. Konvitz, *Bill of Rights Reader: Leading Constitutional Cases,* pp. 468-484, Ithaca, N. Y.: Cornell University Press 1954; Robert E. Summers, ed., *Freedom and Loyalty in Our Colleges,* New York: Wilson, 1954 (pp. 122-153, "The Fifth Amendment Controversy") .

It is commonly said that anyone who joins a totalitarian movement thereby surrenders independence of thought, hence can no longer contribute to a community of free scholars. There is considerable truth in this statement, as shown by the Nazi theories of race under Hitler, and the Lysenko theories of biology under Stalin.

But a partial truth is not a whole truth. The facts show that there are some totalitarians who are brilliant scholars. Nazi Werner Heisenberg, the father of quantum mechanics, was awarded the Nobel Prize in Physics in 1932 for this major contribution to science. Heisenberg subsequently was in charge of the German atomic bomb program. The success of the present Russian efforts in developing the hydrogen bomb shows that Communism and creative thought coexist.

In chemistry, Communists Frederic and Irene Joliet-Curie won the Nobel Prize in 1935; Nazi Richard Kuhn won it in 1938; Nazi Otto Hahn won it in 1944.

In literature, W. B. Yeats was for a time an active member of the fascistic Blueshirts of Ireland. Gabriele D'Annunzio supported Mussolini. Andre Gide and Stephen Spender once belonged to the Communist Party. T. S. Eliot, Roy Campbell, and Wyndham Lewis actively encouraged fascist ideas; while W. H. Auden actively supported the Spanish Loyalists. It is therefore factually incorrect to say that *no* person who embraces totalitarian politics is able to think creatively. Were we to insist on this overgeneralization, we would have to deny that Picasso was a first-rate painter, that Ezra Pound was a true poet, and that Prokofieff was a great musician. We would have to argue that Granville Hicks and Whittaker Chambers were poor journalists while they belonged to the Communist Party, but suddenly gained competence when they resigned.

In listing these examples we do not for a moment suggest that the same degree of creativity exists in totalitarian societies as in democracies. Indeed, most of the persons mentioned grew up in an atmosphere of relative freedom. Nevertheless, if someone says "The exceptions prove the rule," there is only one honest reply: "The exceptions probe (i.e., test) the rule and prove it to be an exaggeration, an example of special pleading."

A university is a community of scholars. True. But it is not necessary for every faculty member to commune with every other faculty member on every subject. Imagine four men working on a research project in physics: a Catholic, a Protestant, a Jew and an Atheist. The Catholic may disagree with his Protestant friend on the theological authority of the Church; with his Jewish friend on the divinity of Christ; with his Atheist friend on the existence of God. Yet all four men may cooperate perfectly in their research in physics. And experience testifies that such men often work together better if they are *not* compelled to discuss their religious or political differences. The very same man who is aboveboard and objective in physics may be secretive and prejudiced in politics or religion. Sometimes such compartmentalized thinking may have definite psychological value. While in the medical school, an anatomist dissects cadavers in a cool, heartless manner. We could hardly expect him to carry this "objectivity" home with him when he greets his wife and family!

It is very flattering to suppose that all of us except those under Communist influence are completely free of prejudice. The plain truth is that we are not. The scientist, in his special field of competence, learns to conquer doubt by cultivating it until it finds its natural limits and can go no further. But "doubting Thomases" are rare creatures even in science. Complete scientific objectivity is so difficult, that it is seldom attained except in a few special areas even by the great scientists. The marvelous thing about a university is that a group of finite, fallible scholars—including even an occasional crackpot—through cooperative effort can attain results which exceed the competence of any single individual. In this sense, says Pratt,

> The chain is stronger than the weakest link. . . . The work of scientists is constantly subjected to the fire of criticism. In this fire the errors and prejudices in the work of single individuals are burned away, leaving an intact and purified remainder. The destruction of a theory . . . may be mourned by the individuals who developed and supported it, but the group as a whole sheds no tears over the loss.[15]

---

[15] Carroll C. Pratt, *The Logic of Modern Psychology*, New York: Macmillan, 1948, p. 61. By permission.

In short, universities consist of scholars who are more or less competent in a few restricted areas. The mature thinker does not claim to be completely enlightened and detached in all things.

A prolonged period of war has drawn many people into the dungeon of friend-enemy, cops-robbers, all-none, black-white thinking. But a calm appraisal of facts proves that democracy and totalitarianism do not exist as blacks and whites[16]—and that there are many degrees of freedom, innumerable varieties of people, including split personalities and compartmentalized minds. Occasionally a man is a veritable genius in one field, while almost completely devoid of common sense in others.[17] The diseased oyster may produce the pearl. So the real question is this: How can our society gain the benefit of every citizen's creative abilities—including those with ambivalent personalities? Of course, other things being equal, sociability and common sense are desirable, and often indispensable. But other things are not always equal. And when they are not, it is not Emily Post, but intellectual competence in one's special field, which becomes the primary criterion for employment.

Because there are many shades and varieties of "subversion" and "communism," there can be no mechanical formula which will apply to every specific case. We all agree that conspirators and traitors should be punished. We all agree that anyone whose party membership impairs his teaching should be dismissed. But surely there are differences between the various individuals who are tagged as "communist." It is simply not accurate to say "They are all alike." Innumerable shades of attitudes exist both within the American Communist Party itself, and among various "front" organizations; between "hard shell" and casual members; "short-term" members and "lifers"; past and present members; officers and "mailing-list members." A unanimous decision of the United States Supreme Court declared that in any organization listed as subversive, ". . . membership may be innocent. A state servant may have joined a proscribed organization unaware of its activities and pur-

---

[16] Compare David Spitz, *Patterns of Anti-Democratic Thought,* New York: Macmillan, 1949, Chapter 1; and Herrlee G. Creel, *Confucius: The Man and the Myth,* New York: Day, 1949, Chapter 10.

[17] A generation ago one of the University of Wisconsin's most eminent English professors had a phobia about railroads. Read William Ellery Leonard, *The Locomotive-God,* New York: Century Co., 1927, p. 298 f.

poses." [18] Because there are such differences in persons and in situations, each case must be judged on its own merits. Universities should be the last institutions to solve problems in terms of scapegoats or panaceas.

1.6. COMMUNISM AND THE SCHOOLS[19]
Lawrence H. Chamberlain

Many who accept without reservation the doctrine of a free intellectual market when applied to any other subject feel that in the case of communism the thesis must be revised. They take this view on the ground that intellectual integrity, the good which is to be preserved through the free-market formula, has already been destroyed in the case of a Communist, therefore he has nothing to contribute and nothing to protect because his mind is no longer free.

To the writer this argument is dangerous because it misses the main point and concentrates upon a minor issue. To argue that a Communist has already lost his freedom of choice and is, accordingly, unable to participate in the quest for truth is to state a thesis that may or may not be true depending upon the individual concerned. Certainly some Communists have freed their minds from the shackles of party dogma and dominance; experience offers proof that such a course of action is possible. It is not only a theoretical possibility; by the hard test of empirical evidence the claim stands up.

From a source which affords every reason to believe the facts are accurate the statement has been made that since 1919 more than one million persons have gone in and out of the Communist Party

---

[18] Tom Clark, *Wieman v. Updegraff,* 344 U.S. 183 (1952); read also William O. Douglas, concurring opinion, *Joint Anti-Fascist Refugee Committee v. McGrath,* 341 U.S. 123, 174 (1950); J. Edgar Hoover, "Civil Liberties and Law Enforcement," 37 *Iowa Law Review* 177: 186-189 (1952); Harold Taylor, *On Education and Freedom,* New York: Abelard-Schumann, 1954, p. 284 f.

[19] From Lawrence H. Chamberlain, *Loyalty and Legislative Action: A Survey of Activity by the New York State Legislature 1919-1939,* Ithaca, N. Y.: Cornell University Press, 1951, pp. 216-221. By permission.

Mr. Chamberlain is Dean, Columbia College, Columbia University.

in the United States. The magnitude of this startling figure has been explained by the contradictory nature of two of the basic operating principles of the Communist Party in this country: heavy emphasis upon recruitment in order to obtain a mass organization; a parallel emphasis upon uncompromising acceptance of party discipline. In furtherance of the first objective, each local unit was always confronted with the necessity of meeting its assigned quota of new membership. As a consequence, the party could not afford to be too rigid in its eligibility requirements. On the other hand, political independence or deviation from the official party line handed down from above was not tolerated.

Under these circumstances a rapid turnover in party membership was to be expected, and the one million figure cited above becomes understandable. Such an unstable membership reduces sharply the force of the current argument that a person who joins the Communist Party has lost his freedom. Apparently freedom is a more hardy plant than many people are willing to believe. At any rate a million ex-Communists in this country is heartening evidence to this effect.

If the channels in and out of the party are sufficiently open to permit the entry and exit of a million persons in the course of the past thirty years, the concept of party members' becoming prisoners intellectually, hence no longer free, needs serious qualification. The conclusion seems inescapable that if the number of ex-Communists in the United States far outweighs the number of active members, the traditional principle of the free market still provides the most effective instrument for counteracting communism. It should be emphasized that this statement is made solely with reference to the United States. Where the long arm of the secret police can snatch offending or apostate party members and condemn them to death or to the living death of a labor camp, the chances of a party member's ever regaining his intellectual freedom are small. No evidence has come to light that such conditions are operative in the United States, however. Instances of persons who have left the Communist Party without bodily harm or other punishment more serious than castigation in the party press are too well known to permit acceptance of the proposition that coercion is of major importance so far as Communist membership in the United States is concerned. One must conclude that American Communists are not beyond possible redemption.

So long as there remains some uncertainty as to the futility of the free-market formula, so long as it may work in some cases, even though it is likely to fail in others, and so long as acute considerations of military security cannot be cited as justification for its suspension in favor of more extreme remedies, the arguments for its application to Communists seem just as strong as for any other dissident group.

There is something particularly offensive in the idea of permitting Communists to use the schoolroom as a vantage point from which to poison the minds of innocent and unsuspecting children. Anyone who would so prostitute the principles of the teaching profession as to use his classroom for proselytizing his students has undoubtedly forfeited the right to claim any constitutional protection on his own behalf. But there is a danger that by concentrating too sharply upon the offending teacher one loses sight of the deeper issue. Certain assumptions need to be clarified.

In the first place, the general acceptance of the effectiveness of the indoctrinating Communist teacher calls for further examination than it has yet received. Surprisingly little factual information has been assembled to document the general assumption that a Communist teacher can actually convert his students to communism. It is not the intention here to argue the point one way or the other, but the fact remains that our information on this question is far too meager to provide an adequate basis for judgment. Until we possess more factual data to test the popular assumption that Communist teachers are actually as dangerous as they are supposed to be, it can be argued that this assumption has been overplayed. In the absence of the information needed, one can offer certain a priori reasons for questioning the validity of the assumptions usually taken for granted. How often does a single teacher make such a deep impact upon his students that his views become a controlling influence on their minds? Under modern city school conditions—and it is reasonable to assume that Communist teachers would operate there rather than in the rural areas—no single teacher has uncontested monopoly over the students' minds. He is one of several persons from whom the student receives instruction.

ments may achieve stability temporarily but they inevitably result in disaffection among the people which leads to instability. The reason is clear. Repression ignores the values of freedom and the salient fact that the desire for freedom is strong and widespread, and that when this desire is repressed a conflict is created that is irrepressible. What are the values of freedom that make for stability? Freedom encourages individual responsibility, repression irresponsibility. Freedom creates an atmosphere conducive to the development of wholesome character and normal personality. Repression warps character and personality. Freedom encourages forthrightness, honesty, and confidence in justice. Repression invites conspiracy and deceit. Individual responsibility, wholesome character, normal personality, forthrightness, honesty, and confidence in justice—all these attributes are essential to stability. The road of freedom is the road to stability. It is the road away from revolution. That at least is the theory of our Constitutional system which, incidentally, it is well to remind ourselves, is one of the oldest and the strongest in the world. In devising our Constitutional system, the founding fathers were fully aware of the risks of freedom. They were students of history. They chose freedom because of their awareness of the greater risks of repression. In choosing freedom they provided appropriate safeguards against the abuse of freedom, safeguards that assure the individual, whose exercise of freedom is called in question, the protection of due process of law. In our institutions of higher education, in addition to the Constitutional safeguards against the abuse of freedom, there are the safeguards provided by the principles of academic freedom that have been developed by the custom and usage of the academic world: principles that have the support of a responsible profession prepared to apply appropriate restraints to a misuse of freedom. To these principles, both Constitutional and academic, the American Association of University Professors is deeply committed.

Academic Freedom (1940 Statement of Principals)[21]

(a) The teacher is entitled to full freedom in research and in

---

[21] *American Association of University Professors Bulletin* 36: 46-47, Spring 1950. The Spring AAUP *Bulletins* list the 1940 *Statement of Principles* concerning both *Academic Freedom* and *Academic Tenure,* and, commencing in 1951, concerning *Academic Retirement.*

the publication of the results, subject to the adequate performance of his other academic duties; but research for pecuniary return should be based upon an understanding with the authorities of the institution.

(b) The teacher is entitled to freedom in the classroom in discussing his subject, but he should be careful not to introduce into his teaching controversial matter which has no relation to his subject. Limitations of academic freedom because of religious or other aims of the institution should be clearly stated in writing at the time of the appointment.

(c) The college or university teacher is a citizen, a member of a learned profession, and an officer of an educational institution. When he speaks or writes as a citizen, he should be free from institutional censorship or discipline, but his special position in the community imposes special obligations. As a man of learning and an educational officer, he should remember that the public may judge his profession and his institution by his utterances. Hence he should at all times be accurate, should exercise appropriate restraint, should show respect for the opinions of others, and should make every effort to indicate that he is not an institutional spokesman. . . .

(1950)[22]: Members of . . . [the first 1915] Committee[23] felt that "dangers to academic freedom" in their day were from some of "the more conservative classes," from influential political groups when there was "a definite governmental policy or a strong public feeling on economic, social, or political questions," and from an aroused popular feeling. "Public opinion," the Committee continued, "is at once the chief safeguard of a democracy, and the chief menace to the real liberty of the individual. . . . In a political autocracy, there is no effective public opinion, and all are subject to the tyranny of the ruler; in a democracy, there is political freedom, but there is likely to be a tyranny of public opinion."

---

[22] Committee on Academic Freedom and Tenure, William T. Laprade, Chairman, "Report," AAUP *Bulletin* 36: 33-42, Spring 1950. By permission. Mr. Laprade is Professor of History, Duke University.

[23] The statement of the first Committee on Academic Freedom and Academic Tenure is known to the profession as the *1915 Declaration of Principles*. It was published in the December 1915 AAUP *Bulletin*, Vol. 1, No. 1, and has been reprinted several times, most recently in the AAUP *Bulletin* 40: 90-112, Spring 1954.

Though writing in 1915, in the midst of a world at war, the Committee declared: "An inviolable refuge from such tyranny should be found in the university. It should be an intellectual experiment station, where new ideas may germinate and where their fruit, though still distasteful to the community as a whole, may be allowed to ripen until finally, perchance, it may become a part of the accepted intellectual food of the nation or of the world." It is the duty of the university also to conserve "all genuine elements of value in the past thought and life of mankind which are not in the fashion of the moment." Nevertheless, it would be a mistake to assume, as many of the uninformed did then and do now, that the faculties of colleges and universities are a refuge for irresponsible radicals. This Committee went on to observe that a university "by its nature is committed to the principle that knowledge should precede action, to the caution . . . which is an essential part of the scientific method, to a sense of the complexity of social problems, to the practice of taking long views into the future, and to a reasonable regard for the teachings of experience." Furthermore, the Committee continued, one of the most characteristic functions of a university "in a democratic society is to help make public opinion more self-critical and more circumspect, to check the more hasty and unconsidered impulses of popular feeling, to train the democracy to the habit of looking before and after. It is precisely this function of the university which is most injured by any restriction upon academic freedom; and it is precisely those who most value this aspect of the university's work who should most earnestly protest against any such restriction." . . .

(1951)[24]: A free society cannot avoid an element of risk. It will search in vain for absolute security. It is based on the assumption that people can be trusted to be free, that a majority of them will not in the long run persist in acting to their own disadvantage, that, given freedom to think, to act, and to influence each other, they will on the whole do better for themselves than if their direction were entrusted to a few, however wise, not subject to popular control. This is the traditional faith at the heart of our political society. . . .

---

[24] Committee on Academic Freedom and Tenure, William T. Laprade, chairman, "Report," AAUP *Bulletin* 37: 72-91, Spring 1951, p. 73. By permission.

(1953)[25]: It would be one of the supreme ironies of history and one of the greatest tragedies if the confidence we exhibited in the weakness of youth should be destroyed through fear in the strength of our maturity.

But we do not believe that this will happen. In the past the American people have repudiated those who "fear freedom's use but love its useful name" and whose weapons threaten defacement of the temple of liberty itself. We believe they will do so again.

1.8. WE SHALL NOT OVERTHROW COMMUNISM BY SUPPRESSING THE CRITICAL AND THE CREATIVE MIND [26]

Howard Mumford Jones

. . . a psychology of fear and conformity is upon us. How shall we meet it? What is to be done? How shall we encourage a flow of fresh general intelligence into the current of the national life and of mankind? We need some radical alteration in our siege psychology, some change in the theory that man is fundamentally irrational, some fresh faith in the individual, some renewed grasp on the fundamental truth that, even in wartime, if a nation throws away its inheritance, it cannot defend what it has thrown away.

The fundamental principles to which we should return are finely stated in a document that is, unfortunately, subversive. They appear in a statement by a minority group busily engaged in overthrowing by force and violence the government to which they owed allegiance—a government which, competent historians assure us, was neither vicious nor tyrannical, although this document accuses it of being both. The principal writer among them was, not once but many times in his life, called a dangerous radical, an atheist,

---

[25] Excerpt from a resolution endorsed by the Thirty-ninth Annual Meeting of the American Association of University Professors, March 1953. Quoted in full in the AAUP *Bulletin* 39: 94-95, Spring 1953; and in the *Bulletin of the Atomic Scientists* 9: 191-192, June 1953. By permission.

[26] From Howard Mumford Jones, "The Creative Intelligence—The World of Ideas," *Harvard Educational Review* 22: 212-217, Summer 1952. By permission. Mr. Jones is professor of English at Harvard University.

a materialist, a liar, an assassin, and the friend and companion of liars and assassins. Of the group who took their leadership from this man, a president of Yale College said that, were it to triumph, American wives and daughters would be the victims of legal prostitution. A leading young English poet pictured this man as living in uncleanly desolation and as stealing secretly away from public business into a filthy shed to enjoy the embraces of a wench. This man not only actively promoted revolution in the country of his birth, but he did what he could to promote world-wide revolution, notably in friendly countries like France. Today, however, whatever he said is piously preserved, and everything that he wrote is being printed in some fifty expensive volumes under the patronage of one of our conservative newspapers. I refer, of course, to *The Papers of Thomas Jefferson,* now being edited at Princeton University by Julian Boyd and his associates, and I need not say that the document to which I principally refer is the Declaration of Independence.

Here is its most famous passage:

We hold these truths to be self-evident, that all men are created equal, that they are endowed by their Creator with certain inalienable Rights, that among these are Life, Liberty, and the pursuit of Happiness.—That to secure these rights, Governments are instituted among Men, deriving their just powers from the consent of the governed,—That whenever any Form of Government becomes destructive of these ends, it is the Right of the People to alter or to abolish it, and to institute new Government, laying its foundation on such principles and organizing its powers in such form, as to them shall seem most likely to effect their Safety and Happiness. Prudence, indeed, will dictate that Governments long established shall not be changed for light and transient causes; and accordingly all experience hath shewn, that mankind are more disposed to suffer, while evils are sufferable, than to right themselves by abolishing the forms to which they are accustomed. But when a long train of abuses and usurpations, pursuing invariably the same Object evinces a design to reduce them under absolute Despotism, it is their right, it is their duty, to throw off such Government, and to provide new Guards for their future security.

This characteristic production of the Age of Reason assumes that men are rational. To Jefferson and his contemporaries, this seemed merely the common sense of the matter. It is, in the words of one historian, both futile and irrelevant to argue that this theory of the origin of government does not square with nineteenth-century experience and twentieth-century anthropological knowledge, because the doctrines are timeless and "the haunting beauty of its phrasing" insures immortality to the great declaration. It is to the timelessness of the doctrine I suggest we recur if we really desire to challenge thought. For a cultural dynamic, for a key to unlock the door which now separates, or seems to separate, the creative intelligence from the world of general ideas, it is to the Declaration that we must go. . . .

American Communists may or may not be persons of the highest intelligence, but the Declaration says not a word about the intelligence of those who consent to be governed, and the question of the intelligence of any minority is, therefore, irrelevant to the Declaration. American Communists, having had some experience with violation of what they claim as inalienable rights, principally the right to liberty and the pursuit of happiness, say that a long course of years now shows that the government in power ought to be overthrown, but the government refuses to be overthrown and would like to prevent the Communists from existing at all, if it could. Shall we appeal to the Declaration? The Declaration lays down the right of the people to alter or abolish government and to institute new government in such form as to the people shall seem most likely to effect their safety and happiness. Is the Declaration wrong? I think not. Are the Communists right? I think not. Are we, therefore, to follow Senator McCarthy? I think not. For the Declaration does not stop there. It is not a mere statement of grievances. It says that governments long established shall not be changed for light and transient causes, and until the radical left can demonstrate more persuasively than it has yet done that the evils of American life are intolerable, we may, I think, continue to trust to good sense and the Jeffersonian philosophy. If we are to face the challenge flung down by the Communists, we must meet it with less hysteria, with some more philosophical statement of what we believe in and why we believe in it. We shall not overthrow communism by suppressing the critical or the creative mind. . . .

If it be said that a time of war is no time to raise fundamental questions, I reply that the Declaration was written and adopted during war. If it was right for the creators of this nation to turn to fundamental principles in their struggle against monarchy, it is right for us not to lose sight of fundamental principles in our struggle against totalitarianism. In time of war prepare for peace. We cannot postpone the theory of democracy. We must either halt our flight from reason or be content to be ruled by authority. If our artists cannot be brought to believe in the general intelligence of mankind today, we shall not come ourselves to that belief tomorrow. If we cannot respect the individual, we shall have to suffer the tyranny of the mass. You cannot conquer hysteria with cynicism. The soul of the nation, if it is to go marching on, requires that we believe in the dignity of the individual, in the capacity of most individuals in their better moments to be reasonable beings, and in the possibility in practical measure for right reason and the creative intelligence still to bring forth ideas that shall enrich the nation with all good gifts.

1.9. THE TRIUMPH OF WISDOM[27]

Learned Hand

The subject matter of science is recorded observation of the external world; the subject matter of the statecraft is the Soul of Man, and of that too there are records. . . . The imagination can be purged and the judgment ripened only by an awareness of the slow, hesitant, wayward course of human life, its failures, its successes, but its indomitable will to endure.

---

[27] Learned Hand, Address delivered at the 86th Convocation of the Board of Regents of the University of the State of New York, Albany, October 24, 1952. Reprinted by permission of Learned Hand. Mr. Hand was judge of the United States Circuit Court, 2nd Circuit, from 1924 until his retirement in 1951.

For a more complete reproduction of this address, read the *Saturday Review* 35: 9 f, Nov. 22, 1952.

Compare Erwin N. Griswold, "By the Law of the Land," *Vital Speeches* 20: 442-446, May 1, 1954; William O. Douglas, "The Essence of Due Process," *Vital Speeches* 19: 554-557, July 1, 1953.

I cannot but think that we of this generation are politically in especial need of such education. Our nation is embarked upon a venture, as yet unproved; we have set our hopes upon a community in which men shall be given unchecked control of their own lives. That community is in peril; it is invaded from within, it is threatened from without; it faces a test which it may fail to pass. The choice is ours whether, when we hear the pipes of Pan, we shall stampede like a frightened flock, forgetting all those professions on which we have claimed to rest our polity.

God knows there is risk in refusing to act till the facts are all in; but is there not greater risk in abandoning the conditions of all rational inquiry?

Risk for risk, for myself I had rather take my chance that some traitors will escape detection than spread abroad a spirit of general suspicion and distrust, which accepts rumor and gossip in place of undismayed and unintimidated inquiry. I believe that that community is already in process of dissolution where each man begins to eye his neighbor as a possible enemy, where nonconformity with the accepted creed, political as well as religious, is a mark of disaffection; where denunciation, without specification or backing, takes the place of evidence; where orthodoxy chokes freedom of dissent; where faith in the eventual supremacy of reason has become so timid that we dare not enter our convictions in the open lists to win or lose.

Such fears as these are a solvent which can eat out the cement that binds the stones together; they may in the end subject us to a despotism as evil as any that we dread; and they can be allayed only in so far as we refuse to proceed on suspicion, and trust one another until we have tangible ground for misgiving.

The mutual confidence on which all else depends can be maintained only by an open mind and a brave reliance upon free discussion. I do not say that these will suffice; who knows but we may be on a slope which leads down to aboriginal savagery. But of this I am sure: if we are to escape, we must not yield a foot upon demanding a fair field, and an honest race, to all ideas.

"Blame not before thou hast examined; understand first and then rebuke. Answer not before thou hast heard; interrupt not in the midst of speech." Those words were written nearly 2000 years ago; they came out of an experience already long, and refined in the fires of passion and conflict; they are the product of a wisdom bought by ages of bitter trial; and by that wisdom alone shall we be saved, we, who boast ourselves to be the apostles of a faith in the eventual triumph of Wisdom.

Section C: Freedom of Assembly—and the Right to Public Employment

1.10. INTRODUCTION: FREEDOM OF ASSOCIATION

The First Amendment joins freedom of religion, speech, press and assembly into a single sentence. The reason why they all belong together was stated by de Tocqueville nearly a century ago:

> The right of association is almost as inalienable as the right of personal liberty. . . . In countries where these associations do not exist, if private individuals are unable to create an artificial and a temporary substitute for them, I can imagine no permanent protection against the most galling tyranny; and a great people may be oppressed with impunity by a small faction or by a single individual.[28]

If there were no freedom of association for groups holding divergent views, the ability of men to correct their mistakes by free and rational discussion would soon be lost.

Nevertheless it is not the organized group, but only individual members of that group who may be punished for crime. This long-

---

[28] Alexis de Tocqueville, *Democracy in America*, Vol. 1, Chapter 12 (1862). Compare Anatol Rapoport, *Operational Philosophy*, New York: Harper, 1953, p. 140.

standing democratic tradition was reaffirmed in 1943 when Mr. Justice Murphy insisted that—

> under our traditions beliefs are personal and not a matter of mere association, and . . . men in adhering to a political party or other organization notoriously do not subscribe to all of its platforms or asserted principles.[29]

But in 1950 Mr. Justice Jackson wrote that "Every member of the Communist Party is an agent to execute the Communist program." [30]

Here we have two generalizations: One by Mr. Justice Murphy declares that few men subscribe to *all* the asserted principles of *any* organization or party to which they belong. The other by Mr. Justice Jackson says that *every* member of the American *Communist* Party is a conspirator. Is there any way to decide which of these two statements is the more accurate? Is each and every member of the American Communist Party a "clear and present danger" [31] to our society? Or are American Communists for the most part "miserable merchants of unwanted ideas"? [32]

If we attempt to decide such a question without factual evidence, we never reach a conclusion: we merely have a clash of values. Those whose primary value is the order and stability of society will tend to exaggerate anything that might challenge that order; those whose primary values center around the First Amendment tend to overemphasize anything which challenges freedom of religion, speech, press or assembly.

Fortunately, factual studies are now available which make serious attempts to report the truth about specific cases. One such study

---

[29] Frank Murphy, majority opinion, *Schneiderman v. United States,* 320 U.S. 118, 136 (1943). The same opinion rejected the contention that "one who advocates radical changes is necessarily not attached to the constitution."

[30] Robert H. Jackson, partly concurring and partly dissenting opinion, *American Communications Association v. Douds,* 339 U.S. 382, 431 (1950); reprinted in the *New York Times Magazine,* May 21, 1950, p. 12 f, and in *Harper's* 201: 21-27, September 1950.

[31] Majority opinion of Chief Justice Vinson, *ibid.;* also of Judge Learned Hand, *United States v. Dennis,* 183 2nd, 201 (1950). These opinions, however, do not say that *every* member of the American Communist Party is a "clear and present danger"; they refer only to the leaders of that party.

[32] William O. Douglas, dissenting opinion, *ibid.,* at 589.

is based on interviews with individual members, or former members, of the American Communist Party. It concludes that over the past twenty years there have been about twenty members who left the party for every one who remains a member today. Except for a rather small group of about 5000-8000 hard-shell Communists, the great majority tried the party and found it wanting. Our traditional "free trade of ideas" took care of about nineteen of every twenty of even the small group who were foolish enough to join the American Communist Party.[33]

Yet the threat remains, and in times of national crisis it is met by attempts to control all groups of doubtful loyalty. The current practice of listing "subversive" organizations began in 1939 with the Hatch Act. The Attorney General's first list contained six organizations, including the German-American Bund and the Communist Party. The list was later expanded, on orders from the President, until in 1950 it totalled 197 organizations. In 1953 the list was further expanded and reclassified to total 254. Meanwhile, the House Un-American Activities Committee issued a list of 624 subversive and Communist-front organizations.

In order to be listed, the Justice Department first ruled that any organization must, first, advocate subversive doctrine, and second, have reasonable ability to make this doctrine effective. But before long the second qualification was dropped, and organizations were listed on the basis of doctrine alone.

The Attorney General's list was intended to aid loyalty review boards in screening federal employees. The list was sent to these boards with the caution that "no conclusions whatsoever are to be drawn from membership in any such organization." The list might give the loyalty board reasonable cause to suspect an employee's loyalty; but final decisions were to be made, not on the basis of the listings, but only on the basis of the individual's proven subversive activities. But as time went on, this important provision

---

[33] Morris L. Ernst and David Loth, *Report on the American Communist*, New York: Holt, 1952; reviewed by Daniel Bell, *Saturday Review* 35: 17, Dec. 20, 1952; Gabriel A. Almond and others, *The Appeals of Communism*, Princeton, N. J.: Princeton University Press, 1954; reviewed by Sidney Hook, *New York Times Book Review*, Sept. 19, 1954, p. 3 f; by Michael Harrington, *Commonweal* 61: 22, Oct. 8, 1954; by Martin Ebon, *Saturday Review* 37: 13-14, Oct. 9, 1954; and by Morris L. Ernst, *Progressive* 18: 38, November 1954.

was ignored, and the lists themselves became "objective evidence" of a suspect's guilt. Associations which had been *clues* to *possible* guilt now became *proof* of *actual* guilt.

Our Anglo-Saxon tradition holds that a person is innocent until proven guilty and that criminal guilt can be established only by due process of law. In the light of this tradition it is significant that in 1951 the Executive Order concerning loyalty of government employees was amended to change the standard for disqualification from government employment from "reasonable grounds . . . for belief that a person is disloyal" to one of "reasonable doubt" as to his loyalty.[34]

It was against this background that three of the listed "subversive" organizations brought suit against the Attorney General in the *Anti-Fascist* case. The majority opinion by Mr. Justice Burton declared: "The issue is whether . . . the Attorney General of the United States has authority to include the complaining organization in a list of organizations designated by him as Communist and furnished by him to the Loyalty Review Board of the United States Civil Service Commission." [35] The Court by a vote of five to three qualified the Attorney General's authority to prepare such arbitrary lists of subversive organizations. ". . . such acts violate each complaining organization's common-law right to be free from defamation." [36] Hereafter, the Court ruled, the Attorney General's listings were to be made only after full notice and hearing, so as to provide listed organizations a right to review. This decision somewhat limits the legality of the Attorney General's list—and also the House Un-American Activities Committee's list—of "subversive" and "front" organizations.

Nevertheless, the Court ruled that the constitutional provisions concerning free speech and assembly were never intended to guar-

---

[34] Executive Order No. 10241, *Federal Record* 3690 (1951). See John Lord O'Brian, "New Encroachments on Individual Freedom," 66: *Harvard Law Review* 1-27, November 1952; Eleanor Bontecou, *The Federal Loyalty-Security Program,* Ithaca, N. Y.: Cornell University Press, 1953, p. 170 f; C. Herman Pritchett, *Civil Liberties and the Vinson Court,* Chicago: University of Chicago Press, 1954, pp. 66-75 and p. 266, note 8.

[35] Majority opinion of Mr. Justice Harold Burton in *Joint Anti-Fascist Refugee Committee v. McGrath,* 341 U.S. 123, 124-125 (1950).

[36] *Ibid.,* p. 139.

antee employment. Any employer, public or private, has the right to set up qualifications for hiring or firing employees. The distinction should be clearly drawn between (1) criminal guilt, as determined by an official court or jury, and (2) qualifications for employment by a state, a school or a business. Suspension from employment because of subversive activities may indeed imply a very real *suspicion* of guilt; but under our system of law *actual* guilt can be established only by a judge and jury.[37]

So the question arises: Under what circumstances may school authorities disqualify teachers from employment because of membership in "subversive" organizations? In the *Adler* case, the majority opinion written by Mr. Justice Minton defends the use of association as a means of establishing qualifications for employment in public schools; argues that the constitutional guarantee of free speech and assembly is no guarantee of school employment; and concludes that school officials may use "association" with listed "subversive organizations" as a criterion of tenure, provided full notice and hearing is allowed. However, as the footnote referring to the *Oklahoma* case indicates, public employees are not subject to arbitrary or wilful dismissal. In this 1952 case the court ruled, by an 8-0 decision, that it is unconstitutional to establish guilt by associating a person with an organization, or by listing any organization, without full opportunity for hearing and review.

The majority opinion in the *Adler* case is further qualified by the minority opinion of Mr. Justice Douglas, who points out that, where serious personal injury results, public employees cannot be arbitrarily dismissed.[38] Furthermore, the attempt to do so would soon make our schools undemocratic institutions, where there could be no exercise of the free intellect, and where supineness and dogmatism would take the place of inquiry. Mr. Justice Douglas would say of the New York *Feinberg* laws what other students have said

[37] Reasons for popular confusion concerning this distinction are brought out by Judge Curtis Bok, "Tightening the Sinews of Procedure," *New Republic* 130: 10-12, Feb. 15, 1954. See also Mark De Wolfe Howe's review of Sidney Hook's *Heresy, Yes—Conspiracy, No!*, New York: Day, 1953, *Yale Law Journal* 63: 132-137, November 1953.

[38] On August 6, 1953, a lower court sustained this opinion. See Harry A. Fosdick, "A Victory for Every Teacher," *National Education Association Journal* 42: 397, October 1953.

about similar legislative measures: ". . . as an unintended consequence of their operation Federal loyalty and security measures
are undermining the great traditions of American democracy which
they seek to preserve;" [39] "They who would give up essential liberty
to purchase a little temporary safety deserve neither liberty nor
safety;" [40] "The best thing to oppose communism is non-commu-
nism—'All the liberty possible—material and spiritual—to all human
beings. That is the only way.' " [41]

1.11. ONE'S ASSOCIATES, PAST AND PRESENT, AS WELL AS ONE'S CONDUCT, MAY PROPERLY BE CONSIDERED IN DETERMINING FITNESS AND LOYALTY [42]

Sherman Minton

The preamble of the Feinberg Law, [43] §1, makes elaborate findings that members of subversive groups, particularly of the Communist Party and its affiliated organizations, have been infil-
trating into public employment in the public schools of the
State; that this has occurred and continues notwithstanding the
existence of protective statutes designed to prevent the appointment to or retention in employment in public office, and particularly in the public schools, of members of any organizations
which teach or advocate that the government of the United States
or of any state or political subdivision thereof shall be overthrown
by force or violence or by any other unlawful means. As a result,
propaganda can be disseminated among the children by those who

---

[39] Maria Jahoda and Stuart W. Cook, "Security Measures and Freedom of
Thought: An Exploratory Study of the Impact of Loyalty and Security Programs," *Yale Law Journal* 61: 312-330, March 1952, p. 330.

[40] Benjamin Franklin, Motto to Historical Review of Pennsylvania.

[41] Albert Schweitzer, as interviewed by the *Christian Science Monitor*, June 30,
1949.

[42] Majority (6-3) opinion, *Adler v. Board of Education*, 342 U.S. 485 (1952).
The complete court opinion plus related opinions may be found in Thomas I.
Emerson and David Haber, *Political and Civil Rights in the United States*,
Buffalo, N. Y.: Dennis, 1952, pp. 859-876.

[43] Editor's Note: The Feinberg Law deals with "elimination of subversive persons from the public-school system."

teach them and to whom they look for guidance, authority, and leadership. The Legislature further found that the members of such groups use their positions to advocate and teach their doctrines, and are frequently bound by oath, agreement, pledge, or understanding to follow, advocate and teach a prescribed party line or group dogma or doctrine without regard to truth or free inquiry. This propaganda, the Legislature declared, is sufficiently subtle to escape detection in the classroom; thus, the menace of such infiltration into the classroom is difficult to measure. Finally, to protect the children from such influence, it was thought essential that the laws prohibiting members of such groups, such as the Communist Party or its affiliated organizations, from obtaining or retaining employment in the public schools be rigorously enforced. It is the purpose of the Feinberg Law to provide for the disqualification and removal of superintendents of schools, teachers, and employees in the public schools in any city or school district of the State who advocate the overthrow of the Government by unlawful means or who are members of organizations which have a like purpose.

Section 3022 of the Education Law, added by the Feinberg Law, provides that the Board of Regents, which has charge of the public-school system in the State of New York, shall, after full notice and hearing, make a listing of organizations which it finds advocate, advise, teach, or embrace the doctrine that the government should be overthrown by force or violence or any other unlawful means, and that such listing may be amended and revised from time to time.

It will be observed that the listings are made only after full notice and hearing . . . so as to provide listed organizations a right of review.

The Board of Regents is further authorized to provide in rules and regulations, and has so provided, that membership in any listed organization, after notice and hearing, "shall constitute prima facie evidence for disqualification for appointment to or retention in any office or position in the school system"; but before one who is an employee or seeks employment is severed from or denied employment, he likewise must be given a full hearing with the

privilege of being represented by counsel and the right to judicial
review. . . .

It is clear that such persons have the right under our law to
assemble, speak, think and believe as they will. *Communications
Assn. v. Douds*, 339 U.S. 382. It is equally clear that they have no
right to work for the State in the school system on their own terms.
United Public Workers v. Mitchell, 330 U.S. 75. They may work
for the school system upon the reasonable terms laid down by the
proper authorities of New York. If they do not choose to work
on such terms, they are at liberty to retain their beliefs and associations and go elsewhere.[44] Has the State thus deprived them of
any right to free speech or assembly? We think not. Such persons
are or may be denied, under the statutes in question, the privilege
of working for the school system of the State of New York. . . .

A teacher works in a sensitive area in a schoolroom. There he
shapes the attitude of young minds towards the society in which
they live. In this, the state has a vital concern. It must preserve
the integrity of the schools. That the school authorities have the
right and the duty to screen the officials, teachers, and employees
as to their fitness to maintain the integrity of the schools as a part
of ordered society, cannot be doubted.[45] One's associates, past and

---

[44] Editor's Note: It should be remembered that the courts are primarily concerned with the constitutionality, not the wisdom, of legislation being reviewed.
This is the major argument in the *Bailey* case, where Judge Prettyman wrote:
". . . the reason [that the spoils system has largely been replaced by a system
of civil service] . . . is because the people became convinced that it was not
good government and the Congress and the President wrote that view into
statutes and regulations. They, not the Constitution, give Government employees
such protection as they have against dismissal for political reasons. . . . The
Constitution did not write political miscellany of personnel into the structure of
the executive branch; Congress has done that. The First Amendment guarantees
free speech and assembly, but it does not guarantee Government employ. It does not
say that if the people elect an executive and legislature with specified political ob-
jectives, those officials must work through subordinates of other political tenets,
if, perchance, such are then in office."—Judge E. B. Prettyman, majority opinion,
Bailey v. Richardson, 182 Fed., 2nd, 46, 59 (1950).

[45] Editor's Note: "That utterances inciting to the overthrow of organized government by unlawful means, present a sufficient danger of substantive evil to bring
their punishment within the range of legislative discretion, is clear. Such utterances,
by their very nature, involve danger to the public peace and to the security of the
State. They threaten breaches of the peace and ultimate revolution. And the
immediate danger is none the less real and substantial, because the effect of a

present, as well as one's conduct, may properly be considered in determining fitness and loyalty. From time immemorial, one's reputation has been determined in part by the company he keeps. In the employment of officials and teachers of the school system, the state may very properly inquire into the company they keep, and we know of no rule, constitutional or otherwise, that prevents the state, when determining the fitness and loyalty of such persons, from considering the organizations and persons with whom they associate.

If, under the procedure set up in the New York law, a person is found to be unfit and is disqualified from employment in the public school system because of membership in a listed organization, he is not thereby denied the right of free speech and assembly. His freedom of choice between membership in the organization and employment in the school system might be limited, but not his freedom of speech or assembly, except in the remote sense that limitation is inherent in every choice. Certainly such limitation is not one the state may not make in the exercise of its police power to protect the schools from pollution and thereby to defend its own existence.[46]

---

given utterance cannot be accurately foreseen. The State cannot reasonably be required to measure the danger from every such utterance in the nice balance of a jeweler's scale. A single revolutionary spark may kindle a fire that, smouldering for a time, may burst into a sweeping and destructive conflagration. It cannot be said that the State is acting arbitrarily or unreasonably when in the exercise of its judgment as to the measures necessary to protect the public peace and safety, it seeks to extinguish the spark without waiting until it has enkindled the flame or blazed into the conflagration. It cannot reasonably be required to defer the adoption of measures for its own peace and safety until the revolutionary utterances lead to actual disturbances of the public peace or imminent and immediate danger of its own destruction; but it may, in the exercise of its judgment, suppress the threatened danger in its incipiency."—Mr. Justice Edward T. Sanford, majority opinion, *Gitlow v. New York,* 268 U.S. 652, 669 (1925). This opinion was the occasion for one of Mr. Justice Holmes' famous dissenting opinions.

[46] Editor's Note: In a later decision, the U.S. Supreme Court held an Oklahoma statute unconstitutional because it did not grant full right to hearing and review:

"[In the *Adler* case] . . . the New York courts had construed the statute [Feinberg Law] to require knowledge of organizational purpose before the regulation [which disqualified teachers of their positions] could apply. . . . [But in the *Oklahoma* case] the fact of membership alone disqualifies. . . .

"But membership may be innocent. A state servant may have joined a proscribed organization unaware of its activities and purposes. In recent years,

1.12. WHERE SUSPICION FILLS THE AIR AND HOLDS SCHOLARS IN LINE FOR FEAR OF THEIR JOBS, THERE CAN BE NO EXERCISE OF THE FREE INTELLECT [47]

William O. Douglas

I have not been able to accept the recent doctrine that a citizen

---

many completely loyal persons have severed organizational ties after learning for the first time of the character of groups to which they had belonged. 'They had joined, [but] did not know what it was, they were good, fine young men and women, loyal Americans, but they had been trapped into it—because one of the great weaknesses of all Americans, whether adult or youth, is to join something' [said J. Edgar Hoover]. At the time of affiliation a group itself may be innocent, only later coming under the influence of those who would turn it toward illegitimate ends. Conversely, an organization formerly subversive and therefore designated as such may have subsequently freed itself from the influences which originally led to its listing. . . .

"We are referred to our statement in *Adler* that persons seeking employment in the New York public schools have 'no right to work for the State in the school system on their own terms. . . . They may work for the school system upon the reasonable terms laid down by the proper authorities of New York.' . . . To draw from this language the facile generalization that there is no constitutionally protected right to public employment is to obscure the issue. . . . We need not pause to consider whether an abstract right to public employment exists. It is sufficient to say that constitutional protection does extend to the public servant whose exclusion pursuant to a statute is patently arbitrary or discriminatory."—Mr. Justice Tom C. Clark, Majority (8-0) opinion, *Wieman v. Updegraff* (the *Oklahoma* case) 344 U.S. 183 (1952) .

[47] William O. Douglas, dissenting opinion, *Adler v. Board of Education,* 342 U.S. 485 (1952) . Mr. Justice Black added the following short dissent:

"While I fully agree with the dissent of Mr. Justice Douglas, the importance of this holding prompts me to add these thoughts.

"This is another of those rapidly multiplying legislative enactments which make it dangerous—this time for school teachers—to think or say anything except what a transient majority happen to approve at the moment. Basically these laws rest on the belief that government should supervise and limit the flow of ideas into the minds of men. The tendency of such governmental policy is to mould people into a common intellectual pattern. Quite a different governmental policy rests on the belief that government should leave the mind and spirit of man absolutely free. Such a governmental policy encourages varied intellectual outlooks in the belief that the best views will prevail. This policy of freedom is in my judgment embodied in the First Amendment and made applicable to the states by the Fourteenth. Because of this policy public officials cannot be constitutionally vested with powers to select the ideas people can think about, censor the public views they can express, or choose the persons or groups people can associate with. Public officials with such powers are not public servants; they are public masters.

"I dissent from the Court's judgment sustaining this law which effectively penalizes school teachers for their thoughts and their associates."

who enters the public service can be forced to sacrifice his civil rights.[48] I cannot for example find in our constitutional scheme the power of a state to place its employees in the category of second-class citizens by denying them freedom of thought and expression. The Constitution guarantees freedom of thought and expression to everyone in our society. All are entitled to it; and none needs it more than the teacher.

The public school is in most respects the cradle of our democracy. The increasing role of the public school is seized upon by proponents of the type of legislation represented by New York's Feinberg law as proof of the importance and need for keeping the school free of "subversive influences." But that is to misconceive the effect of this type of legislation. Indeed the impact of this kind of censorship on the public-school system illustrates the high purpose of the First Amendment in freeing speech and thought from censorship.

The present law proceeds on a principle repugnant to our society —guilt by association. A teacher is disqualified because of her membership in an organization found to be "subversive." [49] The finding

---

[48] *United Public Workers v. Mitchell*, 330 U.S. 75; *Garner v. Board of Public Works of Los Angeles*, 341 U.S. 716.

[49] Editor's Note: In 1950, Mr. Justice Douglas wrote:

"Does it [the word 'subversive'] mean an organization with socialist ideas? There are some who lump Socialists and Communists together. Does it mean an organization that thinks the lot of some peasants has been improved under Soviet auspices? Does it include an organization that is against the action of the United Nations in Korea? Does it embrace a group which on some issues of international policy aligns itself with the Soviet viewpoint? Does it mean a group which has unwittingly become the tool for Soviet propaganda? Does it mean one into whose membership some Communists have infiltrated? Or does it describe only an organization which under the guise of honorable activities serves as a front for Communist activities?

"No one can tell from the Executive Order what meaning is intended. No one can tell from the records of the cases which one the Attorney General applied. The charge is flexible; it will mean one thing to one officer, another to someone else. It will be given meaning according to the predilections of the prosecutor: 'subversive' to some will be synonymous with 'radical'; 'subversive' to others will be synonymous with 'communist.' It can be expanded to include those who depart from the orthodox party line—to those whose words and actions (though completely loyal) do not conform to the orthodox view on foreign or domestic policy. These flexible standards, which vary with the mood or political philosophy of the prosecutor, are weapons which can be made as sharp or as blunt as the occasion requires. Since they are subject to grave abuse, they have no place in our system of law. When we employ them, we plant within our body politic the virus of the totalitarian ideology which we oppose.

as to the "subversive" character of the organization is made in a proceeding to which the teacher is not a party and in which it is not clear that she may even be heard. To be sure, she may have a hearing when charges of disloyalty are leveled against her. But in that hearing the finding as to the "subversive" character of the organization apparently may not be reopened in order to allow her to show the truth of the matter. The irrebuttable charge that the organization is "subversive" therefore hangs as an ominous cloud over her own hearing. The mere fact of membership in the organization raises a prima facie case of her own guilt. She may, it is said, show her innocence. But innocence in this case turns on knowledge; and when the witch hunt is on, one who must rely on ignorance leans on a feeble reed.

The very threat of such a procedure is certain to raise havoc with academic freedom. Youthful indiscretions, mistaken causes, misguided enthusiasms—all long forgotten—become the ghosts of a harrowing present. Any organization committed to a liberal cause, any group organized to revolt against an hysterical trend, any committee launched to sponsor an unpopular program becomes suspect. These are the organizations into which Communists often infiltrate. Their presence infects the whole, even though the project was not conceived in sin. A teacher caught in that mesh is almost certain to stand condemned. Fearing condemnation, she will tend to shrink from any association that stirs controversy. In that manner freedom of expression will be stifled.

"It is not enough to know that the men applying the standard are honorable and devoted men. This is a government of *laws,* not of *men.* . . . When the Government becomes the moving party and levels its great powers against the citizen, it should be held to the same standards of fair dealing as we prescribe for other legal contests. To let the Government adopt such lesser ones as suits the convenience of its officers is to start down the totalitarian path. . . . Guilt under our system of government is personal. When we make guilt vicarious we borrow from systems alien to ours and ape our enemies. Those short-cuts may at times seem to serve noble aims; but we depreciate ourselves by indulging in them. When we deny even the most degraded person the rudiments of a fair trial, we endanger the liberties of everyone. We set a pattern of conduct that is dangerously expansive and is adaptable to the needs of any majority bent on suppressing opposition or dissension. . . .

"Of course, no one has a constitutional right to a government job. But every citizen has a right to a fair trial when his government seeks to deprive him of the privileges of first-class citizenship."—William O. Douglas, concurring opinion, *Joint Anti-Fascist Refugee Committee v. McGrath,* 341 U.S. 123, 174-184 (1950) .

But that is only part of it. Once a teacher's connection with a listed organization is shown, her views become subject to scrutiny to determine whether her membership in the organization is innocent or, if she was formerly a member, whether she has *bona fide* abandoned her membership.

The law inevitably turns the school system into a spying project. Regular loyalty reports on the teachers must be made out. The principals become detectives; the students, the parents, the community become informers. Ears are cocked for tell-tale signs of disloyalty. The prejudices of the community come into play in searching out the disloyal. This is not the usual type of supervision which checks a teacher's competency; it is a system which searches for hidden meanings in a teacher's utterances.

What was the significance of the reference of the art teacher to socialism? Why was the history teacher so openly hostile to Franco Spain? Who heard overtones of revolution in the English teacher's discussion of the *Grapes of Wrath*? What was behind the praise of Soviet progress in metallurgy in the chemistry class? Was it not "subversive" for the teacher to cast doubt on the wisdom of the venture in Korea?

What happens under this law is typical of what happens in a police state. Teachers are under constant surveillance; their pasts are combed for signs of disloyalty; their utterances are watched for clues to dangerous thoughts. A pall is cast over the classrooms. There can be no real academic freedom in that environment. Where suspicion fills the air and holds scholars in line for fear of their jobs, there can be no exercise of the free intellect. Supineness and dogmatism take the place of inquiry. A "party line"—as dangerous as the "party line" of the Communists—lays hold. It is the "party line" of the orthodox view, of the conventional thought, of the accepted approach. A problem can no longer be pursued with impunity to its edges. Fear stalks the classroom. The teacher is no longer a stimulant to adventurous thinking; she becomes instead a pipe line for safe and sound information. A deadening dogma takes the place of free inquiry. Instruction tends to become sterile; pursuit of knowledge is discouraged; discussion often leaves off where it should begin.

This, I think, is what happens when a censor looks over a teacher's shoulder. This system of spying and surveillance with its accompanying reports and trials cannot go hand in hand with academic freedom. It produces standardized thought, not the pursuit of truth. Yet it was the pursuit of truth which the First Amendment was designed to protect. A system which directly or inevitably has that effect is alien to our system and should be struck down. Its survival is a real threat to our way of life. We need be bold and adventuresome in our thinking to survive. A school system producing students trained as robots threatens to rob a generation of the versatility that has been perhaps our greatest distinction. The Framers knew the danger of dogmatism; they also knew the strength that comes when the mind is free, when ideas may be pursued wherever they lead. We forget these teachings of the First Amendment when we sustain this law.

Of course the school systems of the country need not become cells for Communist activities; and the classrooms need not become forums for propagandizing the Marxist creed. But the guilt of the teacher should turn on overt acts. So long as she is a law-abiding citizen, so long as her performance within the public-school system meets professional standards, her private life, her political philosophy, her social creed should not be the cause of reprisals against her.

1.13. TEACHER LOYALTY OATHS

Editorial Essay

Ideally, there is only one oath any teacher in a democratic society should ever need or wish to take:

In all my efforts to comprehend what truth is, and to teach what is true, I shall follow only the guidance of my own conscience, without fearing or favoring any creed, or doctrine, or person.[50]

This ideal is most nearly achieved during times of domestic and international good will. It is then that our courts, in cases involv-

---

[50] Alexander Laing, "Three Ways of Swearing," *New Republic* 129: 9-12, Dec. 28, 1953.

ing civil liberties, have stressed the First Amendment with its emphasis on individual freedom.

But during periods of social crisis such as we are experiencing, governments naturally redouble their efforts to protect schools from subversive influences. The courts permit laws and oaths restricting cherished liberties, and membership in formerly respectable organizations now becomes a reason for excluding teachers from public office.

Here we should distinguish two types of oaths, affirmative and negative. The *affirmative* oath reads something like this:

I will support and defend the Constitution of the United States (and that of this state or municipality). I will bear true faith and allegiance to the same. I take this obligation freely and without any mental reservations. I will faithfully discharge the duties of the office to which I am appointed.

The *negative* type of oath reads somewhat as follows:

I do not advocate, nor am I a member of any organization (e.g., the Communist, Fascist or Nazi party) which advocates the overthrow of the government of the United States. I further swear and affirm that I will not advocate such overthrow, nor become a member of such an organization while I am employed in this public office.

Affirmative oaths have long been recognized as fair and reasonable, and the practice of exacting such pledges from those about to enter public service has seldom been questioned. But the more recent negative oath has provoked storms of criticism, such as the following by Alan Barth:

If we do not believe a man when he swears to uphold the Constitution, why, in the name of common sense, should we be any more disposed to take his word when he swears that he will not attempt to destroy the Constitution? The answer, of course, is that we have lost all faith in what he says in either case. But we insist on his saying it over and over again in the blind, unreasoning way that primitive tribes insisted upon rites of purification and blood sacrifices that had no relation to reality. . . . So far as catching real enemies of the country is concerned, this ritual procedure is about as effectual as a requirement that all criminals register with their local police departments—or a requirement that all citizens take an oath they will do nothing unjust, unethical, or unpatriotic.[51]

Perhaps the most widely publicized instance occurred in California where a book was written on "The Year of the Oath."[52] The California constitution prescribes an oath form for all public officials, and expressly provides that no other oath may be required for any office or public trust. Yet the University of California Regents required faculty members not only to execute the constitutionally prescribed oath, but also to add a statement by letter denying membership in the Communist Party or any similar organization. After prolonged controversy, the California courts ruled this added requirement unconstitutional. The court agreed that loyalty to government and its free democratic institutions is a first requisite for the exercise of the teaching function, but it felt that any loyalty test narrower than the constitutional oath might reduce the University to ". . . an organ for the propagation of the ephemeral political, religious, social and economic philosophies, whatever they may be, of the majority of the Board of Regents at that moment."[53]

Herein lies the nub of the issue: Are the organizations listed as "subversive" (a) detrimental to the American nation, or (b) detrimental only to certain powerful groups within our nation? Do

---

[51] Alan Barth, "The Loyalty of Free Men," *American Association of University Professors Bulletin* 37: 5-16, Spring 1951. By permission. See also Barth's book, *The Loyalty of Free Men*, New York: Viking and Mentor, 1951; and Francis Biddle, *The Fear of Freedom*, New York: Doubleday, 1951, p. 171.

[52] George R. Stewart and others, *The Year of the Oath*, New York: Doubleday, 1950.

[53] *Tolman et al. v. Underhill et al.*, 229 P (2nd) 447 (1951). Other court cases are listed by Barrett A. Hess, "Teacher's Loyalty Oaths in the Courts," *American School Board Journal* 127: 31-32, November 1953. See also William O. Penrose, "Let's Examine Teacher Loyalty Oaths," *School Executive* 73: 46-49, November 1953; E. Edmund Reutter, Jr., "Another Look at Teacher Loyalty Oaths," *Educational Leadership* 9: 193-195, December 1951; Nathaniel Wehl, *Treason: The Story of Disloyalty and Betrayal in American History*, Washington, D. C.: Public Affairs Press, 1950; Elmer Davis, review of Wehl's book, *Saturday Review* 33: 8 f, April 1, 1950; Robert E. Summers, ed., *Freedom and Loyalty in Our Colleges*, New York: Wilson, 1954 (pp. 106-121, "The Loyalty Oath Battle").

oaths restrict and weaken the real secret weapon of democracy—the formation of policy through open controversy and debate? If they do, they restrict and weaken our free society. If they do not, every American teacher should welcome the opportunity to dedicate himself, after the manner of Thomas Jefferson: "I have sworn upon the altar of God eternal hostility against every form of tyranny over the mind of man." [54]

Section D: Questions and Readings for Study and Discussion

1.14. INTRODUCTION

As a general procedure for reviewing each chapter, the following plan may be helpful: Let each reader select any sentence or paragraph with which he finds himself very much in agreement (or disagreement). Let the reader then state the reasons for his agreement (or disagreement), either verbally or in the form of a short essay. Follow by class discussion.

To maintain a reasonable degree of unity, the editor found it necessary to extract only those portions of books or articles which seemed relevant to the issue raised in the chapter. Readers are therefore encouraged to consult the full book or article from which each selection in this anthology was taken.

But review is not enough. The contrasting selections should raise more questions than they answer. To stimulate further reading and discussion, each chapter is followed by five or ten questions for study and discussion, with suggested readings. Where a minimum of collateral reading is to be done, the asterisks indicate those references which the editor happens to prefer. It is hoped that

[54] Thomas Jefferson, Letter to Benjamin Rush, Sept. 23, 1800.

this combination of questions and readings may serve as an annotated bibliography to guide the student in areas in which he is interested.

Most of the questions and readings in Chapter 1 deal with broad problems concerning democracy and civil liberties. Questions and readings more specifically related to education will be found in later chapters.

1.15. The Meaning of Democracy

List some characteristic features of "democracy" and "the American Way of Life."

* Bohlman, Edna McCaull, "Democracy and Its Competitors" (Pamphlet), Columbus, Ohio: Merrill (American Education Press), 1952. (For secondary schools.)

Bowles, Chester A., "The Five Liberties of True Democracy," *New York Times Magazine,* p. 13 f, May 28, 1950.

* Merriam, Charles E., *The New Democracy and the New Despotism,* New York: McGraw-Hill, 1939 (Part I).

Mill, John Stuart, *On Liberty* and *Considerations on Representative Government* (McCallum, R. B., ed.), Oxford: Blackwell, 1946.

* Riker, William H., *Democracy in the United States,* New York: Macmillan, 1953 (Chapter 1, Appendix I).

Smith, T. V., and Lindeman, Eduard C., *The Democratic Way of Life,* rev. ed., New York: New American Library (Mentor #59), 1951.

Wit, Daniel, *Comparative Political Institutions,* New York: Holt, 1953 (Chapter 4).

1.16. Similarity of Liberalism and Conservatism;
of Fascism and Communism

Which of the following two diagrams provides the best analogy to show the relation of Liberalism to Communism? of Conservatism to Fascism? Discuss.

(A)	Extreme Left	Left	Right	Extreme Right
	Communist	Liberal	Conservative	Fascist

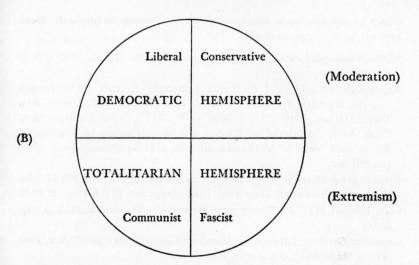

(B)

Baldwin, Leland Dewitt, *Best Hope of Earth,* Pittsburgh, Pa.: University of Pittsburgh Press, 1948 (pp. 23-27).

* Cohen, Morris R., *The Faith of a Liberal,* New York: Holt, 1946 (pp. 449-464).

* Kirk, Russell A., *The Conservative Mind: From Burke to Santayana,* Chicago: Regnery, 1953 (Chapters 1 and 13). (Reviewed by Francis Biddle, *New Republic* 129: 17-19, Aug. 24, 1953).

Oakeshott, Michael, ed., *The Social and Political Doctrines of Contemporary Europe,* London: Cambridge University Press, 1941 (Selected primary source materials on Democracy, Catholicism, Communism, Fascism and National Socialism).

Philbrick, Herbert, "Sixteen Differences Between Liberalism and Communism," an editorial-interview, *Christian Science Monitor,* Feb. 9, 1952; reprinted in *Congressional Record,* Feb. 11, 1952, Vol. 98, Part 8, Appendix, p. A770.

* Schlesinger, Arthur M., Jr., *The Vital Center,* New York: Houghton, 1949 (p. 145 f).

Weldon, Thomas D., *States and Morals,* New York: McGraw-Hill, 1947 (pp. 32-33).

1.17. Other Misunderstood Ideas and Movements

What is meant by each of the following phrases: "Christian democracy"? "Collectivism"? "Socialism"? "The social welfare state"? Are persons who advocate such doctrines necessarily Communist-inspired? Members of "front" organizations?

*Allen, Frederick Lewis, *The Big Change,* New York: Harper, 1952 (Chapter 3).

Amsterdam Assembly (of Protestant Churches) Reports, "The Church and the Disorder of Society" in *Man's Disorder and God's Design,* New York: Harper, 1949 (III: 197-205 or V: 74-82) (also London: SCM Press, 1948); reprinted in *Western Political Heritage* by William Y. Elliott and Neal A. McDonald, eds., New York: Prentice-Hall, 1949, pp. 981-985.

Byrd, Senator Harry F. *versus* Douglas, Senator Paul H., "Are We Headed Toward Collectivism?" *New York Times Magazine,* p. 7 f, Dec. 18, 1949.

Carr, Edward H., *The New Society,* New York: Macmillan, 1951 (Chapter 6).

Crowther, Geoffrey, "Must Capitalism and Communism Clash?" *New York Times Magazine,* p. 5 f, Aug. 6, 1944.

Dunne, George H., "Why Christian Democrats and Socialists Should Get Along," *Commonweal* 43: 134-139; 236-238; 307-308; Nov. 23, 1945; Dec. 14, 1945; and Jan. 4, 1946.

Flynn, John T., "Twenty-Four Steps to Communism," *American Mercury* 77: 3-6, December 1953.

Haber, William, and Cohen, Wilbur J., eds., *Readings in Social Security,* New York: Prentice-Hall, 1948 (Chapters 1 and 2).

Hayek, Friedrich von, *The Road to Serfdom,* Chicago: University of Chicago Press, 1944 (Chapter 2, "The Great Utopia").

* Laski, Harold, "It's Socialism, Not Communism," *New York Times Magazine,* p. 9 f, Aug. 26, 1945.

Lilienthal, David E., *This I Do Believe,* New York: Harper, 1949 (pp. 20-21).

Lindsay, A. D., *The Modern Democratic State,* London: Oxford University Press, 1943 (p. 183 f).

Manly, Chesly, "The Twenty-Year Revolution," *American Mercury* 78: 146-156, July 1954 (Summary of book by same title, with reactionary viewpoint).

Matthews, J. B., "An Anti-Communist's Guide to Action," *American Mercury* 78: 21-28, May 1954. (This article lists 50 books of the past decade which generally defend "McCarthyism" and claim to point to many so-called "Christian" and "social welfare" groups which are Communist-inspired.)

National Council of [Protestant] Churches, "Norms for Guidance: A Declaration of Christian Principles and Their Relation to Social and Economic life," *New York Times,* Sept. 16, 1954, p. 1, 26.

Peck, W. G., *The Social Implications of the Oxford Movement,* New York: Scribner's, 1933 (p. 276 f).

Pope Leo XIII, Encyclical, *Rerum Novarum,* "On the Condition of the Working Classes," May 15, 1891.

Pope Pius XI, Encyclical, *Quadragesimo Anno,* "On the Reconstruction of the Social Order," May 15, 1931.

Pope Pius XII, Christmas Radio Broadcasts, reprinted in *Vital Speeches* 19: 209-214, Jan. 15, 1953; 20: 196-200, Jan. 15, 1954.

Poynter, J. W., *The Popes and Social Problems,* London: Oxford, 1948 (Brief summaries of the above two encyclicals, and others.)

1.18. The Paradox of Freedom

It is sometimes said that liberty, if carried to excess, leads to its own destruction; for it then permits the enemies of liberty to gain power. The great "paradox of freedom" is that complete absence of restraint may lead to the greatest of all restraint, for it may permit the bully to enslave the meek, and allow the intolerant to destroy both the tolerant and tolerance itself.

Should democratic moderation include tolerance of ideas and organizations which do not believe in liberty? Can a reasonably clearcut distinction be made between "conspiracy" and "heresy"? between "conspiring to overthrow the government" and "trying to overthrow the party in power"?

American Bar Association, "Brief on Communism" (Pamphlet), South Bend, Ind.: Ave Maria Press, University of Notre Dame, 1953.

Coker, Francis W., "Some Present-Day Critics of Liberalism," *American Political Science Review* 47: 1-27, March 1953.

Hawkins, Carroll, "Communism: Challenge to Americans" (Pamphlet), East Lansing, Michigan: Governmental Research Bureau, Michigan State College, 1953 (bibliography).

* Hook, Sidney, *Heresy, Yes—Conspiracy, No!,* New York: Day, 1953 (Chapters 1 and 12).

Kintner, William R., *The Front is Everywhere,* Norman, Okla.: University of Oklahoma Press, 1950 (Chapters 3 and 14).

Meiklejohn, Alexander, "Freedom and the People," *Nation* 177: 500-503, Dec. 12, 1953.

Popper, Karl R., *The Open Society and Its Enemies,* Princeton, N. J.: Princeton University Press, 1950 (pp. 348-350; 546-547) (London: Routledge, 1945, I: 265-266, II: 160-162).

Salvadori, Massimo, *The Rise of Modern Communism,* New York: Holt, 1952. (Pages 92-95 summarize the Communist ideology.)

* Spitz, David, *Patterns of Anti-Democratic Thought,* New York: Macmillan, 1949 (especially Chapter 3).

1.19. "Temporary" Suppression of Liberties

If we suppress liberty now in order to make freedom secure until some future time when international tensions may have subsided, is there a likelihood that we shall have gradually acquired habits of submissiveness, types of leadership, and methods of thought-control completely alien to the democracy which we seek to preserve?

(Note that questions 1.18 and 1.19 represent two different ways of approaching the same problem. Does the manner in which a question is formulated tend to determine the kind of answer likely to be reached?)

Biddle, Francis, *The Fear of Freedom,* New York: Doubleday, 1951 (pp. 182-196).

Brubacher, John S., "Loyalty to Freedom," *School and Society* 70: 369-373, Dec. 10, 1949.

* Commager, Henry Steele, ed., *Living Ideas in America,* New York: Harper, 1951. (Read especially Chapter 5, "Democracy, or Majority Rule and Minority Rights," and Chapter 8, "Liberty and Order.")

* Fleming, D. H., "Are We Moving Toward Fascism?" *Journal of Politics* 16: 39-75, February 1954.

Hallowell, John H., "The Meaning of Majority Rule," *Commonweal* 56: 167-169, May 23, 1952.

Lipp, Solomon, "A 'Categorical Imperative' for Democratic Educators," *Harvard Educational Review* 24: 118-121, Spring 1954.

Perry, Ralph Barton, "Academic Freedom," *Harvard Educational Review* 23: 71-76, Spring 1953.

* Sears, Laurence, "Security and Liberty," *American Scholar* 20: 137-149, April 1951.

* Woody, Thomas, "Affirmation *versus* Negation in American Education," *School and Society* 79: 33-39, Feb. 6, 1954.

1.20. Other Selected References, Pro and Con

Below is a selected bibliography of books, pamphlets and magazine articles presenting pros and cons on the general subject of this chapter. They are grouped in *pairs,* and if a reading assignment is made, students should read *both.* If your library does not have some of the books or articles listed, you may pair the *upper* of one group against the *lower* of another. At the teacher's discretion, other pairs may be substituted, preferably current ones.

Alexander, Ruth, "A Formula for Freedom: Attack Subversives Wherever Found," *Vital Speeches* 20: 150-153, Dec. 15, 1953.

Fosdick, Raymond B., "We Must Not Be Afraid of Change," *New York Times Magazine,* p. 7 f, April 3, 1949; reprinted as Chapter 3 of R. B. Fosdick, *Within Our Power,* New York: Longmans, 1952.

Bendiner, Robert, "Has Anti-Communism Wrecked Our Liberties?" *Commentary* 12: 10-16, July 1951.

Siegel, Kalman, *"New York Times* Survey of Major U.S. Colleges Shows Curb on Free Inquiry," *New York Times,* May 10, 1951, pp. 1, 26; May 11, 1951, p. 26, 29, 49.

Buckley, William F., "Freedom to Agree," *American Mercury* 76: 101-107, June 1953 (Restatement of a portion of his book *God and Man at Yale,* Chicago: Regnery, 1951).

Hutchins, Robert M., "What Price Freedom?" *American Association of University Professors Bulletin* 35: 211-215, Summer 1949; same under the title "The American Way of Life," *School and Society* 70: 129-131, Aug. 27, 1949; also published in pamphlet form by the American Civil Liberties Union, New York.

Buckley, William F., and Bozell, L. Brent, *McCarthy and His Enemies,* Chicago: Regnery, 1954.

Wechsler, James, *Age of Suspicion,* New York: Random House, 1953 (Part III).

Budenz, Louis, *Men Without Faces,* New York: Harper, 1950.

McWilliams, Carey, *Witch Hunt: The Revival of Heresy,* Boston: Little, 1950.

Burnham, James, *The Web of Subversion: Underground Network in the United States Government,* New York: Day, 1954.

Commager, Henry Steele, *Freedom, Loyalty, Dissent,* New York: Oxford, 1954.

California Senate Investigating Committee on Education, Ninth Report, "Are Loyalty Oaths Effective?" (Pamphlet), Regular Session, 1951, Senate, Sacramento, Calif., 1952.

Woody, Thomas, "Why Raise an Oath-Umbrella?" *School and Society* 74: 33-38, July 21, 1951.

Chambers, Whittaker, *Witness,* New York: Random House, 1952 (pp. 195-197, 451-525, 768-799).

Hicks, Granville, *Where We Came Out,* New York: Viking, 1954 (Chapter 12). (This book might also be paired against an extremely liberal one. See Chapter 11, "The Liberals Who Haven't Learned.")

Jackson, Robert H., "Communists in America," *New York Times Magazine,* p. 12 f, May 21, 1950; also in *Harper's* 201: 21-27, September 1950.

Douglas, William O., "The Black Silence of Fear," *New York Times Magazine,* p. 7 f, Jan. 13, 1952.

Jenner Committee Report, Summary, "How Communists Try to Influence American Teachers," *U.S. News* 35: 75-87, July 31, 1953.

Chase, Stuart, *Power of Words,* New York: Harcourt, 1954 (Chapter 21, "Guilt by Association").

Kristol, Irving, "Civil Liberties, 1952—A Study in Confusion," *Commentary* 13: 228-236, March 1952.

Kirchwey, Freda, and others, "How Free is Free?" *Nation* 174: 615-670, June 28, 1952.

Matthews, J. B., "Communism and the Colleges," *American Mercury* 76: 111-144, May 1953.

Davis, Jerome, *Character Assassination,* New York: Philosophical Library, 1950 (Chapter 10, "Who is Un-American?").

1.21. Selected General References

The above pairs of books and magazine articles represent opposing viewpoints. Below are some books which most reviewers consider scholarly and objective. Read at least one of them (or a portion thereof), and try to judge whether it seems to be fair and impartial. Can a reader make such a judgment if he has not previously heard or read conflicting views and prejudices on the subject?

Bontecou, Eleanor, *The Federal Loyalty-Security Program*, Ithaca, N.Y.: Cornell University Press, 1953. (This is one of seven factual studies on various aspects of civil liberties, under the general editorship of Professor Robert E. Cushman.)

Cushman, Robert E., "American Civil Liberties in Mid-Twentieth Century," in "Civil Rights in America," edited by Robert K. Carr, *Annals of the American Academy of Political and Social Science*, Volume 275 (entire issue), May 1951.

* Emerson, Thomas I., and Haber, David, eds., *Political and Civil Rights in the United States*, Buffalo, N.Y.: Dennis, 1952 (legal).

* Konvitz, Milton R., ed., (Robert E. Cushman, general editor), *Bill of Rights Reader*, Ithaca, N. Y.: Cornell University Press., 1954.

Palmer, Edward E., ed., *The Communist Problem in America: A Book of Readings*, New York: Cromwell, 1951.

Pritchett, C. Herman, *Civil Liberties and the Vinson Court*, Chicago: University of Chicago Press, 1954.

Summers, Robert E., ed., *Freedom and Loyalty in Our Colleges*, New York: Wilson, 1954.

Wahlke, John C., ed., *Loyalty in a Democratic State (Problems in American Civilization* series), New York: Heath, 1952.

1.22. A Question for Educators:
How Teach Controversial Issues?

What are the best methods of handling controversial issues in the social studies?

Brickman, W. W., "Criticism and Defense of American Education," *School and Society* 77: 390-395, June 20, 1953; "Attack and Counterattack in American Education," *ibid.* 74: 262-269, Oct. 27, 1951; and "Communism and American Education," *ibid.* 71: 180-188, March 25, 1950. (Annotated bibliographies.)

* Brubacher, John S., "Education in an Era of Revolution," *Educational Forum* 15: 271-281, March 1951.

* Butts, J. Freeman, and Cremin, Laurence A., *A History of Education in American Culture*, New York: Holt, 1953. (Pages 542-546), "The Social Role of the Educational Program," summarize five approaches to the teaching of controversial issues. Bibliography.)

Crary, Ryland W., and Steibel, Gerald L., "How to Teach About Communism," Freedom Pamphlet, New York, Anti-Defamation League of B'Nai-B'Rith, 1951. (Bibliography.)

Kehoe, R. E., and Stephenson, O. W., "Free Inquiry into Controversial Issues," *Clearing House* 25: 110-111, October 1950.

McGrath, Earl J., "Academic Freedom and Academic Responsibility," *School and Society* 79: 65-67, March 6, 1954; reply, H. B. Davis, *ibid.* 79: 188-189, June 12, 1954.

* Scott, C. Winfield, and Hill, Clyde M., *Public Education Under Criticism*, New York: Prentice-Hall, 1954 (especially Chapters 6 and 10).

2. FREEDOM FOR LEARNERS

Section A: The Case for Censorship

2.1. INTRODUCTION

By the term *censorship* we mean restraint applied by individuals or institutions (such as government or church) against speech, the press and other forms of expression, with a view to suppressing certain ideas. The case for censorship is based on a defense of values which conflict with freedom of expression. Few who advocate censorship deny openly the values of individual freedom. Many would even agree with Mr. Justice Black in esteeming freedom of expression the central value of our democratic society:

> I view the guarantees of the First Amendment as the foundation upon which our governmental structure rests and without which it could not continue to endure as conceived and planned. Freedom to speak and write about public questions is as important to the life of our government as is the heart to the human body. In fact, this privilege is the heart of our government. If that heart be weakened, the result is debilitation; if it be stifled, the result is death.[1]

The unity of a free society is based on the faith that friendship, reason and justice may draw men together when there is a minimum of external impositions and a maximum of personal liberties. Jefferson believed that ". . . error of opinion may be tolerated

---

[1] Hugo L. Black, *Milk Drivers Union v. Meadowmoor Dairies,* 312 U.S. 287, 301-302, (1941).

where reason is left free to combat it." [2] Emerson said, "Whoso would be a man, must be a nonconformist. . . . Nothing is at last sacred but the integrity of your own mind." [3] Innumerable other statements in the same vein could be cited.

But an examination of specific cases reveals that freedom is not an "absolute" (i.e., a goal to be pursued without any limitations whatsoever). For example, freedom of speech and press does not justify libel or abusive language:

> . . . the right of free speech is not absolute at all times and under all circumstances. There are certain well-defined and narrowly limited classes of speech, the prevention and punishment of which have never been thought to raise any Constitutional problem. These include the lewd and obscene, the profane, the libelous, and the insulting or "fighting" words—those which by their very utterance inflict injury or tend to incite an immediate breach of the peace. It has been well observed that such utterances are no essential part of any exposition of ideas, and are of such slight social value as a step to truth that any benefit that may be derived from them is clearly outweighed by the social interest in order and morality. "Resort to epithets or personal abuse is not in any proper sense communication of information or opinion safeguarded by the Constitution, and its punishment as a criminal act would raise no question under that instrument." [4]

Likewise, freedom of assembly may be restricted if its abuse leads to riots or other serious disturbances of peace and order:

> It is one thing to say that the police cannot be used as an instrument for the suppression of unpopular views, and another to say that, when . . . the speaker passes the bounds of argument or persuasion and undertakes incitement to riot, they are powerless to prevent a breach of peace. [5]

---

[2] Thomas Jefferson, *First Inaugural* (1801).

[3] Ralph Waldo Emerson, *Self-Reliance* (1841).

[4] *Chaplinsky v. New Hampshire,* 315 U.S. 568 at 571-572 (1942). The quotation is from *Cantwell v. Connecticut,* 310 U.S. 296 at 309-310 (1940).

[5] *Feiner v. New York,* 340 U.S. 315 (1951). Compare *Terminiello v. Chicago,* 337 U.S. 1 (1949); *Douglas v. Jeannette,* 319 U.S. 157 (1943).

Again, freedom of religion is not an absolute. In a judgment concerning polygamy, or bigamy, the U. S. Supreme Court declared:

> It was never intended or supposed that the (First) Amendment could be invoked as a protection against legislation for the punishment of acts inimical to the peace, good order and morals of society. . . . Laws are made for the government of actions, and while they cannot interfere with mere religious beliefs and opinions, they may with practices. Suppose one believed that human sacrifices were a necessary part of religious worship, would it be seriously contended that the civil government under which he lived could not interfere to prevent a sacrifice? . . . To permit this would be to make the professed doctrines of religious belief superior to the law of the land, and in effect to permit every citizen to become a law unto himself. Government could exist only in name under such circumstances.[6]

Peace and order, domestic tranquility and national security are so vital that individual actions impairing the realization of these values may on occasion be restrained. If abusive language leads to a riot, it may be curtailed. But the mere *advocacy* of unpopular ideas—even treasonous ideas—may be allowed so long as such advocacy does not seem to threaten the stability of our society. Here we should make a distinction between (a) the right to think, and (b) the right to act. The tradition of free thought in democratic society insists that there must be no attempt at control over the individual's ideas, no matter how dangerous they may seem. Overt actions, however, may be curbed if they seriously menace public welfare. Laws may not dictate beliefs: but laws may govern actions. Between thought (completely free) and action (subject to restriction) lie the doubtful areas of speech, press, religion and assembly with which this chapter is concerned.

Concerning freedom for learners, i.e., freedom for citizens, there are two competing schools of thought. One school insists that our democratic faith is based on a foundation that is both positive and absolute, namely, faith in the primacy of the individual, belief in the inalienable rights of man; and that anything which weakens or

---

[6] *Davis v. Beason*, 133 U.S. 333 at 342-344 (1890).

threatens this basic pillar of our society weakens or threatens democracy itself. The other school of thought emphasizes democracy as a method rather than as an ideal. It affirms that, whereas extreme individualism may lead to anarchy and extreme group pressures may lead to totalitarianism, democracy provides a system of checks and balances by which our society is able to steer a happy middle course between these two extremes. As spokesmen for these competing schools of thought we cite Hugo L. Black and Ralph Henry Gabriel:

(1) Governments need and have ample power to punish treasonable acts. But it does not follow that they must have a further power to punish thought and speech as distinguished from acts. Our own free society should never forget that laws which stigmatize and penalize the thought and speech of the unorthodox have a way of reaching, ensnaring and silencing many more people than at first intended. We must have freedom of speech for all or we will in the long run have it for none but the cringing and the craven. And I cannot too often repeat my belief that the right to speak on matters of public concern must be wholly free or eventually be wholly lost.

It seems self-evident that all speech criticizing government rulers and challenging current beliefs may be dangerous to the status quo. With full knowledge of this danger the Framers [of the U.S. Constitution] rested the First Amendment on the premise that the slightest suppression of thought, speech, press, or public assembly is still more dangerous. This means that individuals are guaranteed an undiluted and unequivocal right to express themselves on questions of current public interest. It means that Americans discuss such questions as of right and not on sufferance of legislatures, courts or other governmental agencies. It means that courts are without power to appraise and penalize utterances upon their notion that these utterances are dangerous. In my view this uncompromising interpretation of the Bill of Rights is the one that must prevail if its freedoms are to be saved. Tyrannical totalitarian governments cannot safely allow their people to speak with complete freedom. I believe with the Framers that our free Government can.[7]—Hugo L. Black.

---

[7] Hugo L. Black, dissenting opinion, *Wieman v. Updegraff*, 344 U.S. 183, 193-194 (1952).

(2) Realistic democracy provides a middle-of-the-road solution for problems which arise from conflicts among interests or pressure groups. Its method is give-and-take. Its normal solutions are compromises. Extreme solutions are rare. . . . The American democratic faith is a system of checks and balances in the realm of ideals. It asserts the possibility of a balance between liberty and authority, between the self-expression of the free individual and the necessary coercion of the organized group. The democratic faith is, then, in essence, a philosophy of the mean.[8]—Ralph Henry Gabriel.

Because democracy is a mode of operation as well as a standard of perfection—a means as well as an end—the contrast between the above two attitudes may seem somewhat academic. As a working institution, American democracy provides for a balance of power between federal, state and local authorities, and between the legislative, executive and judicial branches of government. Were there no such restraint on authority, the contrasts between the ideal and the real would be more definite. To bring the basic issue raised by this chapter into sharper focus, compare the following two statements. Please note that those who defend censorship proclaim the sanctity of the individual as zealously as any libertarian. It is in the *means* by which this ideal is to be attained that the two schools of thought are in opposition.

(1) *The American Method of Unification by Agreement and Representation.*

. . . proclaimed the fundamental principles of democracy, namely that authority in government was vested in the people and not in the king, that authority in knowledge was founded on reason and not in sacred lore, and that authority in religion and morals was vested in the conscience of the individual and not in any pope or sacred book. These are the three fundamental propositions on which democracy is based and which are certain to overcome any patriarchal government when they are accepted. When adopted they must mean freedom of thought, speech, and action,

---

[8] Ralph Henry Gabriel, *The Course of American Democratic Thought,* New York: Ronald, 1940, p. 418.

save as such freedom is voluntarily renounced for the sake of unity.[9]—John Hopkins Denison.

(2) But the supreme teacher in the Church is the Roman Pontiff. Union of minds, therefore, requires, together with a perfect accord in the one faith, complete submission and obedience of will to the Church and to the Roman Pontiff, as to God Himself.[10]

. . . To whatever opinion a man's judgment may incline, if the matter is yet open to discussion let him keep it, provided his mental attitude is such that he is ready to yield if the Holy See should otherwise decide.[11]—Pope Leo XIII.

The selections to follow do not deal with specific examples of censorship in education, but set forth the broad principles necessary to an understanding of the entire controversy. In the first selection, Father Connell defends censorship by the Roman Catholic Church on the ground that the values for which that church stands

---

[9] Reprinted from *Emotion as the Basis of Civilization* by John Hopkins Denison, copyright 1928 by Charles Scribner's Sons; used by permission of the publishers.

[10] Pope Leo XIII, "On the Chief Duties of Christians as Citizens" (1890), Rev. John J. Wynne, S.J., ed., *The Great Encyclical Letters of Leo XIII*, New York: Benziger, 1903, p. 193.

[11] Pope Leo XIII, "Christian Democracy" (1901), *ibid.*, p. 491.

Although these contrasting quotations point up two opposing views concerning censorship, it should be recognized that in their practical application the statements need modification and qualification. Thus, the present Pope declared in 1944: "By reason of the extent and nature of the sacrifices demanded of all citizens, in our time when the activity of the State is so vast and decisive, the democratic form of government seems to many as a natural postulate imposed by reason itself. Yet the cry 'more and better democracy' is a demand which can have no other meaning than to place the citizen more and more in a condition that permits him to have his own opinion, to express it and make it effective in a manner compatible with the common good."—Pope Pius XII, *"Il sesto Natale,"* Dec. 24, 1944, cited by Rev. Gustave Weigel, S.J., "The Church and the Democratic State," *Thought: Fordham University Quarterly* 27: 165-184, Summer 1952, p. 180.

Further treatment of this problem may be found in John A. Ryan and Francis J. Boland, *Catholic Principles of Politics*, New York: Macmillan, 1940, p. 319; Rev. John A. Ryan, "The Protesting Church," *Catholic World* 136: 458-460, January 1933; James Hastings Nichols, *Democracy and the Churches*, Philadelphia: Westminster Press, 1949, p. 194; Edgar L. Allen, *Existentialism from Within*, New York: Macmillan, 1953, pp. 129-133; "Stirrings at the Vatican," *Time* 64: 59, Nov. 15, 1954.

are often weakened or lost for Catholics (and for others) who read certain types of literature.

The second selection by Margaret Culkin Banning deals with a somewhat related conflict of values, though on a more popular level, as it applies to comic books.

The final selection by Professors McClure and Lockhart restates the basic conflict of Chapter 1—freedom versus security—and weighs the traditions built around the First Amendment as against the "clear and present danger" of conspiracy, sedition, and the destruction of our democratic society.

2.2. CENSORSHIP AND THE PROHIBITION OF BOOKS IN THE CATHOLIC CHURCH [12]
Francis J. Connell, C.SS.R.

The Catholic Church approaches the problem of man's right to knowledge with the realization that in settling concrete problems relative to human freedom two fundamental principles must be observed: First, liberty is a most precious possession, based on the dignity of every human person as a creature of God destined to an everlasting existence; hence it must be respected and protected. Second, for the good of society as well as for the welfare of individuals, personal liberty must be curtailed in certain circumstances. This is particularly true when the limitation of liberty is required as a means of protecting individuals from sin or moral evil, which would constitute an impediment to the attainment of their final goal, eternal happiness with God. In determining the extent of man's rights in particular cases a just and reasonable mean must be observed between these two principles. If the first is overemphasized, liberty degenerates into license. If the second is stressed too much, authority becomes tyranny and the way is opened to totalitarianism.

[12] Rev. Francis J. Connell, C.SS.R., "Censorship and the Prohibition of Books in the Catholic Church Law," 54 *Columbia Law Review* 699-709, May 1954. By permission.

Father Connell is Dean of the School of Sacred Theology, The Catholic University of America.

These two principles must be properly coordinated in one of the problems which the Church treats in detailed legislation—the problem of the right to read certain books and other forms of published literature, a problem with a direct bearing on the right to knowledge and its free use. . . .

The notion that people should be allowed to read everything they wish is quite common in our land, for we are a freedom-loving people, resenting any restriction of our freedom. How often do we hear the statement that reading will never cause the reader any harm! An example of this is a statement made by Verner W. Clapp, Acting Librarian of Congress:

> The notion that mankind is corrupted by books is, I believe, a notion held by those whose own reading has been largely of that enforced and unselective kind which the mass media provide. Books are corruptive only to those who seek to be corrupted; but they are already corrupt.[13]

Despite the dogmatic assurance with which this statement is made, the fact is that people can be influenced to evil as well as to good by what they read. And while we justly uphold the ideals of freedom we must admit that freedom has its limitations. Catholics believe that the laws of their Church in regard to censorship and the prohibition of books represent a reasonable limitation of their freedom. And before passing an unfavorable judgment on the Church's legislation on this matter, one should examine the principles on which the Church bases its policy in restricting the right to read for those who are subject to the authority of the Church.

The Catholic Church believes that the chief purpose of man's earthly life is to prepare for an eternal life after death. Happiness in this everlasting existence is merited by living in this world a life in conformity with the commands of God; and it is supremely important to live this life in such a manner as to attain this goal. Whatever advantages may accrue through the exercise of personal freedom, they can have no real value if they impede or imperil the attainment of one's eternal destiny. Hence it is not an evil but a good when those in authority, whether parents, civil rulers or ecclesiastical authorities, regulate the exercise of freedom by those

---

[13] *Washington Sunday Star,* Dec. 6, 1953.

subject to their jurisdiction so as to aid them to observe God's law and to reach the eternal happiness which the Creator has appointed to every human being.

Everyone admits that it is perfectly reasonable to limit the freedom of individuals when the purpose of such limitations is to prevent them from doing physical harm to themselves or to others. If I refuse to give a person a gun with which he is likely to shoot himself or others I am indeed limiting his freedom, but no reasonable person will accuse me of doing wrong. Instead of hampering his proper use of freedom, I am preventing him from abusing it. The Catholic Church applies this same principle to the unrestricted right to read. There are books which would cause spiritual and moral harm to many persons if they were permitted to read them indiscriminately; hence the Church forbids the reading of such books.

Naturally it will be asked by what authority the Church claims the right to do this. The Church replies that it has received from God Himself the right to teach officially the truths of religion and morality and the right to legislate on matters pertinent to the spiritual welfare of those subject to its jurisdiction. . . .

Anyone who admits the existence of an intelligent and all-powerful Deity must grant that if He wills, He can authorize an organization on earth to represent Him in proposing to mankind the doctrines of religion and the principles of morality. For such a person, therefore, the vital question is whether or not the Almighty has acted thus in respect to the Catholic Church. . . .

As to the matter of religious belief, the Catholic Church is convinced that its duty of preserving in its members the faith in the truths which God has communicated to men calls for legislation against books that might endanger that faith. The Church is not motivated by a fear that the arguments brought against its teachings are sufficiently cogent in themselves to discredit Catholic teaching. Rather, the Church recognizes that many Catholics do not possess sufficient technical knowledge of Catholic doctrine or of history to meet all the arguments that can be brought against Catholic belief; hence the Church legislates against books with such a purpose. . . .

2.3. FILTH ON THE NEWSSTANDS[14]

Margaret Culkin Banning

• • • •

We have in this country some of the most beautiful, thoughtful, amusing and informative magazines in the world. Among the pocket books on the newsstands are some of the best reading values ever offered: Bibles, atlases and geographies, books on child care, reprints of the great novels and short stories.

But crowding all these enjoyable and useful magazines and books are publications which can have no possible effect except to misinform the reader, debase his thoughts and degrade his emotions. The publishers of such material will stop at nothing to catch the eye. . . .

By actual count, the trash and smut on the stands now have the advantage of numbers. More than 1200 magazines, including comics, are being regularly distributed among retailers who handle periodicals. Of these, only 210 or so are magazines of healthy interest, acceptable to discriminating readers. The rest are crime and love comics of a low type, fly-by-nights which usually fold after a few issues, and the salacious girly magazines.

In a New York town of 20,000, magazines of this type sold 1719 copies in a single month, or nearly one copy for every ten men, women and children in the town. In a Massachusetts city of 163,000 the same group of sexy magazines sold 13,266 copies on the average every month, which is about the same proportion of readership.

The unpleasant and shocking truth is that our newsstands are beginning to reflect an acceptance of and growing concentration on lewdness. . . .

Is censorship the answer? Many indignant Americans appear to have reached that conclusion.

More than fifty American cities have recently passed new ordinances, with real teeth in them, prohibiting obscene publications on their local newsstands. St. Cloud, Minn., not only passed such

---

[14] Margaret Culkin Banning, "Filth on the Newsstands," *Reader's Digest* 61: 115-119, Oct. 1952. By permission.

an ordinance but created a board of review to pass on such material. In Trenton, N. J., on March 20, 1952, there was a city-wide police raid on all newsstands, and by nightfall what was called "a ton of smut" was stacked in police headquarters. In Ottumwa, Iowa, more than 3000 magazines were removed from the racks at the request of the local Ministerial Association. In Chicago, in Winona, Minn., and in Rhinelander, Wis., organized groups are issuing lists of "approved" and "disapproved" periodicals and pocket books to dealers, with the request—which approximates a demand—that offending titles be taken off sale.

A large portion of the public, however, objects to being told what it can read, whether the dictum comes from Protestants, Catholics, librarians, a mayor's committee or a committee of Congress. There will always be disputes as to the merits of books and other publications, suspicion of favoritism, accusations of proselytizing. There is no way to make political censorship more than the restrictive judgment of individuals whose predilections, prejudices and competence are bound to be challenged. More than is gained by political censorship in a community might easily be lost by the growth of intolerance or bitterness.

In American communities which are at present under censorship such books have been put on disapproved lists as James Michener's *Tales of the South Pacific,* Lillian Smith's *Strange Fruit,* and the novels of de Maupassant, John Steinbeck and Nobel Prize-winner William Faulkner—all of which were issued in cheap form so that people who could not afford cloth-bound books might read the works of these famous authors. I am reliably informed that Jane Austen's *Pride and Prejudice* was included on one master list of disapproved books because the word "adultery" appeared in it.

Nonetheless, many good citizens, though they regret censorship, fearing its effect on a free press, do not believe that constitutional protection should be thrown around obvious filth. If they get a cleanup of newsstands without censorship, they will be satisfied. Otherwise, censorship is on its way.

There are two ways to avoid it. The first is for the publishers and distributors to withhold objectionable material at the source. Such self-discipline has worked well for motion pictures, radio and television, and it could be made to work for magazines. The second is for the public deliberately and consciously to destroy the market for such stuff. To do so, the private citizen need not and must not impetuously seek to usurp police, postal or judicial functions. He can make his protests against printed obscenity felt through his business and professional clubs, his parent-teacher group, the lay association of his church. At the ballot box he can elect those who will prosecute degeneracy and carry out present laws which need to be better enforced. Lists and book-burning only drive lewdness underground.

At best, local censorship will always be an uneasy and unsatisfactory solution, and a constant bone of contention. This country will not tolerate thought control. But neither will it tolerate, as begins to be evident in every section of the land, pollution of its thought supply. It is not necessary to make new laws. All that is needed is to enforce what laws we have, to assert what we believe and to maintain what we have achieved in human dignity and decency.

2.4. BALANCING OF INTERESTS: FREEDOM OF EXPRESSION VERSUS CLEAR AND PRESENT DANGER [15]

William B. Lockhart and Robert C. McClure

Freedom of expression guaranteed by the First and Fourteenth Amendments is not absolute, for despite its great importance in a democratic society, it must on occasion be subordinated to other interests of high value. In the past three decades the Supreme Court has repeatedly had to determine the extent to which freedom of expression must give way to other interests. Gradually the Court has evolved an approach to these problems that often makes use of a deceptively simple phrase—"clear and present danger"—as the framework for important policy judgments. For the purpose of this article, it is necessary to emphasize the factors that enter into those judgments.[16]

---

[15] William B. Lockhart and Robert C. McClure, "Literature, the Law of Obscenity, and the Constitution," 38 *Minnesota Law Review* 295: 295-422, 363-368, March 1954. By permission. Most footnotes omitted here. This article will be expanded into book form and published by the University of Minnesota Press in 1956. Professors Lockhart and McClure teach at the law school of the University of Minnesota.

While the phrase "clear and present danger" had its origin in an opinion by Mr. Justice Holmes for a unanimous court in 1919, it did not become a tool used by a majority of the Court for resolving freedom of expression issues until 1940. Meanwhile it was kept alive by dissenting and concurring opinions of Justices Holmes and Brandeis. Beginning with *Thornhill v. Alabama* in 1940, it frequently though not invariably came to be used by the majority of the Court in deciding freedom of expression issues. It is significant that with one exception since 1940 the Supreme Court has always used the "clear and present danger" test in determining the validity of governmental regulation interfering with the *content* of an utterance, as distinct from the *manner* or *means* of its expression.[17] That exception occurred in the majority opinion in the *Beauharnais* group libel case, where Mr. Justice Frankfurter pushed the test aside saying it was "unnecessary . . . to consider the issues behind the phrase 'clear and present danger' " because libelous utterances are not "within the area of constitutionally protected speech." . . .

The first clear statement of the issues behind the phrase was made in 1927 in a separate concurring opinion by Mr. Justice Brandeis, in which Mr. Justice Holmes joined. In approving a conviction under a criminal syndicalism act in *Whitney v. California*,[18] Mr. Justice Brandeis stressed the values and necessities of freedom

---

[16] To trace the evolution of "clear and present danger" would be a complete article in itself. This has been well done in recent years, permitting us, for the purposes of this article, to build largely on the scholarship of others. See Antieau, " 'Clear and Present Danger'—Its Meaning and Significance," 25 *Notre Dame Law* 603 (1950) ; Corwin, "Bowing Out 'Clear and Present Danger,' " 27 *Notre Dame Law* 325 (1952) ; Gorfinkel and Mack, "*Dennis v. United States* and the Clear and Present Danger Rule," 39 *California Law Review* 475 (1951) ; Mendelson, "Clear and Present Danger—from Shenck to Dennis," 52 *Columbia Law Review* 313 (1952) ; Richardson, "Freedom of Expression and the Function of the Courts," 65 *Harvard Law Review* 1 (1951) ; (Notes) "Clear and Present Danger Re-examined," 51 *Columbia Law Review* 98 (1951) .

[17] See Note, "Clear and Present Danger Re-examined," 51 *Columbia Law Review* 98, 99-100 (1951) . *But* cf. *United Public Workers v. Mitchell,* 330 U.S. 75 (1947) , which sustained the Hatch Act depriving federal civil service employees of the right to take an active part in political campaigns. While no mention was made of the "clear and present danger" test, the opinions are openly an attempt to "balance the extent of the guarantees of freedom against . . . the supposed evil of political partisanship of classified employees of government." *Ibid.,* p. 96.

[18] 274 U.S. 357, 372-380 (1927) .

of expression in a democratic society and emphasized three factors essential to state interference with this fundamental freedom:

1. There must be a "clear" danger that the speech will produce a serious substantive evil that the state has power to prevent. It is not enough simply to "fear" serious injury, but there must be "reasonable grounds" to fear that serious evil will result if free speech is practiced. It is obvious in this opinion that in the thinking of Brandeis and Holmes the single word "clear" connotes a close causal relationship between the prohibited speech and the evil sought to be prevented.

2. There must be a "present" or "imminent" danger. Again, "reasonable grounds" are necessary for believing the danger to be imminent, and that it may result before there is opportunity to avert it by full discussion and the processes of education.

3. The substantive evil to be prevented by suppressing speech must be a "serious" one. Prohibition on freedom of expression is not permissible "unless the evil apprehended is relatively serious." It can never be appropriate to avert "a relatively trivial harm to society." While the meaning of the term "relatively" is not spelled out here, its most likely meaning is that the seriousness of the harm must be weighed in relation to the importance and value of the freedom of expression being interfered with, and the extent of that interference. Consistent with this interpretation is Mr. Justice Brandeis' later statement in the same opinion that one of the issues in a freedom of expression case is "whether the evil apprehended was one so substantial as to *justify* the stringent restrictions interposed by the legislature." Indeed, in an earlier dissenting opinion joined in by Mr. Justice Holmes, Mr. Justice Brandeis emphasized the "clear and present danger" test as "a rule of reason," a "question of degree."

These three factors became and remained the backbone of the "clear and present danger" test as applied by the Supreme Court beginning in 1940, though two substantial modifications were made. (1) The Court came to recognize openly the policy-making, interest-balancing nature of the judicial function in these cases, and (2) the *Dennis* case in 1951 minimized or subordinated the "present" or "imminent" factor, merging it into the "clear" or "probable danger" factor.[19] . . .

At the present time there remain three significant factors that must be considered in appraising governmental interference with freedom of expression, disregarding what may be left of the "present" or "imminent" factor. The first is the "clear" or "probable" danger factor. This necessity for a probable-causal relationship between the forbidden expression and the evil sought to be prevented has been a significant factor since 1940 in determining the validity of interferences with freedom of expression. *Dennis* made no change in this; indeed, in accepting Judge Learned Hand's reformulation of the "clear and present danger" test the plurality opinion expressly indicated that the probability or improbability of the danger was one of the relevant factors. It must be borne in mind, as so well expressed in Richardson's masterful summation of this factor, that what is required is not simply the probability that the evil will occur, but a probability that the forbidden utterance will be a substantial factor in bringing about the evil.

The second factor is the relative seriousness of the evil sought to be prevented by the interference with freedom of expression. Re-

---

[19] For a treatment of this issue see Gorfinkel and Mack, *supra*, at 492-496; Richardson, *supra*, at 8-9.

The plurality opinion, representing the views of Chief Justice Vinson, and Justices Reed, Burton, and Minton, found the meaning of the phrase "clear and present danger" "squarely presented" and accepted the Learned Hand interpretation of the phrase as follows:

"Chief Judge Learned Hand, writing for the majority below, interpreted the phrase as follows: 'In each case [courts] must ask whether the gravity of the evil, discounted by its improbability, justifies such invasion of free speech as is necessary to avoid the danger.' 183 F. 2d at 212. We adopt this statement of the rule. As articulated by Chief Judge Hand, it is as succinct and inclusive as any other we might devise at this time. It takes into consideration those factors which we deem relevant, and relates their significance. More we cannot expect from words." *Dennis v. United States*, 341 U.S. 494, 508, 510 (1951).

Separately concurring, Mr. Justice Frankfurter's long opinion indicates impatience with attempts to use the phrase "clear and present danger" as a formula, or as a "substitute for the weighing of values," and repeatedly stresses that in freedom of expression cases the problem before the Court is a "careful weighing of conflicting interests." *Ibid.*, p. 519 ff. Mr. Justice Jackson would not apply the phrase to cases of communist propaganda like the *Dennis* case, but would "save it, unmodified, as a 'rule of reason' in the kind of case for which it was devised." *Ibid.*, p. 568.

peatedly since 1940 the Court has stressed the necessity for a grave
or serious evil to justify such an interference. Neither of these factors is an absolute. Each must be considered in relation to the
other. The more serious the threatened evil, the lower the required
degree of probability. This seems clearly indicated in the *Dennis*
opinion accepting Judge Hand's reformulation of the clear and
present danger test. Presumably the converse is also true: the less
serious the threatened evil, the higher the required degree of
probability.

But these two factors must not only be weighed in relation to
each other, but in the relation to the *third* significant factor, implicitly though not expressly spelled out in the Brandeis formulation
of "clear and present danger"—the value of freedom of expression
in the context of this utterance, and the effect the challenged suppression may have on freedom of expression on this and similar
occasions. Brandeis made clear that in determining whether a danger was sufficiently "clear" or "imminent" or "serious," it is necessary to consider the importance of freedom of expression in a democratic society; this was not lost on the Court when it began using
the "clear and present danger" test in 1940. Repeatedly it weighed
the factors of "clear" or "probable" danger and the "seriousness" of
the evil against this third significant factor— the value of freedom
of expression on this subject and in this context.[20]

Whether the Court invokes "clear and present danger" or not, in
all freedom of expression cases it inevitably must grapple with
fundamental policy questions as it seeks to balance two significant
interests—the public interest in preventing the supposed evil and
the public interest in preserving freedom of expression. In each
such case the Court must decide whether the seriousness of the evil,
and the probability that the utterance under attack may cause or

---

[20] See, *e.g., Dennis v. United States,* 341 U.S. 494, 508-510 (1951); *Communications Ass'n v. Douds,* 339 U.S. 382, 397, 399-400 (1950); *Pennekamp v. Florida,*
328 U.S. 331, 346-347 (1946); *Thomas v. Collins,* 323 U.S. 516, 530-532 (1945);
Bridges v. California, 314 U.S. 252, 268-271 (1941); *Cantwell v. Connecticut,*
310 U.S. 296, 310-311 (1940); *Thornhill v. Alabama,* 310 U.S. 88, 104-105 (1940).
In others the Court has engaged in this same process of weighing the supposed
evil against the importance of freedom of expression without using "clear and
present danger" talk. See, *e.g., Breard v. Alexandria,* 341 U.S. 622, 643, 644
(1951); *United Public Workers v. Mitchell,* 330 U.S. 75, 96 (1947); *Prince v.
Massachusetts,* 321 U.S. 158, 165 (1944).

substantially contribute to that evil, are sufficiently great to justify the interference with freedom of expression in this particular case and the resulting suppression of freedom of expression in similar situations. The "clear and present danger" phrase helps to point up the factors that enter into that determination, but in the last analysis each such determination has to be a policy judgment in which all of these factors are brought into balance.[21]

Section B: The Case Against Censorship

2.5. INTRODUCTION

"Martha, methinks the whole world is queer except thou and me," said the old Quaker to his wife, "and sometimes, Martha, methinks even thou art a bit peculiar." Every person, every group, is more or less like this. We all tend to become narrow, provincial, and so set in our own patterns of belief that we cannot tolerate others. The extreme form of fanaticism or narrow-mindedness was parodied by Lord Macaulay:

> I am in the right and you are in the wrong. When you are stronger, you ought to tolerate me, for it is your duty to tolerate truth. But when I am the stronger, I shall persecute you, for it is my duty to persecute error.[22]

---

[21] Qualified commentators have repeatedly noted that whatever formula is used, the Court's function in freedom of expression cases is to balance competing interests in reaching a policy judgment. See e.g., 1 Chafee, *Government and Mass Communications* 36 (1947); Chafee, *Free Speech in the United States* 31-35 (1941); Freund, *On Understanding the Supreme Court* 27-28 (1949); Antieau, *supra*, at 639-645; Corwin, "Bowing Out 'Clear and Present Danger,'" 27 *Notre Dame Law*, 325, 359 (1952); Donnelly, "Government and Freedom of the Press," 45 *Illinois Law Review* 31, 53 (1950); Emerson and Helfeld, "Loyalty Among Government Employees," 58 *Yale Law Journal* 1, 86 (1948); Wechsler, "Symposium on Civil Liberties," 9 *American Law School Review* 881, 889 (1941).

[22] Attributed to Thomas Babington Macaulay by David Spitz in *Patterns of Anti-Democratic Thought*, New York: Macmillan, 1949, p. 283. Compare "Holy Willie's Prayer" by Robert Burns.

To see democracy in action is to see hundreds of such zealous minorities clamoring for power, each sure of its own truth and righteousness.

With so many conflicting ideas, how can we decide which shall prevail? On the one hand, society must have unity—"order is heaven's first law"—and the power to manage must ultimately rest in someone's hands. Otherwise we find ourselves like Stephen Leacock's horseman, riding not one horse but many horses—each one galloping wildly in a different direction. To prevent such disunity, democracy accepts majority rule as a working principle.

On the other hand, if the power to manage is not limited, justice will be destroyed. For this reason democracy guarantees two fundamental liberties: First, the rulers themselves must be subject to replacement according to the changing attitudes of the people who elect them. Second, there must be genuine freedom for such attitudes to change by allowing lone thinkers and minority groups the right to challenge prevailing beliefs. Unless minority groups have full rights to speak and organize, majority rule will soon degenerate into mob rule, and enlightenment and reason will be lost to passion and prejudice. The whole strength of reason, and of government based on reason, depends on the condition that reason can be set right when it is wrong—that people hear all sides of an issue. Otherwise errors harden into prejudices; the will of the stronger soon overcomes the judgment of the wiser; those in power close the avenues of communication so that rulers cannot be replaced; and there is no protection for minority groups to inquire, criticize and organize.

Democracy and science are able to progress because they embrace principles of self-alteration which permit the correction of error and partial truth without an overthrow of the system that makes such correction possible. These systems are based on deep humility on the part of the individual, coupled with a faith that, through rational accommodation and collaboration among individuals, a living body of common thought may be created which will more adequately answer the problems of an age or society, than can any individual, whether he be a scientist, a prophet or a dictator.[23]

---

[23] This paragraph borrows from Morris R. Cohen, *The Faith of a Liberal*, New York: Holt, 1946, pp. 449-464; M. R. Cohen, *Reason and Nature: An Essay*

But all too many minority groups within our democracy refuse to abide by these rules of open-mindedness and honest objectivity; instead they attempt to gain their own ends by whatever means are available. Consequently, everyone who reads a newspaper or watches TV is confronted with a constant barrage of exaggerated statements and half-truths. Under such circumstances, how can we disentangle fact from fancy? How can we distinguish honest speech from concealed propaganda? We teach our children the dangers of crossing against a red light; we teach them about the contagion of physical disease; but we have not found an effective way to prevent anyone from being hoodwinked by slick salesmen who "sell the sizzle, not the steak;" or by smooth-talking purveyors of religious or political panaceas. In general, we Americans lightheartedly accept P. T. Barnum's dicta that "a sucker is born every minute" and "people like to be fooled."

In certain areas we have made men responsible for what they say or do. We require newspaper and magazine publishers to identify themselves, and thus become subject to laws against libel. We have pure food and drug laws requiring that the contents of packaged foods be clearly labeled. We have security and banking regulations requiring the registration of stocks and bonds. We require our citizens to register as lobbyists when appearing before certain Congressional committees. In all such cases, we try to establish responsibility for goods sold, or for statements made.

But many organizations which influence public opinion are not held accountable by any legal regulations. The question arises whether the free and open market place of democratic thought can operate as our founding fathers intended if anonymous groups are allowed to corrupt the market place by pumping in unidentified ideas and unlabeled propaganda. Morris Ernst has stated the problem thus:

> The greatest single contribution to our history may well be the gamble we took and wrote into the First Amendment of the Constitution. In simple terms, we said that we will stake our all on a wager that truth will win out in an *open* market place of thought. If ideas are pumped into the market place stealthily,

---

on the Meaning of Scientific Method, 2nd ed., Glencoe, Ill.: Free Press, 1953 (p. 83 f, "The Ideal of Science") .

with vast quantities of pamphlets, etc., anonymously distributed and richly financed, maybe we will have to modify our gamble and admit that the odds are only one out of three that truth can win out against the organized secret sending of ideas to the mind of man by material financed by people who either haven't the courage to stand up and say whom they are financing, or who have such a lack of faith in our national gamble that they know they cannot succeed in winning favor in the market place unless they operate under nightshirts or the equivalent.[24]

Some have supposed that the problem may be solved by censorship. They suggest that closer surveillance can purge the media of communication—newspapers, magazines, books (including textbooks), radio, movies, TV—of undesirable or untruthful material inserted by dangerous pressure groups. In some cases those who support such a policy have actually succeeded in setting up agencies of censorship.

But the use of censorship always poses new problems of its own. Which ideas are "untruthful"? "subversive"? Which forms of expression are "immoral"? "sacrilegious"? Which are "dangerous"; which merely "different"? Above all, who is to be given the tremendous responsibility of deciding these questions? Careful consideration will reveal that censorship itself is a form of secret propaganda, for its results are bound to favor to some degree the per-

---

[24] Morris L. Ernst, "Miasma of Suspicion," *Saturday Review* 32: 18-19, Dec. 24, 1949. By permission. Read also Morris L. Ernst, "Some Affirmative Suggestions for a Loyalty Program," *The American Scholar* 19: 452-460, Autumn, 1950; Senator Karl Mundt, "The Case for the McCarran Act," U.S. Senate, Sept. 6, 1950, *Congressional Record*, No. 177, 96: 14415-14416; Morris L. Ernst and Joel Katz, "Speech: Public and Private," 53 *Columbia Law Review* 620-632, May 1953; Joseph W. Barker, "Faith in an Atomic Age," *Vital Speeches* 19: 585-588, July 15, 1953; Robert K. Carr, *Federal Protection of Civil Rights,* Ithaca, N. Y.: Cornell University Press, 1947 (Consult especially Chapter 7, though the entire book is devoted to the problem). For bibliography of legal cases, read Thomas I. Emerson and David Haber, *Political and Civil Rights in the United States,* Buffalo, N. Y.: Dennis, 1952, pp. 645-646.

In the field of education, Virgil Rogers has suggested that the holding of secret, off-the-record sessions, apart from school administrators and PTA groups, is a criterion by which to distinguish trouble-making "pressure groups" from honest, constructive critics of the public schools. Read C. Winfield Scott and Clyde M. Hill, eds., *Public Education Under Criticism,* New York: Prentice-Hall, 1954, pp. 237, 353.

sonal views and prejudices of the censors, no matter how well-intentioned they may be.

The power of censorship along these lines is amply demonstrated by its use under dictatorship, where secrecy and censorship are necessary to maintain a minority group in power. But our American democracy was established on the assumption that truth and justice would prevail in a free and open competition of ideas. In the words of Walter Lippmann:

> It seems to me perfectly clearly established that no official yet born on this earth is wise enough or generous enough to separate good ideas from bad ideas, good beliefs from bad beliefs, and that the utmost that anyone can ask of a government, is that if it is efficient it should detect and run down criminal acts; that beyond reaching words which are the direct and immediate incitement to criminal acts, no government dare go; and finally, that the man who is not willing to defend the freedom of ideas with which he profoundly disagrees, has not the soul of a free man.[25]

The answer to secrecy is not more secrecy (i.e., censorship) but less secrecy. Only by encouraging the free exchange and examination of all ideas can we truly judge the good and the bad. Such, at least, are the conclusions of the selections that follow.

2.6. DON'T JOIN THE BOOK BURNERS [26]

Dwight D. Eisenhower

. . . Don't join the book burners. Don't think you are going to conceal faults by concealing evidence that they ever existed. Don't be afraid to go in your library and read every book as long as any

---

[25] Walter Lippmann, "Free Speech and Free Press," *The Bulletin* (of) *the League of Free Nations Association,* Vol. 1, No. 1, March 1920. By permission.

[26] The first paragraph is from the President's address at Dartmouth College, June 14, 1953, *New York Times,* June 15, 1953, L 10. The next three paragraphs are from a letter to the American Library Association meeting at Los Angeles, June 26, 1953, *New York Times,* June 27, 1953, L 16. The concluding paragraph is an excerpt from the President's address, "Man's Right to Knowledge and the Free Use Thereof," Columbia University, May 31, 1954, *Vital Speeches* 20: 514-517, June 15, 1954.

document does not offend your own ideas of decency. That should
be the only censorship. . . .

* * *

Our librarians serve the precious liberties of our nation: Freedom of inquiry, freedom of the spoken and written word, freedom of the exchange of ideas.

Upon these clear principles, democracy depends for its very life,
for they are the great sources of knowledge and enlightenment. And
knowledge—full unfettered knowledge of its own heritage, of freedom's enemies, of the whole world of men and ideas—this knowledge is a free people's surest strength.

The converse is just as surely true. A democracy smugly disdain-
ful of new ideas would be a sick democracy. A democracy chronic-
ally fearful of new ideas would be a dying democracy. . . .

* * *

Whenever, and for whatever alleged reason, people attempt
to crush ideas, to mask their convictions, to view every neighbor
as a possible enemy, to seek some kind of divining rod by which to
test for conformity, a free society is in danger. Wherever man's
right to knowledge and the use thereof is restricted, man's freedom
in the same measure disappears. . . . Our dedication to truth and
freedom, at home and abroad, does not require—and cannot tolerate
—fear, threat, hysteria and intimidation. . . .

2.7. FREEDOM TO READ [27]

American Library Association
and
American Book Publishers Council

The freedom to read is essential to our democracy. It is under
attack. Private groups and public authorities in various parts of

[27] "The Freedom to Read," a declaration approved by the American Book
Publishers Council and adopted by the American Library Association, *Library
Journal* 78: 1272-1274, August 1953; *Saturday Review* 36: 24-27, July 11, 1953;
New Republic 128: 5-6, July 6, 1953. By permission.

Compare "Library Bill of Rights," *American Library Association Bulletin*
42: 285, July-August 1948.

the country are working to remove books from sale, to censor text-books, to label "controversial" books, to distribute lists of "objectionable" books or authors, and to purge libraries. These actions apparently arise from a view that our national tradition of free expression is no longer valid; that censorship and suppression are needed to avoid the subversion of politics and the corruption of morals. We, as citizens devoted to the use of books and as librarians and publishers responsible for disseminating them, wish to assert the public interest in the preservation of the freedom to read.

We are deeply concerned about these attempts at suppression. Most such attempts rest on a denial of the fundamental premise of democracy: that the ordinary citizen, by exercising his critical judgment, will accept the good and reject the bad. The censors, public and private, assume that they should determine what is good and what is bad for their fellow-citizens.

We trust Americans to recognize propaganda, and to reject obscenity. We do not believe they need the help of censors to assist them in this task. We do not believe they are prepared to sacrifice their heritage of a free press in order to be "protected" against what others think may be bad for them. We believe they still favor free enterprise in ideas and expression.

We are aware, of course, that books are not alone in being subjected to efforts at suppression. We are aware that these efforts are related to a larger pattern of pressures being brought against education, the press, films, radio and television. The problem is not only one of actual censorship. The shadow of fear cast by these pressures leads, we suspect, to an even larger voluntary curtailment of expression by those who seek to avoid controversy.

Such pressure toward conformity is perhaps natural to a time of uneasy change and pervading fear. Especially when so many of our apprehensions are directed against an ideology, the expression of a dissident idea becomes a thing feared in itself, and we tend to move against it as against a hostile deed, with suppression.

And yet suppression is never more dangerous than in such a time of social tension. Freedom has given the United States the elasticity to endure strain. Freedom keeps open the path of novel and creative solutions, and enables change to come by choice. Every silencing of a heresy, every enforcement of an orthodoxy, diminishes the toughness and resilience of our society and leaves it the less able to deal with stress.

Now as always in our history, books are among our greatest instruments of freedom. They are almost the only means for making generally available ideas or manners of expression that can initially command only a small audience. They are the natural medium for the new idea and the untried voice, from which come the original contributions to social growth. They are essential to the extended discussion which serious thought requires, and to the accumulation of knowledge and ideas into organized collections.

We believe that free communication is essential to the preservation of a free society and a creative culture. We believe that these pressures toward conformity present the danger of limiting the range and variety of inquiry and expression on which our democracy and our culture depend. We believe that every American community must jealously guard the freedom to publish and to circulate, in order to preserve its own freedom to read. We believe that publishers and librarians have a profound responsibility to give validity to that freedom to read by making it possible for the reader to choose freely from a variety of offerings.

The freedom to read is guaranteed by the Constitution. Those with faith in free men will stand firm on these constitutional guarantees of essential rights and will exercise the responsibilities that accompany these rights.

We therefore affirm these propositions:

1. *It is in the public interest for publishers and librarians to make available the widest diversity of views and expressions, including those which are unorthodox or unpopular with the majority.*

Creative thought is by definition new, and what is new is different. The bearer of every new thought is a rebel until his idea is refined and tested. Totalitarian systems attempt to maintain themselves in power by the ruthless suppression of any concept which challenges the established orthodoxy. The power of a democratic system to adapt to change is vastly strengthened by the freedom of its citizens to choose widely from among conflicting opinions offered freely to them. . . .

2. *Publishers and librarians do not need to endorse every idea or presentation contained in the books they make available. It would conflict with the public interest for them to establish their own political, moral or aesthetic views as the sole standard for determining what books should be published or circulated.*

Publishers and librarians serve the educational process by helping to make available knowledge and ideas required for the growth of the mind and the increase of learning. . . . It is wrong that what one man can read should be confined to what another thinks proper.

3. *It is contrary to the public interest for publishers or librarians to determine the acceptability of a book solely on the basis of the personal history or political affiliations of the author.*

A book should be judged as a book. No art or literature can flourish if it is to be measured by the political views or private lives of its creators. No society of free men can flourish which draws up lists of writers to whom it will not listen, whatever they may have to say.

4. *The present laws dealing with obscenity should be vigorously enforced. Beyond that, there is no place in our society for extra-legal efforts to coerce the taste of others, to confine adults to the reading matter deemed suitable for adolescents, or to inhibit the efforts of writers to achieve artistic expression.*

To some, much of modern literature is shocking. But is not much of life itself shocking? We cut off literature at the source if we prevent serious artists from dealing with the stuff of life. Parents and teachers have a responsibility to prepare the young to meet the diversity of experiences in life to which they will be exposed, as they have a responsibility to help them learn to think critically for themselves. These are affirmative responsibilities, not discharged simply by preventing them from reading works for which they are not yet prepared. In these matters taste differs, and taste cannot be legislated; nor can machinery be devised which will suit the demands of one group without limiting the freedom of others. We deplore the catering to the immature, the retarded or the maladjusted taste. But those concerned with freedom have the responsibility of seeing to it that each individual book or publication, whatever its contents, price, or method of distribution, is dealt with in accordance with due process of law.

5. *It is not in the public interest to force a reader to accept with any book the prejudgment of a label characterizing the book or author as subversive or dangerous.*

The idea of labeling supposes the existence of individuals or groups with wisdom to determine by authority what is good or bad for the citizen. It supposes that each individual must be directed in making up his mind about the ideas he examines. But Americans do not need others to do their thinking for them.

6. *It is the responsibility of publishers and librarians, as guardians of the people's freedom to read, to contest encroachments upon that freedom by individuals or groups seeking to impose their own standards or tastes upon the community at large.*

It is inevitable in the give and take of the democratic process that the political, the moral, or the aesthetic concepts of an individual or group will occasionally collide with those of another individual or group. In a free society each individual is free to determine for himself what he wishes to read, and each group is free to determine what it will recommend to its freely associated members. But no group has the right to take the law into its own hands, and to impose its own concepts of politics or morality upon other members of a democratic society. Freedom is no freedom if it is accorded only to the accepted and the inoffensive.

7. *It is the responsibility of publishers and librarians to give full meaning to the freedom to read by providing books that enrich the quality of thought and expression. By the exercise of this affirmative responsibility, bookmen can demonstrate that the answer to a bad book is a good one, the answer to a bad idea is a good one.*

The freedom to read is of little consequence when expended on the trivial; it is frustrated when the reader cannot obtain matter fit for his purpose. What is needed is not only the absence of restraint, but the positive provision of opportunity for the people to read the best that can be thought and said.

Books are the major channel by which the intellectual inheritance is handed down, and the principal means of its testing and growth.[28] The defense of their freedom and integrity, and the enlargement of their service to society, requires of all bookmen the utmost of their faculties, and deserves of all citizens the fullest of their support.

We state these propositions neither lightly nor as easy generalizations. We here stake out a lofty claim for the value of books. We do so because we believe that they are good, possessed of enormous variety and usefulness, worthy of cherishing and keeping free. We realize that the application of these propositions may mean the dissemination of ideas and manners of expression that are repugnant to many persons. We do not state these propositions in the comfortable belief that what people read is unimportant. We believe rather that what people read is deeply important; that ideas can be dangerous; but that the suppression of ideas is fatal to a democratic society. Freedom itself is a dangerous way of life, but it is ours.

2.8. TO MAKE MEN FREE[29]

Archibald MacLeish

Freedom, in American usage, means the freedom of the individual human being to think for himself and to come to the truth by the light of his own mind and conscience. It is the freedom defined by the American Constitution. Congress is forbidden to make any law abridging the freedom of speech. There is to be no establishment of religious authority or supervision. There is to be no meddling, in other words, by state or by church with a man's thoughts or what he chooses to say about them. When it comes to thoughts,

[28] Editor's Note: Motion pictures, like newspapers and radio, are now included in the press whose freedom is guaranteed by the First Amendment. *United States v. Paramount Pictures*, 334 U.S. 131 (1948); *Burstyn v. Wilson*, 343 U.S. 495 (1952); W. P. Clancy, "Freedom of the Screen," *Commonweal*, 59: 500-502, Feb. 19, 1954; 57-58, March 12, 1954.

[29] Archibald MacLeish, *Freedom is the Right to Choose*, Boston: Beacon, 1951, pp. 173-175, 178, 182. By permission. Under the title "To Make Men Free," this article appeared in the *Atlantic* 188: 27-30, November 1951.

Mr. MacLeish has been a Pulitzer Prize winner in poetry, Librarian of Congress, Assistant Secretary of State, Assistant Director of the Office of War Information, and a member of the executive board of UNESCO, and is now Boylston professor at Harvard.

when it comes to ideas, when it comes to opinions and their expression, a man is free. His freedom is guaranteed by the fundamental law of the Republic. The opinions of others are not to be imposed upon him, no matter whose opinions they may be—the opinions of a church or the opinions of the government or the opinions of his fellow citizens—even the opinions of a majority of his fellow citizens.

A man's freedom to believe, that is to say, does not depend on *what* he believes. It does not depend on his being "right" as others see the right, no matter how numerous they may be or how well entrenched or how powerful. Right and wrong as others judge the right and wrong are irrelevant to the American conception of freedom to think and believe and say. That, of course, is the nub of the whole matter, and the essential distinction between freedom as we mean it and freedom as it is meant in certain other quarters of the earth. In the American conception of freedom, the man and his conscience come first and the established opinions, the accepted verities, the official views come after.

Strangers to the American tradition find this aspect of our historical belief in freedom difficult, if not impossible, to accept. Their inclination is to interpret freedom to mean freedom to think *right* thoughts. Which means, freedom to think as they think, and, by enlargement, freedom to think as their friends think, or their party, or their church, or their veterans' organization, or their union, or their professional association, or whatever. The majority, the institution, the accepted opinion comes first with them and the man and his conscience nowhere. Freedom is freedom to be like everybody else, to think as the majority in the town or state or country thinks, to teach what the legislature or the dominant political or religious opinion wants taught, to conform.

The pressure which the word freedom has been under in the past few years is a pressure of this character: a pressure from those who have never really accepted or wholly understood the meaning of the word in its American use. There are some, of course, who deliberately reject the American meaning—who would destroy it if they could, replacing it with an interpretation more amenable to their own beliefs—but they are not numerous as yet. The real danger to freedom in the United States—to the word and to the thing—is the danger of the impairment of the American usage by negligence and default. Unless we can maintain the pure traditional meaning of the word—unless we can understand in common and as a nation that the only opinion established in this country by the American Constitution is the opinion that a man is free to hold *any* opinion unless we can agree among ourselves that by freedom we mean precisely *freedom*, we may end by finding ourselves "free" in the sense in which the Russians now find themselves "democratic." . . .

The American Proposition is the proposition, advanced at the beginnings of the Republic and enacted into law when the Constitution was adopted, that a man's freedom to be a man, and to find and speak the truth that is in him, is more important than the protection of any accepted belief, and official verity, against criticism, against challenge, against dissent. More important not only to that man but to all men, to the society which all men compose, to the nation, to the world, to life itself. It is a proposition, in other words, which rests upon an act of faith, the most courageous of all earthly acts of faith—an act of faith in man and in the God whom man, in the freedom of his conscience and his thought, can find.

When it was first enacted into law the American Proposition was new. It is still new: the one wholly new and revolutionary idea the modern world has produced, for all its triumphs in science and technique—an idea so new and so revolutionary in its literal and explicit meaning that half the patriotic societies which celebrate their attachment to the American Revolution have yet to understand it or accept it. But it is new and revolutionary, not solely because it proclaims human liberty, nor solely because it founds its conception of human liberty on the freedom of the individual human mind, defending that freedom in the most explicit and peremptory terms against the tyranny of organized opinion. It is new and revolutionary because of the act of faith which it expresses.

Our reliance in this country is on the inquiring, individual human mind. Our strength is founded there: our resilience, our ability to face an ever-changing future and to master it. We are not frozen into the backward-facing impotence of those societies, fixed in the rigidness of an official dogma, to which the future is the mirror of the past. We are free to make the future for ourselves. And we are free because it is the man who counts in this country: always and at every moment and in any situation, the man.

Not the Truth but the man: not the truth as the state sees the truth or as the church sees the truth or as the majority sees the truth or as the mob sees the truth, but the truth as the man sees it, as the man finds it, for himself as man. Our faith is in the infinite variety of human beings and in the God who made them various and of many minds; in their singularity, their uniqueness, the creativeness of the differences between them. Our faith, in simple, sober truth, is in the human Being, the human spirit, the hungers and the longings that lead it toward its images of truth, its perceptions of the beauty of the world.

Those who launched the great human adventure which this Republic is, dared to put their trust in the individual man, the man alone, the man thinking for himself. They dared to believe in a *people,* which is a nation of individual men constituting among themselves a society; for a people is not what the totalitarians call "the masses"; a people is an agreement of many alone to make together a world in which each one of them can live as himself. The founders of the American Republic believed in a people. They not only provided no censors for the thoughts of those who were to come after them: they prohibited censors. They not only provided no moral or intellectual or religious authority to govern the beliefs of their successors: they rejected forever the establishment of any such authority. They trusted men.

It is in that trust that the Republic can still be defended. Indeed it is only in that trust that it can be defended as the kind of country it is. To attempt to defend it otherwise—to attempt, above all, to defend it by debasing the coinage of meaning in which its nature is expressed—is to lose both the country itself and the struggle against Communism which is cited as justification of the fraud. If freedom can come to mean something less than freedom in the general mind, it can come to mean the opposite of freedom. If freedom ceases to express the American faith in man and in man's unqualified right to find the truth for himself, it will shortly express a faith in established truth, in the rightness of official opinion. When that happens we shall have lost both the American Proposition and the fight against Communism. For the one idea that can triumph over the police-state notion that the truth is already known, once for all, and that the truth is therefore entitled to impose itself by force, is the American Proposition that a man is free to find the truth for himself. It is the one idea that can triumph because, as long as it is held, man himself is the cause of those who hold it. And against that cause no enemy has prevailed for long.

2.9. COMMENTS ON NEW YORK TEXTBOOK CENSORSHIP[30]

The New Yorker

The Board of Education has twenty-three criteria for selecting textbooks, library books, and magazines for use in the public schools. We learned this by reading a fourteen-page pamphlet published by the Board explaining how it makes its choice. One criterion is: "Is it [the book or magazine] free from subject matter that tends to irreverence for things held sacred?" Another criterion is: "Are both sides of controversial issues presented with fairness?" Another: "Is it free from objectionable slang expressions which will interfere with the building of good language habits?"

These three criteria by themselves are enough to keep a lot of good books from the schools. Irreverence for things held sacred has started many a writer on his way, and will again. An author so little moved by a controversy that he can present both sides fairly is not likely to burn any holes in the paper. We think the way for school children to get both sides of a controversy is to read several books on the subject, not one. In other words, we think the Board should strive for a well-balanced library, not a well-balanced book. The greatest books are heavily slanted, by the nature of greatness.

As for "the building of good language habits," we have gone carefully through the pamphlet to see what habits, if any, the Board itself has formed. They appear to be the usual ones—the habit of untidiness, the habit of ambiguity, the habit of saying everything the hard way. The clumsy phrase, the impenetrable sentence, the cliché, the misspelled word. The Board has, we gather, no strong convictions about the use of the serial comma, no grip on "that" and "which," no opinion about whether a textbook is a "text book,"

---

[30] Editorial "Notes and Comments," *The New Yorker Magazine, Inc.,* 25: 19, October 9, 1949. By permission.

a "text-book," or a "textbook." (The score at the end of the four-teenth was "text book" 5, "text-book" 11, "textbook" 5.) It sees nothing comical, or challenging, in the sentence "Materials should be provided for boys and girls who vary greatly in attitudes, abilities, interests, and mental age." It sees no need for transposition in "Phrases should not be split in captions under pictures." It sees no bugs in "The number of lines should be most conducive to readability." And you should excuse the expression "bugs"—a slang word, interfering with the building of good language habits.

We still have high hopes of getting *The New Yorker* accepted in the schools, but our hopes are less high than they were when we picked up the pamphlet. We're bucking some stiff criteria—criteria that are, shall we say, time-tested?

Section C: Some Specific Examples

2.10. INTRODUCTION

Except for classified military knowledge, the free world normally has no official censors to examine material in advance of publication and to suppress it if disapproved. Under our traditions an author is relatively free to publish anything, but he must then run the gauntlet of possible prosecution for slander, sedition, immorality and blasphemy.[31] One church may criticize another church. The CIO may differ from the NAM. But the government stands aloof from such controversy unless public peace and order are seriously endangered.

There is a very practical reason for this absence of prior restraint. Censorship laws must be framed either in such explicit terms that any clever writer or artist can get around them, or in such general

---

[31] For leading constitutional cases on "Previous Restraints or Censorship," read Milton R. Konvitz, ed., *Bill of Rights Reader*, Ithaca, N.Y.: Cornell University Press, 1954, pp. 207-232.

terms that their interpretation depends on the whims and prejudices of police officers.[32] And it is a notorious fact that law enforcement officers do not always draw the line wisely.

Suppose it is "indecency" that you dislike. Would you condemn
Esquire? Life? Gone With the Wind? the Kinsey report? the story
of Jezebel? the Song of Solomon? the Book of Ruth? Judges XIX?

If you believe that modern comics are full of gruesome, suggestive
horrors, what will you say concerning the tales of Hercules and
Ulysses? Thor and Woden? Cain and Abel? Hansel and Gretel?
Samson? Ben Hur?

If it is race or religious prejudice you would outlaw, must you
therefore ban *Uncle Tom's Cabin* because it depicts Negroes as
slaves? *The Merchant of Venice* because the characterization of Shy-
lock offends certain Jews? or *The Miracle* because portions of it
seem sacrilegious to Cardinal Spellman?

If it is Communism you fear, does this mean that schools and
libraries shall burn or expurgate Marx and Engel's *Communist
Manifesto? Plato's Republic?* More's *Utopia?* Chapters IV and V of
the Book of Acts in the New Testament? Once you start down this
path, just where do you stop? Because of such difficulties, relatively
few clear-cut examples of legal censorship arise.[33]

But if we use the term censorship broadly to also include undue
restraints and pressures applied by groups other than the legally
constituted authorities, then censorship constitutes a persistent
problem in any free society. When overzealous partisans try to
legislate intelligence, morality and loyalty, such partisanship may
become a threat to democracy. When they "take the law into their
hands" and apply unreasonable pressures to compel uniformity of
thought, speech or action, such so-called defenders of freedom become in fact freedom's worst enemies. All too often such groups,

---

[32] See *Winters v. New York,* 333 U.S. 507 at 525 (1948).

[33] See A. Whitney Griswold, "We Cannot Legislate Intelligence, Morality, or
Loyalty: These Must be Inspired, Not Compelled," *Vital Speeches* 19: 588-590,
July 15, 1953; Sidney Hook, "Cultural Vigilantism," Chapter 2 in *Heresy, Yes—
Conspiracy, No!,* New York: Day, 1953; Fred B. Millett, "The Vigilantees,"
American Association of University Professors Bulletin 40: 47-60, Spring 1954;
W. M. Daniels, ed., *Censorship of Books,* New York: Wilson, 1954.

perhaps led by self-anointed prophets, take on a self-assurance that borders on arrogance—which is a first cousin to ignorance. These attitudes thrive because they appeal to personal pride and to group prestige.[34] When they become dominant, they destroy the give-and-take needed in a free society.

It is precisely at this point that there is a fundamental cleavage between the free world and the Soviet Union. Harold J. Berman, who has spent recent years doing research on the Soviet Union, writes:

> Soviet writers condemn pragmatism and relativism, and insist that there is an absolute and knowable truth. They also insist that the basic content of objective truth is revealed through Marxism-Leninism. Where there is class conflict, so the theory goes, truth is obscured by class interests; under Soviet socialism, the Communist Party as the vanguard of the proletariat can perceive the truth pure and unadulterated through its Marxist-Leninist glasses.[35]

Concerning such ideological arrogance, one of the ablest jurists of our day, Judge Learned Hand, has written:

> . . . wisdom comes as false assurance goes—false assurance, that grows from pride in our powers and ignorance of our ignorance. Beware then of heathen gods; have no confidence in principles that come to us in the trappings of the eternal. Meet them with gentle irony, friendly scepticism and an open soul.[36]

Censorship by group pressure is also encouraged through mis-

---

[34] The theological doctrine of "original sin" is sometimes interpreted to mean that all men are subject to this "sin of pride." See Ward Madden, "Education for Religious Quality in Experience," *Harvard Educational Review* 21: 14-31, Winter 1951, p. 21 f; Reinhold Niebuhr, *Nature and Destiny of Man*, Part I, Chapters 6-10, New York: Scribners, 1941, 1949.

[35] Harold J. Berman, "The 'Right to Knowledge' in the Soviet Union," 54 *Columbia Law Review:* 748-764 at 762, May 1954. By permission.

[36] Learned Hand, "Democracy: Its Presumptions and Realities," *Federal Bar Association Journal* 1: 40-45, March 1932; cited by Irving Dilliard, ed., *The Spirit of Liberty: Papers and Addresses of Learned Hand*, New York: Knopf, 1952, pp. 101-102. By permission.

representation or incomplete presentation of facts to the public. This type is very common in contemporary America. To illustrate, compare the half-truth, "Lawyer X spent time in jail," with the full truth "Lawyer X spent time in jail consulting his client." To cite one more example:

> Two schools of thought prevail on the UNESCO subject. One holds that UNESCO is simply a crackpot organization. . . . The other view holds that UNESCO is a more serious menace to world intelligence.[37]

Strictly speaking, this statement is not false, for it does not say that there are *only* two schools of thought. But it is misleading.

John H. Hallowell has summarized the basic reason why coercion, prejudice, concealment and misrepresentation threaten the existence of democracy:

> . . . Majority rule . . . presupposes widespread discussion and deliberation and presupposes that the discussion will be conducted in the most reasonable manner possible, to the end that policy may be framed in the interests of the common good. . . .

> To the extent, therefore, that the discussion is not as widespread as possible, to the extent that judgment is coerced or cajoled rather than persuaded, to the extent that the instruments of persuasion are used to obscure issues rather than to clarify them, to the extent that the participants make no effort to transcend the motivations of their private interests to contemplate the common good, to the extent that appeals are made to prejudice rather than to reason—to that extent the principle of majority rule is corrupted and debased. It is the reasoned judgment of the majority that obligates our compliance with its decision, not the will of the majority as such. To the extent, therefore, that the rule of the majority becomes more an expression of will and less an expression of reasoned judgment, to that degree does it become less democratic and more tyrannical.[38]

---

[37] Harold Lord Varney, "UNESCO: UN's Brainwashing Apparatus," *American Mercury* 78: 3-8, February 1954.

[38] John H. Hallowell, "The Meaning of Majority Rule," *Commonweal* 56: 167-169, May 23, 1952. By permission.

2.11. THE RIGHT TO FIND OUT: AN ANALYSIS OF THE CRITICISMS OF "BUILDING AMERICA" [39]

Helen Luce, and the Staff of the San Bernardino County Free Library

Introduction

This report is submitted in order that you may have our careful and considered opinion of the *Building America* series. The Los Angeles *Times* for February 25th [1948] carried an article condemning the series as controversial. The article gave the testimony of Richard E. Combs, special counsel for the State Senate Investigating Committee on Education, in which he criticized eleven different titles.

Building America is a series which issues eight numbers a year, and it has been published since 1935. It is published for [a department of] the NEA, . . . [The Association for] Supervision and Curriculum Development. . . .

Librarians in the school department and I have carefully read both the Los Angeles *Times* account of Mr. Combs' findings and the eleven issues of *Building America* which he criticizes as being controversial. We have come to the following conclusions:

We feel that there is no basis for the investigation and that Mr. Combs' criticisms are unfounded. There are four types of criticism or methods which he uses that should be pointed out and denounced.

First, he quotes many statements from the text that are not there at all. We have read the books word for word and in many instances do not find the thing he is quoting. It is possible that he worked with a different edition from ours, but where we have two editions, we have read both. . . .

---

[39] "The Right to Find Out: An Analysis of the Criticisms of *Building America*," by Helen Luce and the Staff of the San Bernardino County (California) Free Library; issued by the Committee on Intellectual Freedom of the California and the American Library Associations, June, 1948. By permission.

Second, by lifting a single sentence out of the context, the meaning and intent are often changed. This is a vicious practice used to put across your own interpretation. In the report to follow, we have endeavored to give full quotations where this has happened. When both good and bad points are mentioned, quoting only the bad, as Mr. Combs frequently does, does not present a true picture of the text.[40]

Third, Mr. Combs employs exaggeration and places false emphasis. When a few pictures are unflattering, he has a tendency to say that a great many or nearly all are. In the same manner, he emphasizes a small portion of the text or illustrations out of all proportion to their real prominence. Specific instances of this type of thing are noted in the report that follows.

Fourth, Mr. Combs seems to have an aversion to unpleasant facts and pictures being used, even though they may be true. The series, on the other hand, has shown the bad, as well as the good, especially for the purpose of indicating progress.

The report which follows lists in one column the issues of *Building America* which Mr. Combs criticized, and in the second column lists our report of the same issues, made after carefully reading each one. . . .

Helen Luce,
and the Staff of the San Bernardino
County Free Library

[40] Editor's Note: Unfortunately, such half-truths are frequently accepted and passed on without qualification, as the following quotation shows:

"In California a series of history textbooks called 'Building America' has been declared 'unfit for use' in public schools because of its communistic leanings, and funds for the purchase of these books has been denied by the State Legislature. There are other textbooks, anti-American in nature, which are in the high schools of this country. . . . In California the committee of the State Legislature which investigated the 'Building America Series' proved that, in the main, those who supported the introduction of these books into the schools were Communists or fellow travellers."—Milo F. McDonald, Ph.D., " 'Progressive' Poison in Public Education," New York: The American Education Association, 1951, p. 23. By permission.

Richard E. Combs report on Building America for State Senate Investigating Committee on Education (taken from the Los Angeles Times, February 25, 1948).

San Bernardino County Library critical estimate of Building America issues attacked by Mr. Combs.

Vol. 13, Russia:

Discussed extensively by Combs. Text and illustrations, he said, portray the Russian people as happy, well-fed and free, and "its cardinal sin is that it propagandizes by omission." The pictures in the volume on Russia, he said, "have been explained as showing plump, well-fed people, fertile farms and a general air of well-being and prosperity. They were obtained from Sovfoto, an official Soviet agency. . . . These pictures should be contrasted with the Farm Security Administration illustrations in "Seeing America." When the two volumes are placed side by side, the contrast is striking. This, too, is propaganda of the most subtle and vicious type."

Russia:

Published 1944 when Russia was our ally. It does not whitewash Russia. Good and bad features of Russian life discussed, poor standard of living described, [as is fact that] people must follow single party line. Pictures portray country in favorable light. Perhaps no other kind available than these from an official Soviet agency. Charts and graphs show failures as well as successes.

Vol. 12, China:

Sharply criticized because part of the text "indicates to the grammar school pupil that the U.S., Germany and Britain refused to help the Chinese people free themselves from the grip of the war lords, but that Russia kindly agreed to assist in this cause. . . .

China:

Running throughout this issue is mention of American and Chinese association. China has tried to take the best from our democratic process, now has a constitution. Whole section "Toward a Genuine, Lasting Friendship." Other authors bear out statement

The writers of this book seem to have avoided with studious care any mention of the fact that the Chinese Communist party was conceived, nurtured, directed and dominated by the Kremlin as a part of its plan for the eventual Communizing of China. There must have been some sources somewhere from which the learned and liberal authors of this volume could have learned the facts of life about the Chinese Communists," Combs commented, and then referred to "the standard work, 'Stalin.' "

of *Building America* that in 1921 America, Britain, and Germany did not send men to fight war lords, but Russia did. This statement, therefore, seems accurate— it appears only once and does not color the entire book. There seems to be a difference of opinion among authorities as to whether Chinese Communists are brothers of Russian Communists. *Building America* makes no statement on this.

Vol. 30, Seeing America:

Seeing America:

". . . being the last and certainly one of the worst books in the series." Criticized was "a picture of a dejected-looking middle-aged man clad in overalls and leaning against a vacant building. Caption: 'As motionless as a cigar-store Indian of old, the despairing figure of a jobless man leans against a vacant store. This might be 'Any Town, U.S.A.' where unemployment is still a problem." Also criticized was a picture showing a horse-drawn water cart portrayed as part of a "typical American town." Combs commented that the nation is shown to a theoretical young couple by way of view of the seamy side, with nowhere a picture of

Published in 1937 when we were emerging from the depression. Purpose stated on p. 2: "It discusses the different problems facing our people in each region and the ways some of these problems are being solved." Purpose to present problems and achievements, not a travelogue. Many pictures of industry and agriculture, but attractive pictures are included. P. 7: Maine lake; p. 11: sun bathing; p. 14: air view of farm land; p. 19: Rocky Mts.; p. 20: Idaho truck farms; p. 21: petrified forest; p. 22: Western wheat farm; p. 25: San Francisco and bay; p. 31: picnic grounds. Entire theme is tracing history of regions, stating progress made. Conclusions a beautiful park, other abundant examples of healthful, happy life. "And so the young people have seen America. They have seen its slums, its shanties, its expropriated farms and drouth victims, its hot dog stands, and the shanties of the miners and steelworkers. They have seen its mules, its jackasses, and its jobless. They have [been] shown the class struggle thru pictures and the working of captions. Some day they may take a trip and see a national park, a public library where people can prepare themselves for a better standard of living, a decent residential section. . . ."

present nature-made and man-made problems confronting regions. Purpose of volume seems achieved in objective manner.

Vol. 16, Community Planning:

". . . in the process of pointing out the need for adequate city planning, a sordid picture is painted of the average American community. . . . Only 9 of the 61 photographs are examples of good community planning; there are 23 examples of bad planning, and some of them are horrible."

Community Planning:

Book shows that between 1790 and 1890 no planning led to bad results. Since 1900 more planning. Pictures show both good and bad. Thirty show bad planning and thirty show good planning. Various types of planning discussed, education, recreation, sanitation, business, etc.

Vol. 17, Conservation:

Seventeen pictures show desolated farms, starving cattle, families in broken-down jalopies . . . only 8 pictures . . . showing correct methods. . . .

Conservation:

Twenty-six pictures show correct methods or their results. Only one starving cow and one broken-down jalopy. Book discusses ways in which conservation should be practiced to save soil, forests.

Vol. 14, Social Security:

. . . presents pictures of "Our Homeless Poor," of a typical county poorhouse, of a breadline in 1930, and of a closed factory. This sort of Marxist salesmanship is neatly packaged—but it is there, just as surely as two of the authors of the basic texts for this volume were members of front organizations. . . .

Social Security:

Does not present a "neatly packaged Marxist salesmanship." Picture "Our Homeless Poor" is a drawing made in the 1800's. Many large pictures show better phases than "a typical county poorhouse" and a breadline in 1930 (which is not so labeled). Pictures show housewives buying from well stocked grocery, men depositing money in bank, children supervised by trained worker, etc. Have two editions, one 1937 with more material on depression, other 1947 with information on Social Security Act. On p. 1, new ed., "Compared with most countries of the world, we are extremely fortunate." . . .

2.12. CENSORSHIP OF TEXTBOOKS IN ALABAMA, 1953-1955 [41]

Fred M. Hechinger

. . . Last year in the summer heat, just before the [Alabama] legislature adjourned, a law—Act 888—was hastily passed. It provided, in brief, that every single book used for instruction in Alabama's public schools and colleges bear a label on which the publishers certified that they knew the author, *or any author or authors mentioned within the book as parallel reading,* as being or not

---

[41] Fred M. Hechinger, "Education 1954-55: A Newscast," reprinted in the *Saturday Review* 37: 21, 59, Sept. 11, 1954. By permission.

Mr. Hechinger is education editor of the *New York Herald-Tribune*.

being a present or past member of the Communist Party, pro-Communist, pro-Marxian Socialist, or belonging to any group that had been considered subversive by any committee of Congress or by the Attorney General.

At first the State Superintendent of Instruction endorsed the law and even said he thought similar laws should be passed elsewhere. But opposition snowballed. The press, led by the *Montgomery Advertiser* and the *Montgomery Examiner,* staged a sustained campaign against the law. A group of publishers, among them the most distinguished names in that American industry, led by the American Textbook Publishers Institute, brought suit, holding that their rights were violated. They referred to the first (freedom of the press) and fourteenth (deprivation of property without due process of law) amendments. Many state educators and college presidents supported the publishers.

The Alabama Polytechnic Institute actually tested what it would mean to comply with the law: to screen and label their own 150,000 books only would have taken more than a million dollars and—since an average book was found to have about 280 cross-references to other authors—the checking of 28,000,000 authors.

The court that heard the publisher's case called the law totally impracticable, said it would rule out all textbooks, and declared it unconstitutional, in violation of the Fourteenth Amendment. The court also hinted strongly that the state legislature had inexcusably interfered with the functions of the executive branch—the education departments and school administrators.

An afterthought: the author of the law was the only incumbent not to be re-elected in the recent primaries. . . .

2.13. HAVE WE THE COURAGE TO BE FREE? [42]

Arthur Hays Sulzberger

. . . Are we [Americans] as free to speak our minds today as twenty years ago? Is thinking and giving expression to thought as unre-

[42] Arthur Hays Sulzberger, Address upon receipt of the Alexander Hamilton award, Columbia University, January 14, 1953; revised as "Have We the Courage to be Free?" *New York Times Magazine,* p. 12 f, Feb. 15, 1953. By permission.

Mr. Sulzberger is president and publisher of the *New York Times.*

stricted as in the past? Most of us . . . will join in saying "no," and we base our judgment on the record. . . .

My thesis is that we cannot have a good public opinion unless there is freedom of expression—freedom of expression in our schools, in our Government, in our assemblies, in our press, in all our walks and ways of life.

How, then, do matters stand today in these areas? In the first instance—our schools—I cannot find any satisfaction as an American citizen when I read that a brochure entitled "The E in UNESCO" was permanently removed from the schools of Los Angeles after it had been acclaimed by the teaching profession.

I do not hold my head any higher when I note that the Board of Education of Houston, Texas, voted not to permit the students under their jurisdiction to participate in an annual school contest conducted by the American Association for the United Nations. The U.N. has been attacked and the Houston Board of Education surrendered to the implications of that assault.

In Rhode Island—the traditional home of free thought—the principal of a Pawtucket high school suspends a club called "The UNESCO Thinkers" because he feels that UNESCO is atheistic and communistic. The action, according to my information, was upheld by those presumed custodians of our freedom—the Pawtucket branch of the Daughters of the American Revolution. As a Son of the American Revolution, I cannot feel too fraternally toward these particular sisters of mine.

Let's go up to the university level. Thirty-five years ago Frank Magruder wrote a book entitled *American Government*. Recently, a critical review of it appeared in *The Educational Reviewer,* which is published by the Committee on Education of the Conference of American Small Business Organizations. The critic said the book had socialistic and communistic overtones. That review was then picked up by a well-known radio commentator.

Reaction came fast: The state of Georgia dropped the book, but, ironically, agreed to sell to the highest bidder the 30,000 copies it had on its hands.

Houston, Texas, banned the book.

Little Rock, Arkansas, dropped it as a text, but retained it for reference.

Attacks were made in other communities—New Haven, Connecticut; Council Bluffs, Iowa; Washington, D. C.; Jackson, Michigan; Trumbull County, Ohio—to name just a few.

Did any of these critics read the book? It is doubtful that one out of a hundred of those attacking this or other books for "subversive" contents actually read the books he—or she—attacks.

I didn't read it either, but wherever *American Government* was examined by impartial committees of educators or responsible citizens, it was given a clean bill of health.

The case of the attacks made on the book *Basic Economics* provides another distressing example. This book was written by four Rutgers professors, was approved by the Phoenix, Arizona, Board of Education, by the President of Phoenix College and the School Superintendent.

Then, from the blue, an anonymous Army corporal in a letter to the *Phoenix Gazette* charged that *Basic Economics* was subversive and should be dropped by the college. The local American Legion post examined the book and called it "socialistically and communistically inclined," and urged that it be dropped.

In the course of the subsequent public hearing it developed that the corporal had said that he had not read the book but merely "glanced through" the 500 pages. The four Rutgers professors properly asked, "Are we to be discredited by the rash complaint of an anonymous person who had 'glanced' at the pages that required years of training and experience, and months of composition on our part?"

One poison-pen letter was enough to smear the book. The President, Superintendent of Schools and the Board of Education capitulated and the book was removed from Phoenix College. The American Legion committee then announced a campaign to remove it from the forty universities and colleges where it then was in use.

The effect of all this is summed up by the principals of four schools in Scarsdale, New York, who said: "We see suspicion, fear and distrust spreading among our neighbors and friends. We see our teachers being affected by the feeling that their loyalty and patriotism are being impugned. . . . Unless the forces that are undermining confidence can be met and resolved there can be no future for the good name of our schools."

Next let us consider briefly restriction on free—and therefore fruitful—thought in government. The most conspicuous aspects of that problem are found in the State Department. Now I am not defending all that has happened in "Foggy Bottom" in recent years. Far from it. I think that too often there have been temporizing and timidity when sternness and strength were required. But when members of the department are attacked now for honest advocacy of policies generally accepted some years ago but presently unpopular, when their assailants say in effect: "The test is not whether you were honest in your opinion, but only whether, in our view, you were right"—then I say that this is doctrine right out of the maw of the Kremlin.

Consider then another area—what might be called the Area of Assembly and Debate. No one will deny that it is vital that the great issues confronting us be argued out fully and freely. Yet there is mounting evidence that such discussion is being restricted and in many instances prevented—in public meetings, on radio and television and other forums—because of the pressures that result from blacklists and irresponsible accusation.

The stringent provisions of the new immigration law have added to this kind of restriction. Many visitors, including scientists who might have contributed to our sum of knowledge, have been kept out. The damage to American prestige abroad is undeniable; the measure of security attained is surely debatable.

Then we come to the area of the press, the area of the printed word, in which of course I include magazines and books and all other printed matter as well as the newspaper.

The effects of these attacks are increasingly apparent. Authors are now required, in effect, to pass loyalty tests; otherwise their publishing houses may find themselves in the midst of blind boycotts. And as for newspapers, the pressures there, too, are great. On the whole they have been admirably resisted, although there are some which have joined, with great hoopla, in the witch-hunts, whether for circulation or ideological reasons I have no means of knowing.

Our book reviewers have had a particularly difficult time, because of the too general assumption that any anti-Communist book is automatically a good book. I should think the fact that Hitler and Mussolini were authors foremost among the foes of communism would be sufficient refutation of that theory.

And so it goes. One begins to wonder whether this is still the "Land of the free and the home of the brave" about which we sing so wholeheartedly. There has been dropped upon utterance and ideas a smoke screen of intimidation that dims essential talk and essential thought. Nor is it the super-zealots who bother me so much in all of this—it is the lack of plain, old-fashioned guts on the part of those who capitulate to them. Surely, such actions must be of great aid and comfort to the Kremlin; these capitulators are, in effect, a *sixth* column which does not even require payment.

Well, what is to be done? In the first place, I do not believe that the picture is either as black or as red as it has been painted. I do not believe, for example, that Messrs. McCarthy and McCarran represent the real feeling of the American people. I have great faith in the basic common sense and the fundamental fairness of the nation.

But there is more fear in the country than the facts warrant. Beset by doubt, the nation listens to those who seem to offer a cure, even though the medicine be more harmful than the disease.

There are times when all of us are oppressed by the magnitude of the problems surrounding us, when we wonder what we as individuals can do to alleviate the situation. I offer four suggestions:

First, let us keep strong; let us never lower our guard.

Second, in the justifiable concern about our own loss of equilibrium, let us keep alert to all aspects of aggressive Communist imperialism.

Third, let us remember that we need spiritual unity in our land. We must not lock our minds with the key of prejudice. We cannot afford senseless fights—they are a luxury based on a security we do not possess.

Finally, I urge that we dedicate ourselves anew to the principles of "Man's Right to Knowledge and the Free Use Thereof." Let us thus help to restore a courage of old to our beloved country.

Section D: Questions and Readings for Study and Discussion

2.14. The History of Censorship

Summarize and discuss the history of censorship.

If the following references were arranged in historical, rather than alphabetical order, the list would perhaps read: Lasswell, Garrison, Cohen, Chafee, Myers, Ernst, Sibley and Cross. Do you think the references concerning "bigotry" and "intolerance" belong here?

Chafee, Zechariah, *Free Speech in the United States,* rev. ed., Cambridge, Mass.: Harvard University Press, 1949.

Cohen, Morris R., "The Dark Side of Religion," pp. 337-361 in *The Faith of a Liberal,* New York: Holt, 1946.

Cross, Harold L., *People's Right to Know: Legal Access to Public Records and Proceedings,* New York: Columbia University Press, 1953.

Ernst, Morris L., and Lindey, Alexander, *The Censor Marches On,* New York: Doubleday, 1940.

Garrison, William E., *Intolerance,* New York: Round Table Press, 1934.

* Lasswell, Harold D., "Censorship," article in *Encyclopedia of the Social Sciences,* New York: Macmillan, 1930 (III: 290-294).

Myers, Gustavus E., *History of Bigotry in the United States,* New York: Random House, 1943.

Sibley, Mulford Q., and Jacob, Philip E., *Conscription of Conscience: The American State and the Conscientious Objector, 1940-1947* (Preface by Robert E. Cushman), Ithaca, N. Y.: Cornell University Press, 1952.

2.15. Some Positive Aspects of Organized Pressure Groups

To most people "censorship" implies the negative and distasteful effects of group pressures. But is there not a positive side? Are not group-imposed disciplines and restrictions necessary for social morality and progress? If there were no organized groups (religious, esthetic, scientific, recreational, etc.) committed to definite values, and eager to share them with others, would not society stagnate into indifference and sloth?

Bell, Bernard Iddings, *Crowd Culture,* New York: Harper, 1952.

Berelson, Bernard, and Janowitz, Morris, eds., *Reader in Public Opinion and Communication,* Glencoe, Ill.: Free Press, 1950 (Chapter 9).

Bernard, L. L., *Social Control in its Sociological Aspects,* New York: Macmillan, 1939 (Part III).

Bryson, Lyman, *The Next America,* New York: Harper, 1952 (Chapters 10 and 11).

* Faris, Robert E. L., *Social Psychology,* New York: Ronald, 1952 (Chapters 1 and 4).

* Krutch, Joseph Wood, ed., *Is the Common Man Too Common?* Norman, Okla.: University of Oklahoma Press, 1954.

Landis, Paul, *Social Control,* New York: Lippincott, 1939 (especially Chapter 25).

Mumford, Lewis, *The Conduct of Life,* New York: Harcourt, 1951 (Chapters 6 and 7).

Young, Kimball, *Personality and Problems of Adjustment,* New York: Appleton-Century-Crofts, 1952 (Chapter 7).

2.16. Censorship for Different Age Levels

Are problems of censorship the same for all age levels? Are they alike for elementary, secondary, college and adult classes? Discuss.

* Bode, Boyd H., *Progressive Education at the Crossroads,* Chicago and New York: Newsom, 1938 (Chapter 5, "Education as Growth").

Bossard, James H. S., *The Sociology of Child Development,* rev. ed., New York: Harper, 1954 (Chapter 27, "The Changing Status of Childhood in the United States").

* Dewey, John, *Experience and Education,* New York: Macmillan, 1939 (Chapter 7, "Progressive Organization of Subject Matter").

Garrison, Karl C., *Growth and Development,* New York: Longmans, 1952 (pages 341-377, 503-507) (bibliography).

Gesell, Arnold, and Ilg, Frances L., *Infant and Child in the Culture of Today,* New York: Harper, 1943 (pages 288-290, "Absolute *versus* Relative Concepts").

* Schneiders, Alexander A., *The Psychology of Adolescence,* Milwaukee: Bruce, 1951 (Chapter 22, "The Development of Intellectual Functions") (bibliography).

2.17. Secrecy and Security

In the context of the current world crisis, most people recognize the need for military secrecy and censorship. Modern military power depends on science, but scientific progress requires free and open communication. **What is the proper relation between science, secrecy and security?**

Conant, James B., *Science and Common Sense,* New Haven, Conn.: Yale University Press, 1951 (Chapter 12) .

Committee of the American Association for the Advancement of Science, Maurice B. Visscher, chairman, "Civil Liberties of Scientists," *Science* 110: 177-179, Aug. 19, 1949.

* Gellhorn, Walter, *Security, Loyalty, and Science,* Ithaca, N. Y.: Cornell University Press, 1948 (Chapters 2 and 3) .

Killian, James R., "The University in a Period of Armed Truce," *Vital Speeches* 16: 252-256, Feb. 1, 1950.

* Painter, Sidney, Meyerhoff, H. A., and Waterman, Alan T., "The Visa Problem," *Scientific Monthly* 76: 11-19, January 1953.

* Smyth, Henry D., "National Security and the Scientist," *Saturday Review* 33: 6 f, July 29, 1950.

Wiener, Norbert, *The Human Use of Human Beings,* Boston: Houghton, 1950 (Chapter 8) .

Wolfe, Bertram D., "Science Joins the Party," *Antioch Review* 10: 47-60, March 1950.

2.18. Education and Propaganda

How is education like and unlike propaganda? Is propaganda always harmful? or is it sometimes necessary and beneficial?

Beardsley, Monroe, *Practical Logic,* New York: Prentice-Hall, 1950 (Part I) .

* Bridgman, Percy W., "The Potential Intelligent Society of the Future," Chapter 11 in F. S. C. Northrop, ed., *Ideological Differences and World Order,* New Haven: Yale University Press, 1949.

Chase, Stuart, *Power of Words,* New York: Harcourt, 1953 (Chapter 16) (bibliography) .

* Doob, Leonard, *Public Opinion and Propaganda,* New York: Holt, 1948 (Chapter 11, pp. 232-250) .

Evans, Bergen, *A Natural History of Nonsense,* New York: Knopf, 1946 (Chapter 1) .

Huse, H. R., *The Illiteracy of the Literate,* New York: Macmillan, 1930 (Chapter 10).

Lee, Alfred McClurg, *How to Understand Propaganda,* New York: Rinehart, 1952 (Chapters 1 and 2).

* Martin, Everett Dean, *Farewell to Revolution,* New York: Norton, 1935 (p. 357 f).

Ruby, Lionel, *Logic: An Introduction,* New York: Lippincott, 1950 (Part I). (Many other logic textbooks also deal with logical fallacies and verbal ambiguities.)

2.19. Competing Values versus Absolute Values

In writing the U. S. Supreme Court's opinion which led to the conviction of the leaders of the American Communist Party, Chief Justice Vinson said concerning the "clear and present danger" doctrine:

> . . . neither Justice Holmes nor Justice Brandeis envisioned that a shorthand phrase should be crystallized into a rigid rule to be applied inflexibly without regard to the circumstances of each case. Speech is not an absolute, above and beyond control by the legislature when its judgment, subject to review here, is that certain kinds of speech are so undesirable as to warrant criminal sanction. Nothing is more certain in modern society than that there are no absolutes, that a name, a phrase, a standard has meaning only when associated with the considerations which gave birth to the nomenclature. . . . To those who would paralyze our Government in the face of impending threat by encasing it in a semantic straitjacket we must reply that all concepts are relative.

For saying ". . . there are no absolutes . . . . all concepts are relative. . . ." the Chief Justice was criticized by Judge Desmond, Father Wise (see references below) and others. **Do you think such criticisms were justified?**

Desmond, J., *Zorach v. Clauson,* 100 N. E. 2nd, 463 at 471 (1951).

Vinson, Chief Justice Fred M., majority opinion, *Dennis v. United States.* 341 U.S. 494, 508 (1951).

Wise, Rev. John E., S.J., "Relativism and the University," *School and Society* 78: 161-166, November 28, 1953.

2.20. A Philosophical Problem: The Relative and the Absolute

Since those who most strongly advocate censorship are generally those who believe in "absolutes," we are led into one of the persistent problems of philosophy—the problem of the Relative and the Absolute. Of the references below, those by Carré, Mannheim and Quine, and perhaps those included in Vivas and Krieger's anthology, are the most abstract and philosophical.

Becker, Carl, *The Heavenly City of the Eighteenth Century Philosophers,* New Haven, Conn.: Yale University Press, 1932 (Chapters 1 and 4).

Carré, Mayrich H., *Realists and Nominalists* (Augustine, Abelard, Aquinas, Occam), New York: Oxford, 1946.

Hook, Sidney, "Can We Trust Our Teachers?" *Saturday Review* 36: 11 f, April 18, 1953.

* Mannheim, Karl, *Ideology and Utopia,* New York: Harcourt, 1936 (Chapters 1 and 2).

Quine, Willard Van Orton, *From A Logical Point of View,* Cambridge, Mass.: Harvard University Press, 1953 (Chapter 1).

Ryan, John A., and Boland, Francis J., *Catholic Principles of Politics,* New York: Macmillan, 1940 (p. 318 f).

Ryan, John K., "Truth and Freedom," *Journal of Higher Education* 20: 349-352, October 1949.

Sellars, Wilfrid, and Feigl, Herbert, eds., *Readings in Philosophical Analysis,* New York: Appleton-Century-Crofts, 1949 (Introduction).

Spalding, Willard B., "Academic Freedom," *Progressive Education* 28: 111-117, February 1951.

* Vivas, Eliseo, and Krieger, Murray, eds., *The Problems of Aesthetics: A Book of Readings,* New York: Rinehart, 1953 (pages 430-479).

3. RELIGION AND PUBLIC EDUCATION

Section A: Religion in a Pluralistic Society

3.1. INTRODUCTION

Although religion has been one of the great social forces of history, today it seems to be more of a divisive element than a unifying cement. Jew and Gentile, Catholic and Protestant, Hindu and Moslem, theist and atheist—such divisions are so pronounced that no one religion seems capable of forming a center for modern society. Most religions have taught that true progress is progress in charity, all other advances being secondary thereto. But because the religions of mankind remain irreconcilably plural, science, art and the secular state have at present taken charge of those interests that alone seem capable of knitting together the many divided groups.

But the state is not almighty, and we should not look to it for everything. In a free society the worth of the individual is supreme, and the great bulk of individual affairs lie outside the province of government. The modern state is indeed a center of unity; but in a free society the state enforces unity only in terms of the practical needs of communal living: Its only obligation is to keep its citizens together in peace and harmony. Citizens may be influenced by their churches, and indirectly churches may thus have an effect on state policies. But the state deals only with its citizens, not with the churches. History affords ample proof that, united with government, religion becomes legalistic or superstitious; united with religion, government becomes despotic or totalitarian.

In the United States, all attempts to set up any one religion as an exclusive faith have met with failure. Since Washington's day, Americans have recognized that ". . . the Government of the United States of America is not in any sense founded on the Christian religion." [1] The United States is not a Christian, a Jewish or a Mohammedan nation; neither is it agnostic nor atheistic. A democratic society is a cooperative, interactive society; and where men cannot agree on a set of beliefs, such beliefs cannot be a part of democracy—except insofar as we agree to disagree. Which is to say: America is religiously pluralistic.

Many Americans look upon religious pluralism, democratic tolerance and scientific open-mindedness as expressions of Christian charity.[2] To be tolerant and open-minded, to be dubious about whatever tradition may insist upon as absolute, to depend on private experience as the ultimate source of social values—these are qualities which any mature civilization demands. Does such tolerance make us indifferent to the values traditionally associated with God and religion? Some people seem to think so. "Liberalism" then becomes only a superficial attitude concerning politics or economics, with no real ethics, philosophy or religion. "Freedom" in education means "just growing up," like Topsy. And "democracy" stands only for an external type of political or geographical organization, with little or nothing to do with basic human values. This unfortunate emptiness may explain why in our century democracy has at times seemed unattractive to people who yearn for some purpose, and who, to borrow Erich Fromm's phrase, seek "escape from freedom." Such "tender-minded" people have sometimes preferred life under a dictator to the nakedness and complete self-reliance which democratic society seems to demand.

---

[1] U. S. Treaty with Tripoli, November 4, 1796, Article XI. Read also James Hastings Nichols, *Democracy and the Churches*, Philadelphia: Westminster, 1951, p. 17 f.

[2] Some, however, take issue with this viewpoint, notably many Catholic philosophers, who base their dissent on the scholastic doctrine that tolerance and charity are "moral" virtues which pertain to the *will*, and which are to be sharply distinguished from dogmatic "truth," which pertains to the *intellect*. On this point, read Etienne Gilson, *Dogmatism and Tolerance: An Address* (Pamphlet) New Brunswick, N. J.: Rutgers University Press, 1952.

Today we realize the need of the individual for attachment to ideals larger than himself, whether they be secular ideals such as "welfare," "security," "truth," "freedom"; or religious ideals such as the "Way and Power" of a Taoist, the "Yoga" (Yoke) of a Hindu, the "Path" of a Buddhist, or the "Fatherhood of God and Brotherhood of Man" of a Hebrew, Christian or Mohammedan.

From the viewpoint of religious faith, the important question arises: Is it necessary for an ideal to be eternal, or for an idea to be infallible, in order that the will may be firmly attached to it? Liberals do not think so. A 1925 car owner may have been as attached to his "Model T" as in 1950 he later becomes attached to his "V-8"; and he is not in the least dismayed because new and better models appear. It is certainly true that our medieval ancestors attained an integrated view of the world and of man's place in it, when they supposed that the earth was flat and stationary, and that intellectual and moral absolutes were indispensable. But countless twentieth-century thinkers attain an equally integrated and satisfactory viewpoint, based on the belief that ours is a spinning planet whose human inhabitants can learn to apply tentative, reconstructive thinking to ethical beliefs as well as to scientific theories. But although such intellectual theories (or car models) may be subject to change, our emotional attachment to them may be very genuine. In sum: It is not necessary to be dogmatic about our intellectual beliefs in order to be firmly attached to them emotionally.

Democracy and civilization thrive on differences. We revert to barbarism when we allow ourselves to be flattered into supposing our own group a "master race," a "chosen people," or an exclusively "divinely inspired faith." Once this happens, other groups and other individuals tend to be rated as inferior; members of the "in-group" are regarded as first-class citizens, others only as second-class citizens. Men are no longer respected as *men:* Respect for a *theory about men* takes precedence over respect for men as men. Since our American democracy contains all types of citizens, with a tremendous variety of cultural and religious backgrounds, it may properly be expected to contain all types of faith (i.e., theories and convictions about Man, God and the Universe).

Does lack of reliance on a single viewpoint mean the absence of any viewpoint? Does loss of "faith" in an exclusive set of beliefs mean the complete lack of faith? Some think so. Others, like Elliot E. Cohen, believe it implies a new type of shared conviction:

> It seems to me that the free citizen, religious or non-religious, does have at least one shared conviction. Whether he professes to believe in God, or professes not to believe in God, he has a conviction that there is no God but God. To put it another way: I think both the religious believer and the man of secular faith in the United States come very close to holding in their hearts the Hebraic commandment "Thou shalt have no other gods before Me." I take this to mean that whether one believes in some transcendent power or not, one does not believe that there is any idea, institution, or individual—a man, a nation, an "ism"—that man can accept as a God.[3]

The democratic citizen should be humble enough not to think of himself as God or as godlike, and he is on eternally safe ground so long as he permits no group to arrogate to itself the attributes of the divine.

This includes the State. The order of a democracy is not a single order of the State: It is a system of orders, some in conflict with others, some even in conflict with the State itself, as presently conceived. Like the lobby of a hotel, the State is a kind of "room" whose function is to connect the more private rooms and thus to serve as a common center of communication. But free men cannot allow the State to claim overriding allegiance in all things. For the religious man, God alone may have the final claim, and he may freely assert: "There is a higher law than the Constitution." For the scientist, Euclid's adage still stands: "There is no royal road to geometry." As for poetry and art, "Art for art's sake" may not represent the entire truth, but it points up the fact that creative endeavors cannot be genuine unless free. As Charles Morgan has said: "If art has anything to teach it is . . . that to mistake one

---

[3] Elliot E. Cohen, "The Free American Citizen, 1952," *Commentary* 14: 219-230, at 225, September 1952. By permission.

Compare Harry Emerson Fosdick, "How Shall We Think of God?" Harper's 153: 229-233, July 1926; St. Thomas Aquinas, "We cannot know what God is, but only what He is not," *Summa Contra Gentiles* 1: 30, 33; and for a more difficult reference: Charles Hartshorne and William L. Reese, *Philosophers Speak of God*, Chicago: University of Chicago Press, 1953.

supposed aspect of truth for Truth itself and so to imprison man's curiosity and aspiration in the dungeon of an ideology, is the unforgivable sin against the spirit of man." [4] If society is to enjoy the maximum benefits of the aspiring saint, the reflective scientist or the creative artist, the State dare not dictate precisely how or what such men shall think or say. The sanctions of religion, the theories of science, and the creations of art cannot be coerced.

Encouraging each citizen to contribute toward and to share in the group pool of talent, democracy has faith that in so doing the various elements (no longer termed "higher" or "lower") will be helped by one another. "Tolerance" in the democratic sense thus means an attitude of creative appreciation, not grudging acceptance, of the diversity of peoples, occupations and interests needed for civilization. In a true democracy every citizen wears a crown.

The contrast between authoritarian and democratic philosophies has been clearly stated by Harold Rugg:

> The Philosophy and Social Order of Authority and the Exploitative Tradition say, "You and I are different. Each is an Individual. I am Superior. You are Inferior. So, I shall dictate to you. The greatest thinking has already been done and has been passed on in the Word. I shall interpret the Word of that thinking for you. And I shall rule you." Thus through most of recorded history the strong and ambitious have ruled the docile and less aggressive.
>
> The Philosophy of Experience, the Social Order of Democracy and the Great Tradition say: "You and I are different, yet we must live together. Each of us is a Person. I am a Supreme . . . but you are a Supreme also. Each has a unique experience and some original power of thought. Together we can distill judgment and decision out of human experience. So we shall rule together.[5]

Does such cooperative self-rule demand open discussion about religion? The editor believes it does. America is a strong nation

---

[4] Charles Morgan, *Liberties of the Mind,* New York: Macmillan, 1951, p. 91. Compare Archibald MacLeish, "The Muses' Sterner Laws," *New Republic* 128: 16-18, July 13, 1953.

[5] Harold Rugg, *Foundations for American Education,* Yonkers, N. Y.: World Book Co., 1947, pp. 35-36. By permission. Compare Robert M. MacIver, *The Ramparts We Guard,* New York: Macmillan, 1950 (Chapter 13).

because its citizens are courageous. They are courageous because they are free to disagree, to quarrel with authority, to challenge orthodoxy. Democratic society does not provide a cloistered world where the opinions or prejudices of any group are shielded from the criticism of others. Democracy is not for weaklings, nor for indoctrinated automatons. It is for citizens of independent convictions, who also have genuine respect and courtesy toward others—including those whose views they detest.

Even if we so desired, we could not avoid discussion of this subject, since education is equally significant to democracy and to religion. In a society which not only tolerates but (by remission of taxes) encourages religion, questions inevitably arise as to the basic authority behind educational institutions. In mid-century America we face such problems as the following: If Communist party members are disqualified from teaching, because of subjection to foreign discipline, what about Catholic priests and nuns? [6] Can religious instruction be made a part of education without substituting indoctrination for learning? Can religion be taught in the public schools without becoming partial to some religions as against others? Can public funds be allocated to parochial schools without breaking down our traditional separation of Church and State? Whether we like it or not, these are issues which face contemporary America. Let us hope we can discuss them openly, fairly, fearlessly and intelligently. If we can, we will have affirmed a basic tenet of our democratic faith, which Horace Kallen has described as follows:

> Democracy is the method by which hitherto inflexible and unadjustable infallibilities may adjust to one another and live together as a communion of the different on equal terms. . . . To paraphrase Edwin Markham: other ways of thought and life draw circles which shut the different out, as heretics, rebels and things to flout, but democracy and science are the methods that win, for the circle they draw brings the differences in.[7]

---

[6] This problem has been quite thoroughly explored in *Zellers v. Huff*, 236 P. 2nd, 949 (N.M. 1951); *Harfst v. Hoegen*, 349 Mo. 808; 163 S.W. 2nd 609 (1942). The other questions will be considered in the selections to follow.

[7] Horace M. Kallen, "Democracy's True Religion" (Pamphlet), Boston: Beacon, 1951, page 10. By permission.

3.2. BASES FOR DEVELOPING RELIGIOUS COMMUNITY [8]

Peter Anthony Bertocci

Is there any way out of the tragic conflicts which seem to spring so inevitably from the religious conviction that without adequate adjustment to God's purpose, every human success is ultimately failure? . . .

The author speaks as one to whom the Judeo-Christian tradition is the most vital source of religious guidance and inspiration. The Christian, he feels, must not belittle or deny the reality of God's concern and respect for the sincere efforts of all other minds —religious and irreligious—to discover and live by the truth. It is the *meaning of God in human experience*—not the meaning of Christ, or Mohammed, or Confucius, or Buddha, or Ramakrishna, or other founders of great religions—which must have primacy. The central loyalty is to God, the father; and the permanent concern is for that love of God which makes all men brothers.

All religious insights should be respected; but none are final. Does this mean that there is no final revelation of the truth to all men through one particular tradition? Does this mean that one religious tradition is just as good or true as another? Does this mean that allegiance to the church is not important?

An adequate answer to these questions, especially to the first two, should be preceded by a careful study of theologies and the religious traditions within which they grow. Yet certain conclusions are suggested by our discussion; these clearly challenge both the claim to finality and the claim to equality.

Voices will be raised from within major traditions against our insistence that however bound each of us may be to his religious tradition, the supreme focus of religious loyalty must be God. Let us simulate a spokesman of the dominant strain in the Christian tradition, representing Roman Catholic and conservative Protestant perspectives, in order that our discussion become relevant, if still too brief.

---

[8] Peter Anthony Bertocci, *Introduction to the Philosophy of Religion,* pp. 506-514. Copyright, 1951, by Prentice-Hall, Inc., New York. Reprinted by permission of the publisher.

Mr. Bertocci is professor of philosophy at Boston University.

"But it is not as easy as that," says the objector. "The God we know through Christ is not, in important respects, the God of the Hindu and Mohammedan. We do not worship God in abstraction from the insights and experience of our religious leaders. Have you yourself not said that in the last analysis, value lies not in 'belief in God' but in belief in the true God? We believe the Christian view of God is valid. The God we worship is the God we see through the life and teachings of Christ, and through the rich experience of our historic community. We believe that only in Jesus' exemplary life, atoning death, and victorious resurrection will men find *the* meaning of God in human experience about which you speak."

We cannot agree with the person who believes that only in Christ and through Christ is there revelation, or that only through an especially inspired Book (or a specifically ordained Church) has God revealed himself supremely and finally to man. But it certainly would be foolish to suggest that any person who so believes stop believing what he honestly does believe about the revelation of God and the proper approach to him. That person ought to proclaim and live conscientiously by that belief until he has substantial reason for changing it. But all who sincerely disagree must be allowed a similar privilege. . . .[9]

Let it be clearly noted that we have not denied categorically that the final truth (that is, the truth upon which none may ever improve) *may* be found within a given tradition. A given tradition may, theoretically at least, have reached the zenith of religious insight. But no human being could ever know this. And all who assert it without carefully understanding the religious experience and thought of others and the formulations of that experience and thought in doctrine, in worship, and in action, are less than fair to their fellowmen. . . .

Convinced that God cares about the spiritual growth of all persons, and realizing that God is doing all he can to work with all lives at their point of growth, the believer will not assume that *his*

[9] Editor's Note: Compare A. K. Coomaraswamy (Hindu), *Am I My Brother's Keeper?* New York: Day, 1946, p. 42; Erich Fromm (Psychologist), *Psychoanalysis and Religion*, New Haven, Conn.: Yale University Press, 1950; Duncan Howlett (Unitarian), *Man Against the Church: The Struggle to Free Man's Spirit*, Boston, Beacon, 1954.

differences from his fellows mark God's special point of growth, while the differences of others betray the weaknesses of human nature! He will rather try to see God working in the differences of others! There is no easy path to tread here. We do not mean to sentimentalize; differences are not necessarily good just because they are differences. But it is only as each person views his own differences and those of others not with pride but with responsible fellow-feeling that he and his critic can come together to live *with* their differences!

We have not, let it be stressed, said that one faith is as good as another and that differences are not important. Disregard of differences is evidence of intellectual irresponsibility and a contemptuous tolerance. Tolerance is properly rooted in the realization that the truth is difficult to find. *The wisdom of tolerance lies in the realization that the insights of others may help to bring new truth. Tolerance is the willingness to bear with differences in the conviction that a deeper truth can be found.* Tolerance is *never* indifference to what other persons believe. It stems not from the certainty that we have already discovered the final truth, but from profound love for truth, and from the humble awareness of the different paths by which men may come to it. Such tolerance is never condescension; it does not wear the mask of "patience with the evildoer." The tolerant person is all too conscious that he may be the one in error.

To say all this is not to provide a formula for solving the concrete issues upon which religions differ both in the realm of theory and in the realm of practice. But it does point the way to the kind of union desirable between all churches and religious bodies. For taking advantage of the unity already present, we recognize the possibility of good and evil in differences, and we set the mind to maximize the good and quarantine the possible evil in differences. We build on the fact that different persons set out to find God with their own particular complex of limitations, needs, and aspirations, and that God meets *them* and works with them in their social and spiritual predicament to do all he can to draw them closer to himself.

The attitude of "live and let live" thus becomes one of "live and help live." The focus is shifted to the common task of helping all men to realize the values God is yearning for them to share with him and with each other. When members of any religious group act as if their corner of the world—and any other they can control or possess—belongs to them and not to God, other persons may well question the reality of their vision and dedication to God. The tolerance of religious persons should have a quality about it which distinguishes it from the tolerance of unbelievers. Believing, as religious persons do, in God's loving respect for all persons, they must order their whole lives, *spiritual, social, economic,* and *political,* so that they may work with God in removing the obstacles to spiritual growth. These obstacles are not so much the differences in specific religious doctrine as the economic, social, and political injustices perpetuated or encouraged by members of one religious group or culture upon another. Religious tolerance must spell helpfulness in every sphere of life, for God does not love the spirit in isolation from the body through which the spirit works.

The dangers of an authoritarian conception of tolerance. But we must come to closer grips with one very serious barrier to mutual confidence between religious groups. This is the claim made by members of any one perspective that God has entrusted them with the whole essential truth about his nature and will. To this essential truth, it is alleged, there is simply nothing to be added or taken away. Tolerance now cannot spring from the realization that the truth is so difficult to find that we need to inspect and protect significant differences in other perspectives. For this is to challenge the thesis which is crucial to the affirmations of such authoritarians: that the revelation made available in their tradition is final. *Tolerance for the authoritarian means, at best, loving concern for the rest of God's children, welcome recognition of agreements, and generous cooperation on all points which do not touch the sacred revelation entrusted to them. But the authoritarian conception of tolerance has no place for the thought that perhaps his revelation might fall short; there is no place for argument and further reasoning about the essentials of the faith as entrusted to him.* He will be willing to work with others who work consistently with his own purposes, but let there be no expectancy that he will gladly study the "untrue" elements in the faith of others or encourage other members of his group to do so.

Freedom of speech must never, in this view, extend to the so-called impartial discussion of untruth. Indeed, any freedom which involves the freedom to be wrong on matters of revelation is not real freedom. For freedom is circumscribed within the dictates of revealed truth. This conception of tolerance and freedom may be called authoritarian in order to distinguish it from the *liberal* conception of tolerance and freedom suggested above.

Religious authoritarians are not necessarily puffed with pride. They are solemn in their sense of obligation to the truth which they believe has been delivered to them. If it is not theirs to argue *with* the revelation, it is not theirs to treat it as *one* among many, or even as a hypothetical best amenable to further substantiation. Theirs it is to oppose all views and persons inconsistent with the revelation; theirs it is to diminish the opportunities of those whose strength is the strength of error. A church with this belief will open doors wide to all who would join *the* faith; at the same time it builds walls thick and strong to preserve its own from the evil influences of members of other faiths. Meanwhile through church and school it will encourage its own members to use their social, economic, and political influence to weaken the political, economic, and social power of those who live outside *the* faith. There is no other way of being consistent and loyal to the belief that God has given unqualified revelation and authority to one religious group and its clergy.

Without denying that, under some circumstances, such authoritarian groups have done their share of good, one may doubt whether that good is not being counterbalanced by an increasing weight of evil. For other religious groups realize that (by hypothesis) argument is of no avail. And those who find belief in God impossible or unnecessary realize that their freedom will be regarded as license and not freedom by these authoritarians who believe that there is no real freedom apart from the truth which their group holds. Suspicion and fear thus permeate the social life of the community, nation, and world to discourage the objective consideration of issues which concern the health and education of the people as a whole. For the nonauthoritarian groups never feel safe when the authoritarians seem to increase in power; and the authoritarians never feel safe when those who do not accept the revelation are on the increase. What is worse, such fear prevents each side from giving due consideration to the reasonable requests of the other.

The author has explicitly refrained from naming specific groups so far because he has been concerned with the psycho-logic of authoritarianism in religion wherever it be found. It may be found in America among Protestants, but they have increasingly come to live with their doctrinal differences and are seeking further bases for cooperation. Each Protestant denomination insists, and implicitly promises every other, that its belief in its own version of God's revelation will not prevent it from guaranteeing the freedom of other religious groups. This, of course, is not to say that individual Protestants are free from bigotry. (The reader should bear in mind that we are not discussing here the actions of particular individuals; our consideration is the logical basis for two different conceptions of tolerance and the outcome of action consistent with those conceptions.) Each Protestant may sincerely believe that the tenets of his denomination are in some respects superior to those of others, but he is being untrue to the basic Protestant conviction that no human being has the final revelation if he denies the validity of the independent search for God by those who cannot agree with him.

It was this conviction which prevailed among Protestants and allowed the establishing of the Roman Catholic Church in America (though, once more, the record is hardly one of consistent, ungrudging welcome). What Protestants now ask is: Can, or will, the authoritarianism of Catholicism also adapt itself to the underlying conviction that freedom of religious belief and unbelief is paramount, as have authoritarian Protestant sects? Or will Roman Catholicism be unyielding in pursuing the logic of authoritarianism with regard to freedom and tolerance? The author does not know the answer to these questions. Certainly doubt on this score is having unfortunate consequences for religious unity among Christians in America and in the world. It seems equally certain that religious conflict adds yearly to the number of those who doubt that religion can save man.

On the other hand, there is reason for supposing that authoritarianism in religion can be fitted into the democratic way of life if, as part of its conviction, it takes seriously the conviction that in matters of religion souls can only be won by persuasion. . . .

3.3. RELIGIOUS TOLERANCE [10]
Victor White
* * * *

The question of tolerance and intolerance drives the theologian and the religious teacher into the deeper question of the truth or falsehood of what he or others believe and teach; and this, in its turn, should lead him to inquire into the character and scope, the *kind* of truth which he is concerned to believe and proclaim. And if he be a Christian, the answer should be plain enough. His professional concern is not with any sort of truth, neither mathematical, nor scientific, nor philosophical, nor social, nor even ethical truth, but with the *verbum salutis,* the message of human healing and salvation, the Gospel, the good news of the Divine offer of human deliverance and the means for its attainment. His message, he believes, is the message of Divine love for mankind, and if he takes at all seriously his own calling as its messenger, he cannot tolerate within the Church, the community of believers, any distortion of that message which would be harmful to its hearers: he must hate heresy because he loves God and his neighbor. Nevertheless, and this he has too often forgotten, it is of the very essence of that message itself that it is a Divine gift of grace and election, that its acceptance means free, individual response and decision, and that discipleship means personal willingness to take up a cross and to follow.

Once these things are really grasped, the pluralist society no longer presents a problem, but rather a welcome opportunity, to the orthodox believer. It needs no justification. The problem now

---

[10] Victor White, "Religious Tolerance," B.B.C. broadcast reprinted in *Commonweal* 58: 531-534, Sept. 4, 1953; discussion, *Commonweal* 59: 450-452, Feb. 5, 1954; 59: 555-556, March 5, 1954. By permission.

Father White is an English Dominican, author of *God and the Unconscious* and other books.

That this is not the official view of Rome may be seen by reading *Time* 51: 70, June 28, 1948; 62: 41, Aug. 3, 1953; 63: 88, Jan. 25, 1954. Read also James Hastings Nichols, *Democracy and the Churches,* Philadelphia: Westminster, 1951.

is rather to justify the former employment of Christianity as the religion of a sacral society. For it at least tacitly assumed that the Christian Church and the human community were coterminous, and that membership of a nation, the habitation of a geographical area, entailed orthodox Christian faith and discipleship. From the outset, Christianity had meant a breakaway from the sacral institutions of Judaism, the formation of an *ecclesia* of the "called," of those who "were born, not of blood . . . nor of the will of man, but of God." And it was from the intolerance of the sacral society of the Roman Empire that the early Christian Church suffered.

The transformation of Christianity itself into the established religion of a sacral society for a millennium after the conversion of Constantine was an anomaly which produced many anomalies, as well as all that we call Christian civilization. Not least of these anomalies was the Inquisition and the *De haeretico comburendo*. The anomaly lay not only in the fact that preachers of Divine love found themselves supporting brutal force to ensure conformity in a matter which their theology told them was an affair wholly of gracious election and individual decision: in the very fact of acting as judges of religious orthodoxy on behalf of the secular power, they cannot easily be absolved of the charge of rendering to Caesar the things that are God's.

Yet the sacral ideal has its attractions, and the medieval ideal of synthesis of Church and State is so impressive that we have been slow to see that it was an anomaly rather than a norm. But its departure should be a matter of rejoicing rather than for the nostalgic regrets of the apologists of the "Europe is the Faith" school. A pluralist society is one in which a Christian must be a Christian indeed; in which even the theologian can breathe more freely, with less temptation to prostitute his craft or distort the teaching committed to him in the interest (however intrinsically legitimate) of social unity and order. Now he is better able to get on with his own job: the job which Aquinas described as the "greater clarification of the content of Divine Teaching" to human minds. Toleration itself opens to him new vistas, presents him with exciting tasks. For toleration brings intercommunication; wider and deeper knowledge of the variety of the needs of the human soul, and of the mysterious and manifold ways of God with man. Christ came not to destroy but to fulfil the old dispensation; and only as the fulfilment of the truths which men already possess can His Gospel still be proclaimed. Idols must still be destroyed; but now men must freely destroy their own idols rather than have them destroyed by *force majeure*. Loving evangelism must replace sectarian proselytization; honest encounter must replace intimidation; the smoking flax must be fanned instead of quenched. To all this the theologian should have much to contribute. Perhaps he may even contribute to laying a firmer foundation for the Western world's precarious experiment in toleration itself.

Section B: Some Contrasting Viewpoints Concerning Religion in Education

3.4. INTRODUCTION

The percentage of church-going Americans is higher today than it has been at any previous time in the entire history of the United States. Most of these church members are products of the public schools. It is surprising, therefore, that the public schools have lately become victims of a widespread attack by persons who fear "secularism," "statism" or "the decline of the family." Perhaps such criticisms are merely an expression of current social anxiety. It may be that "secularism" provides a convenient scapegoat for the many evils of our time. Possibly some schools or teachers are aggressively irreligious. Or perhaps the current attacks are part of an organized drive by groups with special axes to grind. Whatever the reasons, our public schools are being called "godless" and "atheistic," and it is well that American citizens should understand some of the contrasting views concerning the place of religion in education.

The following selection by the American Council on Education will further introduce the problem as it exists today.

3.5. THE FUNCTION OF THE PUBLIC SCHOOLS IN DEALING WITH RELIGION [11]

American Council on Education

Public education in the United States is committed by federal and state law to the general principle that sectarian religious instruction must be excluded from the curriculum. This does not mean, however, that the problem of what to do about religion in the public schools has been solved. On the contrary, there is no clear-cut understanding of what the schools should or should not do in this field.

Some people think that the schools should leave religion completely to organized religious groups and to the home. They fear that any consideration of religion in the school will result in dangerous divisions in the community because of the emotional factors with which religion is surrounded; or they believe that the public school in a democratic society cannot handle religion without violating the religious liberty of minority groups.

Many people, however, are convinced that the public school's program of general education becomes distorted and impoverished when all religious references are excluded. They fear that neglect of religion will undermine the very foundations of individual and social morality. In their opinion the Founding Fathers did not intend to exclude religion from the schools when they restrained Congress from any move toward an "establishment of religion." . . .

In 1947 the Committee on Religion and Education issued our first report, *The Relation of Religion to Public Education: The Basic Principles.* . . . Relevant conclusions from that report may be restated as follows:

1. The problem is to find a way in public education to give due recognition to the place of religion in the culture and in the convictions of our people while at the same time safeguarding the separation of church and state.

[11] American Council on Education, *The Function of the Public Schools in Dealing with Religion: A Report on the Exploratory Study Made by the Committee on Religion and Education,* Washington, D. C.: National Education Association, 1953, Chapter 1, pages 1-7. By permission. (Contains excellent bibliography).

2. The separation of American public education from church control was not intended to exclude all study of religion from the school program.

3. Teaching a common core of religious beliefs in the public schools is not a satisfactory solution.

4. Teaching "moral and spiritual values" cannot be regarded as an adequate substitute for an appropriate consideration of religion in the school program.

5. Teaching which opposes or denies religion is as much a violation of religious liberty as teaching which advocates or supports any particular religious belief.

6. Introducing factual study of religion will not commit the public schools to any particular religious belief.

7. The role of the school in the study of religion is distinct from, though complementary to, the role of the church.

8. The public school should stimulate the young toward a vigorous, personal reaction to the challenge of religion.

9. The public school should assist youth to have an intelligent understanding of the historical and contemporary role of religion in human affairs. . . .

The Educational Policies Commission of the National Education Association of the United States and of the American Association of School Administrators published its report on *Moral and Spiritual Values in the Public Schools* [12] in 1951. The commission maintains that the public schools, in discharging their responsibility for the development of the moral and spiritual values which the American people desire their children to hold, can and should teach *about* religion. . . .

The commission says,

. . . when a point about religious opinion or religious practices arises in a classroom discussion the teacher will not brush it aside with a statement that he is not allowed to discuss this matter in the public school. There can be no doubt that the American democracy is grounded in a religious tradition. While religion may not be the only source of democratic moral and spiritual values, it is surely one of the important sources. For this objec-

---

[12] Washington: National Education Association.

tive reason, if for no other, an attitude of respect toward religion should prevail in the schools. . . .

Under the heading "The Public School Can and Should Teach About Religion" the commission says,

The public schools can teach objectively *about* religion without advocating or teaching any religious creed. To omit from the classroom all references to religion and the institutions of religion is to neglect an important part of American life. Knowledge about religion is essential for a full understanding of our culture, literature, art, history, and current affairs. That religious beliefs are controversial is not an adequate reason for excluding teaching about religion from the public schools. . .

Our position with respect to the problem under study may be briefly summarized as follows:

The public school is limited, as the private institution is not, in its treatment of religion. The constitutions, statutes, and interpretations thereof in the forty-eight states, and the decisions of the Supreme Court of the United States, make it illegal for the public school to teach religion in the sense of the attempt to inculcate sectarian religious beliefs. Even if agreement could be reached among the religiously minded on a "common core" or set of basic propositions common to and acceptable to Roman Catholics, Protestants, and Jews, there would remain the nonreligious groups in the community who would maintain that their rights were violated by any attempt to inculcate general propositions embodying religious beliefs.

On the other hand, to be silent about religion may be, in effect, to make the public school an antireligious factor in the community. Silence creates the impression in the minds of the young that religion is unimportant and has nothing to contribute to the solution of the perennial and ultimate problems of human life. This negative consequence is all the more striking in a period when society is asking the public school to assume more and more responsibility for dealing with the cultural problems of growth and development.

Therefore, it is vitally important that the public school deal with religion. There are many ways in which this may be and indeed is being done. Some are good; others, in our judgment, may be dangerous to a greater or lesser degree. All public schools, however, can provide for the factual study of religion both as an important factor in the historical and contemporary development of our culture and as a source of values and insight for great numbers of people in finding the answers to persistent personal problems of living. Religion can, and in our judgment should, be studied in the same way as the economic and political institutions and principles of our country should be studied—not as something on which the American public school must settle all arguments and say the last word, but as something which is so much a part of the American heritage and so relevant to contemporary values that it cannot be ignored.

3.6. MORAL AND SPIRITUAL VALUES AND THE SECULAR PUBLIC SCHOOL[13]

Cheong Lum, George Kagehiro and Edwin Larm

Few of us would say that the school ought not teach the child honesty, equal regard for individual personality, kindness, cooperation, love, and related values. Yet, there are individuals who believe that moral and spiritual values cannot be taught in the public schools. These values, they maintain, are religious values and cannot be taught by a secular institution. There are others who feel that something must be done to develop the character of our youth and, to accomplish this, a "character training" course is added to the curriculum. In the opinion of many competent educators, the most usual result of such a course is a greater evil of compartmentalized learning and the resultant isolation of learning from practice. Then there are some who prefer to ignore the problem entirely, and others who would institute released-time religious instruction.

[13] Cheong Lum, George Kagehiro and Edwin Larm, "Some Thoughts on Moral and Spiritual Values and the Secular Public School," *Progressive Education* 30: 166-171, 192, April 1953. Slightly revised. By permission.

The three authors are from the University of Hawaii.

Confusion Over Moral Education Is Related To Idea That Values Are Extra-Mundane

It seems that at least part of the reason for this confusion over this question of values can be traced back to the frequently accepted notion that moral and spiritual values are inextricably bound up with a divine authority. This supernatural relation being assumed, the church inherits the responsibility of teaching these values. The secular public school does not teach religion and thereby disqualifies itself from teaching moral and spiritual values. A suggestion might be offered that religion be included in the curriculum of the public school. Such a proposal is out of the question. The only other alternative is not to teach moral and spiritual values. This is an equally unacceptable suggestion. . . .

It would be folly to pit the supernatural against the secular, the church against the state. What is proposed then is a search for a community of agreement in moral and spiritual values. We believe that our democracy is hospitable to cultural variety and differentiation and within its framework we can agree on "values which better organize a community in its cooperative life, which more fully enlist the active energies and interests of the individual or the community in a unified act which results in the continuing integrity of personality or community." [14] . . .

Definition of Some Key Terms

Before we begin a reinterpretation of the concept in question, it may be well to clarify the use of certain key terms such as *secular, value, moral and spiritual values,* and *public school.*

The term *secular* is used to refer to the temporal and earthly as distinguished from the supernatural. It is in no way intended to suggest opposition to or antagonism towards organized religion, nor does it imply a denial of the supernatural.

Public school refers to the peculiarly American type of school which is publicly supported and publicly controlled. This idea of a publicly controlled and publicly supported institution is in consonance

---

[14] G. E. Axtelle, "How Do We Know What Values Are Best?" *Progressive Education* 27: 194, April 1950.

with the doctrine of church and state separation which means that
the "state shall not appropriate money to religious institutions and
shall not prefer one religious outlook as such to another; and that
the state will protect its citizens in the equal free exercise of thought
and choice in matters religious and will require of its schools that
they not teach or act in any way to contravene these principles." [15]
There is no implication whatever that the public school is anti-
religious or atheistic in outlook. Whenever the term *public school*
is employed we mean the secular public school. . . .

A *value* has sometimes been used to mean a *considered* want.
Thus it "implies a good which has passed through the process of
examination and evaluation. . . ." [16]

By *spiritual values,* we mean those values which grow out of the
"aspirations of the human spirit—its love of freedom, its sense of
beauty, its hope of creating a better civilization." [17] "Moral insight,
integrity of thought and act; equal regard for human personality
wherever found, faith in the free play of intelligence both to guide
study and to direct action; and finally, those further values of refined thought and feeling requisite to bring life to its finest quality." [18] These are expressions of the spirit that is distinctively
human; to them we apply the term spiritual values. . . .

It is difficult to draw any clear-cut distinction between moral and
spiritual values. The differentiation we suggest is entirely arbitrary.
For our purposes, we assign the following definition to moral values:
those rules of conduct which man has evolved through his experiences. We consider them to be more strictly regulatory within a
particular community, whereas spiritual values are more pervasive in
character. . . . By spiritual we "mean those ways of living and
thinking which undergird and contribute to the dignity of human
personality. Nothing that degrades the life of the individual man
can be considered spiritual; nothing that enriches it can be unspiri-

---

[15] John Dewey Society, Seventh Yearbook, *The Public Schools and Spiritual
Values,* New York: Harper, 1944, p. 9.

[16] *Ibid.,* p. 29.

[17] Yervant H. Krikorian, ed., *Naturalism and the Human Spirit,* New York:
Columbia University Press, 1944 (Preface).

[18] John Dewey Society, *op. cit.,* p. 2.

tual." [19] Spiritual values refer to the human spirit, that intangible, complex, undefinable potential within man. The realms in which the human spirit finds expression are ethics, aesthetics, intelligence, and religious activity.

We do not hold that all spiritual values are universally accepted. But whether they are or not and whether the naturalists or super-naturalists agree as to the validity of such values, these and other values must be realized in the natural order. With the criteria of whether or not a value contributes to the worth of human personality and whether or not it degrades the life of the individual, we shall proceed to consider a few spiritual values.

It may be surprising to many that knowledge may be considered a spiritual value.

This is true whether knowledge is pursued in the form of science, philosophy, or art. Indeed, naturalists and supernaturalists may find to their surprise that their ultimate aims of education may tend to coincide in this area of knowledge as its own end. Thus Catholic supernaturalists often think of the highest end of man as union with God and this union as a glimpse of the beatific vision. This vision is an essentially intellectual vision since to look upon God is to behold perfect reason or understanding. The pragmatic naturalist, in stating that education is subordinate to nothing save more education, seems to be formulating an ultimate aim of education which is not unlike that of the supernaturalist. Since education can be pursued indefinitely as its own end, the search for education becomes an infinite quest. But since God is infinite, the beatific vision too is without limit. Hence naturalism and supernaturalism do not seem far apart in their ultimate aims of education when these are projected indefinitely into the future.[20]

Self-denial or temperance is another spiritual value. Obviously, if one can restrain himself in situations of conflicting interests, "a clash of interest is avoided and cooperation can go forward. This is a difficult value or virtue to achieve; yet civilized communities

---

[19] John L. Childs, "Spiritual Values in Public Education," *Teachers College Record* 48: 367, March 1947.

[20] John S. Brubacher, *Modern Philosophies of Education*, 2nd Edition, New York: McGraw-Hill, 1950, p. 333.

have been so dependent upon it for their continued existence that it is small wonder it ranks high in the roster of spiritual values. It is also deeply involved in the persistence and tenacity so necessary to achieving good things that are difficult to do. Self-denial is not only a part of moral fiber but it ranks so high with some that they make an absolute of it." [21]

Another spiritual value is kindness. "Kindness is an important lubricant of social contact. It prevents friction when the irregularities of individuality rub against each other. Perhaps it is even more important in the effect it has on the undeveloped potentialities of individual capacity. It tends to draw it out, to encourage it to activate itself. Unlike cruelty or malice, kindness provides the friendly warmth so necessary for all growing things. In intensified form it becomes the spiritual value of charity and love." [22]

These are but a few of many spiritual values. Now we propose to name several we consider as being strategic to democracy and spirituality. These the schools *should* cultivate. First among these is respect for persons, "a sense of their dignity and worth which requires that they be treated as ends, not means merely, as individuals with feelings and preferences and desires, with potentialities to be developed. Each individual . . . is entitled to the right to grow to his best. . . . But as we owe these things to each human being, so he also owes them to all others. As a participant in democratic living he must respect others, show consideration of their rights. . . . The two, then, go together—right of the individual to respect and consideration so long as he does not affect others adversely, and responsibility of the individual to see that each other also receives this respect and consideration." [23]

A second spiritual value of importance is "to help pupils to exercise increasing control over their own destiny. No one whose framework of living is controlled importantly by others can taste life to the full, can attain the full spiritual stature of a free man. To increase such control, then, means increasing self-directiveness; . . . it means development of and use of his own intelligence; . . . it

---

[21] John Dewey Society, *op. cit.*, p. 19.

[22] *Ibid.*, p. 19.

[23] *Ibid.*, p. 125.

equally means growing knowledge to be utilized in exercising control." [24]

Loyalty to democratic group life is a third important spiritual value. "Individuals in the group should see that right to respect and freedom to have one's own values indicate the correlative obligation to maintain a situation in which all, himself and each other, can have the same privilege. . . . Similarly basic in democratic group life is loyalty to the free play of intelligence as a method of determining the values of others and of finding the most effective ways of realizing them." [25]

A fourth spiritual value is developing aesthetic sensitivities and enjoyments. "Acceptance of it places on us the obligation to strive for conditions in which realization of the implied aim is encouraged. Drab schoolrooms, living and teaching methods devoid of encouragement to creativeness, curricula restricted to utilitarian and mechanical pursuits—these deny development of this essentially spiritual quality. On the other hand, enterprises which call forth love and beauty and skill in producing it, joyousness in putting creative effort into what is felt to be meaningful, worthwhile, satisfying—these give aesthetic enjoyments which constitute their own immediate justification and simultaneously build a cumulative resource for continuing satisfaction and enjoyment." [26]

Moral Values and Reflection

Moral values, as previously mentioned, refer to those values which man has experientially evolved and which serve to regulate his conduct. For further clarification we might well consider briefly the nature of such values.

There is general agreement among present-day psychologists that man is equipped with certain original, unlearned tendencies to act, or impulses, and wants, such as love, fear, anger, sex, hunger, thirst, and sympathy. It is also a truism that "men not only live, but live together," and that, as Aristotle said long ago, "man is a social animal." Upon consideration, one can see that the limiting factor

---

[24] *Ibid.*, p. 126.

[25] *Ibid.*, p. 127.

[26] *Ibid.*, p. 127.

to the free expression and satisfaction of impulses and wants is the above fact that man lives not alone but with other men. In the process of satisfying his desires he is destined to come into conflict with other individuals equipped with equally strong desires. To resolve the many conflicting human desires that arise in the process of living together, some sort of cooperative adjustment is needed. And it is this dual fact of conflict and cooperation which arises that is "the root of the moral problem."

Stemming from the necessity for cooperation in living together, certain acts become recognized as approved or disapproved by the group. These sanctioned modes of conduct then serve as controls for individual action—as moral standards, more appropriately called "folkways" or customs. Being moral, in the sense of morality so conceived, subsequently means conforming to the established folkways—oftentimes blind, mechanical obedience to the group ways.

But customs seem never adequate to adjustment for all, and the need for reflection on them, usually by observant individuals, occurs. This reflection should involve two phases: that of pointing out discrepancies and absurdities, and that of deliberate discovery of codes by which men can live together happily, i.e., the reconstruction of existing customs into more effective methods for achieving the good. Out of such reflection and reconstruction, the individual develops a personal morality. Instead of behavior that is custom controlled, he now conducts himself according to principles or moral standards that he consciously acknowledges as good. It is in relation to this reflective personalized morality that the term *moral values,* for our purposes, is most appropriately used.

Undoubtedly, a reflective morality is of moral value and is to be encouraged in a democratic society where moral standards ought to be examined in terms of consequences for the greater good. Taken in this reflective sense, "Actions are not moral or immoral in themselves, but in their consequences or relations, which are only discoverable in experience." [27]

The implications and emphasis are here given that moral standards or values are matters of discovery; that the laws of conduct

[27] Irwin Edman, *Human Traits and Their Social Significance*, Boston: Houghton, 1920, Chapter 15, "Morals and Moral Valuation," p. 452.

must be derived from experience, just as must the laws of the physical sciences. To use the terminology of science, moral values may be viewed as *hypotheses*. The term *hypothesis* is used to emphasize the standing possibility of value modification. It is not to suggest that moral values are transient, transitory, and undependable, or that morality is in a state of constant upheaval akin to chaos. Far from it. For the history of mankind has indicated an essential stability of basic human nature and the recurrence or re-emergence and re-enforcement of basic human values. Consequently, our present values attain a stability and a degree of permanence attributable to the entire accummulated life experiences of mankind.

In the light of the preceding orientation, we can subsequently look upon the emergence of some of our own moral values such as honesty, justice, chastity, respect for private property, and respect for the rights of others, as natural outcomes of the give-and-take of community living. These specific values among many others are pertinent to our type of society and are not intended to be thought of as absolute universal values. (Yet we will, if and when challenged, reaffirm our faith in those values we feel to be conducive to and consonant with that higher quality of living and civilization we call democracy.)

Emerging from cooperative adjustments, moral values become socially and individually useful instruments for the attainment of happiness for all in society. To the extent that they are esteemed and accepted by the group, they may become fixed in law, the degree of moral reflection and reconstruction depending on the nature of the society.

The place of education is then one of developing in the individual those habits of conduct which are both individually and socially useful, a process in which the entire social environment is involved. More specifically, formal education is provided as the "chief means by which society inculcates into its younger members those values, traditions, and customs which its controlling element regard as of the most pivotal importance." [28] "Education, more especially, is the instrument through which the young can be educated not only to ideals and customs already current, but to their

---

[28] Irwin Edman, *op. cit.*, p. 458.

reflective modification in the light of our ever-growing knowledge of the conditions of human welfare." [29]

What the Schools Can Do About Values

We recognize that the public school is the strategic educational instrument of our democratic society; to say then that it must not teach, or cannot teach moral and spiritual values would prohibit fulfillment of its primary function, i.e., to teach the younger members of our society those values, customs, and traditions that we experientially perceive to be of or pertaining to the true spirit of democracy.

To say that moral and spiritual values need necessarily be attributed to a supernatural source is questionable, since they may be practically conceived as natural outcomes of human experiences in community living, these values becoming common values to which all members of the community pay allegiance irrespective of racial origin, creed, or class.

We do not intend to deny the right of any person to ascribe these values to a supernatural source. We rather feel that democracy thrives on the plurality of thought, powers, and beliefs within the group. As Sidney Hook writes:

> The underlying premises, whether theological, metaphysical, or naturalistic, from which different groups justify their common democratic beliefs and practices must not be subject to integration. It is enough, so to speak, that human beings live in accordance with democratic laws; it is foolish intolerance to make only one justification of the laws legal.[30]

And Jacques Maritain, an eminent Catholic philosopher, has aptly put it thus:

> . . . the only solution is of the pluralistic type. Men belonging to most different philosophical or religious creeds and families could and should cooperate in the common task and for the common welfare of the earthly community, provided they similarly assent to the basic tenets of a society of free men. . . .

[29] *Ibid.,* p. 459.

[30] Sidney Hook, "The Dilemma of T. S. Eliot," *Nation* 160: 70, January 20, 1945.

Thus it is that men possessing quite different, even opposite, metaphysical or religious outlooks—materialists, idealists, agnostics, Christians and Jews, Moslems and Buddhists—can converge, not by virtue of any identity of doctrine, but by virtue of an analogical similitude in practical principles, toward the same practical conclusions, and can share in the same practical democratic philosophy, provided that they similarly revere, perhaps for quite diverse reasons, truth and intelligence, human dignity, freedom, brotherly love, and the absolute value of moral good.[31]

In summary we hold that:

Values . . . are the monopoly of no one segment of our society, nor does their validity derive from any one religious faith or philosophic school. They are common values because all recognize them as common essentials of communication and interrelationship. . . . Precisely because the public school is the representative of all the people, it is sacredly obligated to educate for the common values in ways that are exclusively public and nonsectarian.[32]

Moreover, despite the divergent beliefs and ultimate sanctions for moral and spiritual values, one can discern a high degree of agreement on values at the level of conduct or at the level of action, i.e., in those desirable acts that are expressive of moral and spiritual values. In this light, we therefore affirm the right of the public school to teach moral and spiritual values on the basis of human reason and experience without recourse to supernatural authority.

3.7. THE CATHOLIC APPROACH TO RELIGION IN EDUCATION [33]

Francis M. Crowley

Catholic education provides for the education of the whole man, "soul united to body in unity of nature, with all his faculties,

---

[31] Jacques Maritain, "The Foundations of Democracy," *Nation* 160: 440-441, April 21, 1945.

[32] Vivian T. Thayer, "Education in Moral and Spiritual Values," *Hawaii Educational Review* 37: 205, March 1949.

[33] Francis M. Crowley, "The Catholic Approach to Religion in America," reprinted from Ernest O. Melby and Morton Puner, eds., *Freedom and Public*

natural and supernatural, such as right reason and revelation show him to be." The Catholic theory is that the effects of original sin—weakness of will and disorderly inclinations—must be corrected and good habits must be developed. This cannot be done by relying solely on the powers of human nature. The mind must be enlightened and the will strengthened by supernatural truth and the grace of God. This is the same as saying that Catholic philosophy of education is the philosophy of the supernatural; that is, it has not only a sound philosophical but a decidedly positive theological basis. The student is to be prepared for life here and hereafter. "For precisely this reason, Christian education takes in the whole aggregate of human life, physical and spiritual, intellectual and moral, individual, domestic and social, not with a view of reducing it in any way, but in order to elevate, regulate and perfect it, in accordance with the example and teaching of Christ," said the late Pope Pius XI in his great encyclical letter on the Christian Education of Youth. In order to achieve the ends of Christian education, it is necessary that the entire program be dominated by the Christian spirit, so that religion may be "the foundation and crown of the youth's entire training at every level of instruction."

Many years have passed since the late Pope Pius XI published his encyclical letter. He was not the first to speak out on this vitally important question of Christian education. In his encyclical he made it quite clear that he was only repeating the instructions of Pius IX and Leo XIII, and that attendance at public schools is forbidden by Canon Law, thus making the regulation binding in conscience. "The school," he wrote, "if not a temple, is a den." A school from which religion is excluded is contrary to the fundamental principles of education. Such school in time is bound to become irreligious. The only school that is a fit school for Catholic students is a school controlled by the Church, in which religion is the foundation and crown of the youth's entire training, not only in the elementary grades but in the high school and college as well.

American bishops have been just as solicitous as the long line of

Education, published by Frederick A. Praeger, Inc., New York, 1953, pp. 65-72. By permission.

Mr. Crowley is Dean of the College of Education, Fordham University.

Compare Msgr. Paul E. Campbell, "What Makes a Catholic School Catholic?" *Catholic World* 179: 426-430, September 1954.

Holy Fathers. Numerous pastoral letters of the American hierarchy have dealt with the subject of education, and the Decrees of the Third Plenary Council of Baltimore (1884) proclaim in forceful language that the parent must send his child to the Catholic school. The language is quite to the point—in its strictest interpretation the Bishop alone can approve sending a Catholic child to a public school. In the hurly-burly existence which we lead, it is impossible for the average Catholic parent to care for more than the normal demands made on him by his occupation and his home. For those who have been fortunate enough to secure an education under Catholic auspices, the instruction of their offspring in the teachings of the Church is a comparatively easy matter; but we must remember that a great number are only possessed of a rudimentary knowledge of the teachings of the Church, usually secured through Sunday-school instruction, released-time programs, desultory reading and attendance at missions or Sunday services. Thus, the Catholic Church has been obliged, for the sake of principle, to establish a separate system of schools. The chief purpose of these schools is to give to the Catholic child the Catholic training which is his baptismal birthright. Educational institutions functioning under the aegis of the Church in America today provide training adapted to all stages of the student's educational growth.

The Third Plenary Council decrees influenced the growth of parochial schools, since many Catholics were quite dissatisfied with public schools and only needed such counsel to undertake the task of organizing a separate school system. In 1883, the year preceding the Baltimore Council, there were 6,241 churches and 2,491 schools; that is, forty per cent of the churches reported schools. By 1933, the numbers had grown to 12,537 and 7,462 respectively, showing that sixty per cent of the parishes offered education at the elementary level. While this represents a twenty per cent increase during the fifty-year period (1883-1933) in the number of parishes with schools, it falls far short of the ideal set by the Baltimore Council—a school in every parish. . . .

The Catholic Church cares for approximately sixty per cent of all Catholic children in parochial schools. It has not been possible to live up to the ideal set by the Third Plenary Council of Baltimore —a parochial school near each church. Poverty, indifference, widely scattered Catholic groups and the shortage of religious teachers may be cited as some of the reasons for inability to achieve the ideal. Many Catholic parents have been obliged, therefore, to send their children to public schools. The religious instruction of these pupils must be cared for in the home, in Sunday schools or in released-time programs, in keeping with the tradition of the Catholic Church. . . .

The Catholic Church is in favor of any plan which makes it possible to provide for the religious education of Catholic children attending public schools and looks on released-time programs with special favor. Even the perfect program of supplementary instruction, however, would not be considered as a substitute for the Catholic school.

The use of released time makes weekday religious education possible. Children are released during school hours to attend classes in religious education held by the different denominations in churches, schools or halls. The schools thus cooperate with church and home in providing religious education. In the pioneer days programs were conducted before and after school hours. The advantages of using released time have become so evident that the present swing toward this practice is decidedly marked. In 1937, it is reported that released-time schools were conducted under various legal provisions in forty-five states, in more than 2,000 centers, with an estimated enrollment of 265,000 pupils. Returns for 1945 showed a sharp increase. In January of that year 1,500,000 elementary and high-school children were participating in the released time plan. The programs for these students were offered in approximately 2,000 communities in all but two states. In 1952, approximately 2,000,000 students were using the released-time privilege. Since in the better plans, provision is made for qualified teachers, proper equipment, attendance reports, proper grading, standard examinations and activity programs, school leaders have been willing to cooperate, and in many instances have taken the initiative in recommending the adoption of the plan.

The released-time program leads the student to see that religious instruction is an integral part of education. More time is provided for religious instruction, thus making continuity possible. The instruction is unquestionably vested with a certain amount of dignity and higher standards are established. Providing for the instruction elsewhere does away with the criticism of bringing sectarian influence into the public school and removes entirely any possibility of friction or legal action. The weekday religious education program does as much as any plan can to make the religious attitude a part of the learning process. The cooperation of home, Church and school makes education one to the child. The ideal set-up is the denominational school, such as the Catholic parochial school; but funds are not forthcoming for support of a still greater number, so we must do the best we can for the great number of Catholic children now in public schools, and we can do so through the weekday religious education program.

There are some who claim that released time for religious instruction creates a divisive influence in the public school. They hold that group antagonisms are thus promoted with all of their ugly consequences. But the record does not support this claim: in fact, the contrary seems to be true, in the sense that common planning for a worthy purpose promotes cooperation based on sympathy and understanding—the only true basis of tolerance. . . .

Children must be taught that they have a common Father in heaven and that they must love one another as God also loves them. Many Americans are so little concerned over God and the things of God that the concepts of the fatherhood of God and the brotherhood of Christ have little meaning for them. Yet it is these concepts alone which give rise to belief in the sacredness of the human personality. It is the only basis for the American way of life. The wise man makes sure that his fellow enjoys the same rights that he holds sacred. Personality is sacred for all or for none.

The home is the first and holiest school. The attitude of the young toward most of life's activities is determined by the home environment. The prejudices of childhood often shape the thinking of the man. Justice and charity must function in the home training of youth or the promotion of tolerance is a lost cause. Family education of the right sort is then of the very essence. It must have a foundation in the supernatural, for religion is necessary to give social charity form and sanction. This prerequisite gives second place to the church. The third should go to the school and community agencies functioning on a cooperative basis. This order is somewhat at variance with that commonly accepted by the public, calling for the school in first place; the community, second; the home, third; and the church, last. . . .[34]

Society can only be transformed through the individual. At the very moment our problem is "to make America safe for differences." Democracy is after all a religious ideal. A sense of relationship to God, a belief in His Fatherhood and the brotherhood of man contribute greatly to the development of attitudes that will make America safe for differences.

3.8. TAX-SUPPORTED SCHOOLS NEED NOT IGNORE GOD AS THOUGH HE DID NOT EXIST [35]

Canon Bernard Iddings Bell

We need to combat the notion that the only attitude toward God which is legitimate in a tax-supported school is the attitude that ignores God as though He does not exist, or, if He does exist, does not matter.

It is of course proper that atheists should be able to send their children to atheistic schools if they so desire; but it is hard to see

---

[34] Editor's Note: Perhaps the basic reason why Catholics do not trust their children to "lay" or "neutral" (i.e., public) schools, is made evident from the following papal pronouncement:

"In such a [Catholic parochial] school, in harmony with the Church and the Christian family, the various branches of secular learning will not enter into conflict with religious instruction to the manifest detriment of education. And if, when occasion arises, it be deemed necessary to have the students read authors propounding false doctrine, for the purpose of refuting it, this will be done after due preparation and with such an antidote of sound doctrine, that it will not only do no harm, but will be an aid to the Christian formation of youth."—Pope Pius XI, "The Christian Education of Youth," (Encyclical, December 31, 1929), *Catholic Education Review* 28: 157, March 1930; *Current History* 31: 1091-1104, March 1930.

[35] Reprinted from Bernard Iddings Bell, *Crisis in Education*. Published by the McGraw-Hill Book Company, Inc., New York, 1949, pages 221-224. By permission.

Dr. Bell is pastor of Episcopalians, University of Chicago.

Read also Henry P. Van Dusen, "What Should Be the Relation of Religion and Public Education?" *Teachers College Record* 56: 1-9, October 1954; James A. Pike, "Has Pragmatism Undermined Basic Values in Education?" *Teachers College Record* 56: 31-37, October 1954.

why atheists, few in number as they are, should be allowed to force atheistic-by-negation education on the children of the great majority of us who do pay at least theoretical attention to the Deity. As the American school system is now conducted, more and more conducted, there is no such thing as religious liberty in American education. There is liberty only to be unreligious. "In God we trust," we still put on our coins; we cannot entrust our children to Him. If the public schools must "leave religion out," then the only decent thing is to permit religious groups to run their own schools, which of course we now do, and to give them tax money to run them with, which we do not. . . .

If it be contended that multiple school systems divide the body politic, which to some extent they do, then in reply it may be pointed out that the only way to retain complete unity and at the same time give freedom to those who desire that their children shall recognize God is to see to it that time is given in the public schools to a common examination by the growing children of what are the basic religious and moral ideas, all this taught objectively and with no desire to bring about conviction (which is the province of the Church and the home), and also to furnish opportunity in school hours for the various current faiths in a community to teach their own children what they themselves believe.

3.9. PUBLIC SCHOOLS MUST BE SECULAR

Henry H. Hill[36]

1

I feel I must begin by pointing out the danger, in the years ahead, of bitter and disruptive religious divisions and quarrels in America. Such divisions are common in Germany, for example, where religion and politics are frequently identical in the life of the community, where preachers and priests are supported by taxes,

[36] Henry H. Hill, "Public Schools Must be Secular," *Atlantic* 190: 75-77, October 1952. By permission.

Mr. Hill is President of the George Peabody College for Teachers. This article is from his report as chairman of the Educational Policies Commission of the National Education Association, 1952.

and where substantially all schools are confessional and under control either of the Catholic or the Protestant churches. Citizens so divided find it hard to get along together, much less with other nations. What is a local disturbance can in such a case become an international threat. So far we have avoided this particular kind of bitterness in the United States because we remain essentially secular in our political party organization. We do not support our churches by taxes. Being a Republican or a Democrat carries with it as yet little intimation of a man's religion or lack of it. Nearly ninety per cent of all our children attend the public schools, which are secular and not denominational.

There is now in some quarters a demand that the public schools teach religion. Whose religion? What creed or ritual? However much we may like the plan of teaching that religion common to all recognized religions in the United States, the religious leaders have not produced such a text. Nor are they likely to do so. In both Protestant and Catholic bodies there are leaders who insist that truth cannot tolerate error. It seems to be "my truth, your error." These same leaders do not favor or practice interfaith understanding for this and other reasons.

In the opinion of thoughtful observers, religion itself cannot be taught in our public schools. If one religious group will not permit the King James version of the Bible to be read and another will not permit the Douay version, can we expect further excursions into purely religious matters?

When, then, by statute or by public opinion or controversy, the public schools are stopped from teaching religion—we do not here discuss released time and other possible compromises of value which affect a minor fraction of the children—they may be and are occasionally referred to as godless. This charge is misleading, or else there is some peculiar religious alchemy which takes place en route between church and school.

As a former superintendent of public schools in Arkansas, Kentucky, and Pennsylvania it has been, over a period of thirty years, my privilege and duty to recommend to boards of education the appointment of some hundreds of teachers. Without a single exception they have been members of a recognized church—Protestant, Catholic, or Jewish. If we may identify church membership with goodness—and surely most of the good people are in the churches; if we may identify membership in any church or synagogue with godliness as contrasted with godlessness, then how and at what moment do good and perhaps godly teachers become godless as they step from the churches and homes to their posts of duty in the public schools? Are all places of assembly or work—the stores, factories, courts, farms, trains, and market places—to be regarded as godless because in them man does not, through ritual or formal act, worship God or study or recite the dogma of his church? Are the Mohammedans to be regarded as godlier than Christians if they practice their religious devotions daily seven times, stopping their immediate duties at a given time or signal?

To ask these questions is to invite the thesis in which I happen to believe. The good or godly teacher has a quality—let us call it moral and spiritual values—which will "rub off" on her associates wherever she is. Is not this thesis acknowledged in the suspicion—unfounded for the most part—with which denominations sometimes regard teachers who belong to other denominations? The essential question is: can and will this teacher teach by example and precept and through the daily life of the school those abiding values in which all religions believe? If there be no values to rub off, then indeed we should worry.

On rare occasions I have heard what seems to me the irresponsible assertion that our public schools are "as Stalin would have them." I do not believe Stalin would be likely to select Protestants and Catholics and Jews as teachers.

The word "secular" is sometimes substituted for "godless." There is being read into this word, which has been used to designate civil as separated from religious affairs, the pejorative idea that secular is evil.

What else can schools open to all American children be except nondenominational? They must remain secular unless we change those underlying concepts and practices which have to date made and kept America relatively free from the religious quarrels, wars, and intolerances which drove many of our forefathers, fettered by oppressors, to escape to America. Are we willing, as members of church groups, to insist that the homes and churches handle matters of religious beliefs and that the public schools deal with common moral and spiritual values?

2

Let me state candidly my own position. It involves divided allegiance, as is only right and proper. As a Presbyterian I have the responsibility to see that Presbyterian religious values are taught to Presbyterian children. This I believe may be done and has been done by the church through Sunday school and vacation schools and in other ways, leaving the public schools to provide those relatively noncontroversial values and learnings necessary to American citizenship.

As a citizen I have the responsibility of supporting and defending and improving the public schools where, in any now-conceivable future, the great majority of all children will be educated for peace or war.

As an individual I have the responsibility to do what I can to build intercultural understanding and to work constructively for good will and tolerance among all faiths. I have both the freedom and the responsibility to take my stand in behalf of those values and practices in which I believe.

I agree with President James B. Conant, former chairman of the Educational Policies Commission, that both private and denominational schools have a constitutional right to exist. Further, I think both private and public schools provide each other stimuli to better performance. Without specific knowledge I assume the American Catholic schools are in some ways the best Catholic schools in the world, and I would infer that the challenge of good public schools has helped produce this. In a similar way public schools are sometimes challenged by the best practices of private and parochial schools.

The right to do something and the wisdom of doing it are not identical. Lutherans, Catholics, Methodists, Baptists, Episcopalians, and Congregationalists, for example, have the right to establish their own schools from nursery school through the graduate school, or, speaking more practically, for the twelve grades prior to college. Yet I would regret to see the day come when the last Lutheran, Catholic, Presbyterian, Methodist, Baptist, Episcopalian, and Congregationalists disappeared from the public schools. Since it is estimated that ninety per cent of all who attend private and parochial schools are Catholics, I shall be more specific and say I would regret to see the last Catholic child depart from the public schools. There are perhaps four million, or roughly half, who attend public schools now.

It has been my personal experience to know and like many members of other faiths. How do we know them, and hence like them, if we do not associate with them? If, for example, all the eight or nine million Catholic children and youth should go through twelve years divorced in their daily school life from all association with those of other faiths, would we not be taking a step towards the German pattern? Suppose then—to follow the argument further— that all other denominations of substantial size should do the same thing. Would we not, wittingly or unwittingly, have jerked the rug of common integrating experiences out from under our young citizens? Would we not have laid a possible foundation for the spread of the necessary religious diversity to other facets of public life at a time when we need unity in facing a hostile world of Communists?

It is important that parents who exercise their right to provide education for their children through private schools should understand and support the public schools from whence have come, and will continue to come, eighty to ninety per cent of all our armed forces. It is important that parents who exercise their right of choice to provide religious education for their children through schools established to perpetuate their creeds should understand and respect the views of the majority of American citizens, who believe religious education should be cared for by the home and church. It is important that those of us who believe wholeheartedly in the public schools should understand and respect the legitimate rights of other Americans to support other schools. It is, we believe, our privilege to call to the attention of all American citizens what the full and complete exercise of these rights would mean in creating all over again those old religious and class bitternesses so prominent in much of Europe's history.

To guard against increasing tensions between public schools on the one hand and private and parochial schools on the other, there should be a united effort on the part of religious leaders to provide common agreements and sanctions for moral and spiritual values to be taught in the public schools. It is dangerously easy and appallingly irresponsible to voice hurtful and sweeping criticism against the public schools for the very conditions which divergent religions have in part produced. We need not dodge our disagreements, but we may speak quietly and fairly and responsibly, putting the welfare of our great American nation ahead of the complete and ultimate exercise of all our own personal or religious rights. Both churches and state will be served by this.

Perhaps you have read E. M. Forster's *Two Cheers for Democracy*. He gives one cheer for the variety of life and therefore the better opportunity for more individuals to live richer lives. He gives another cheer for criticism—that is, the possibility of free criticism which exists in full measure only in a democracy. Mr. Forster fails to give a third cheer because he thinks democracy deserves only two cheers.

My third cheer is for public education, its unique contribution to a classless society and to a freedom and tolerance largely unknown among countries with class education systems, and for the educational options offered the American people.

I am *for* public education. I am *not* anti-Catholic, anti-private school, or anti-religious, any more than I am anti-chocolate ice cream because I select vanilla. Three cheers for our democracy, our republic, if you prefer, our representative form of government, and for the options which make us free.

Section C: Separation of Church and State: Some Recent Court Decisions

3.10. INTRODUCTION

Most European nations have an established church, and the disestablishment of the various colonial churches in favor of religious pluralism was a major development in the first two hundred years of American history. But the European traditions persist; and ever since the days of Horace Mann, our public schools have been accused of being under the control of "infidel sects" or "unbelievers." In order to keep clear of the bitter controversies between the various religious denominations, the public schools have adopted the policy that it is not their function to teach Protestantism, Catholicism, Judaism, or any other sect or creed. Such instruction is left to the various denominations and private homes. On the other hand, the public schools are not hostile to religions (though an occasional teacher may be). And in some instances local community pressures have sought, in one way or another, to bring definite religious instruction into the public schools.

The selections to follow deal with such problems as they became manifest in three recent cases before the United States Supreme Court, popularly known as the Everson, McCollum and Adler cases. The McCollum and Adler cases are concerned with the problem of released time for religious classes and specify with some measure of accuracy under what circumstances released time for religious instruction may be permitted. In the Everson case, which follows, the Court tried to draw a line between two conflicting sets of values: On the one hand, all citizens have a right to police and fire protection, to the school lunch program, and to other aspects of "general welfare." On the other hand, no church group has a right to receive public tax money for its own sectarian ends. The court opinions not only indicate where the lines were drawn in each particular case, but also indicate the broad points at issue in the general dispute.

3.11. A STATE MAY PROVIDE TRANSPORTATION TO PAROCHIAL AS WELL AS TO PUBLIC SCHOOLS, NOT AS AN AID TO SECTARIAN RELIGION, BUT AS A PHASE OF GENERAL WELFARE [37]

Hugo L. Black and Others

A large proportion of the early settlers of this country came here from Europe to escape the bondage of laws which compelled them

---

[37] Hugo L. Black, Majority opinion (5-4 decision), *Everson v. Board of Education*, 330 U.S. 1 (1946). Footnotes not included in these excerpts.

to support and attend government-favored churches. The centuries immediately before and contemporaneous with the colonization of America had been filled with turmoil, civil strife, and persecutions, generated in large part by established sects determined to maintain their absolute political and religious supremacy. With the power of government supporting them, at various times and places, Catholics had persecuted Protestants, Protestants had persecuted Catholics, Protestant sects had persecuted other Protestant sects, Catholics of one shade of belief had persecuted Catholics of another shade of belief, and all of these had from time to time persecuted Jews. In efforts to force loyalty to whatever religious group happened to be on top and in league with the government of a particular time and place, men and women had been fined, cast in jail, cruelly tortured, and killed. Among the offenses for which these punishments had been inflicted were such things as speaking disrespectfully of the views of ministers of government-established churches, non-attendance at those churches, expressions of non-belief in their doctrines, and failure to pay taxes and tithes to support them.

These practices of the old world were transplanted to and began to thrive in the soil of the new America. The very charters granted by the English Crown to the individuals and companies designated to make the laws which would control the destinies of the colonials authorized these individuals and companies to erect religious establishments which all, whether believers or non-believers, would be required to support and attend. An exercise of this authority was accompanied by a repetition of many of the old-world practices and persecutions. Catholics found themselves hounded and proscribed because of their faith; Quakers who followed their conscience went to jail; Baptists were peculiarly obnoxious to certain dominant Protestant sects; men and women of varied faiths who happened to be in a minority in a particular locality were persecuted because they steadfastly persisted in worshipping God only as their own consciences dictated. And all of these dissenters were compelled to pay tithes and taxes to support government-sponsored churches whose ministers preached inflammatory sermons designed to strengthen and consolidate the established faith by generating a burning hatred against dissenters.

These practices became so commonplace as to shock the freedom-loving colonials into a feeling of abhorrence. The imposition of taxes to pay ministers' salaries and to build and maintain churches and church property aroused their indignation. It was these feelings which found expression in the First Amendment . . . which commands that a state "shall make no law respecting an establishment of religion, or prohibiting the free exercise thereof." . . .

The "establishment of religion" clause of the First Amendment means at least this: Neither a state nor the Federal Government can set up a church. Neither can pass laws which aid one religion, aid all religions, or prefer one religion over another. Neither can force nor influence a person to go to or to remain away from church against his will or force him to profess a belief or disbelief in any religion. No person can be punished for entertaining or professing religious beliefs or disbeliefs, for church attendance or non-attendance. No tax in any amount, large or small, can be levied to support any religious activities or institutions, whatever they may be called, or whatever form they may adopt to teach or practice religion. Neither a state nor the Federal Government can, openly or secretly, participate in the affairs of any religious organizations or groups and *vice versa*. . . .

New Jersey cannot consistently with the "establishment of religion" clause of the First Amendment contribute tax-raised funds to the support of any institution which teaches the tenets and faith of any church. On the other hand, other language of the amendment commands that New Jersey cannot hamper its citizens in the free exercise of their own religion. Consequently, it cannot exclude individual Catholics, Lutherans, Mohammedans, Baptists, Jews, Methodists, Non-believers, Presbyterians, or the members of any other faith, *because of their faith, or lack of it,* from receiving the benefits of public-welfare legislation. While we do not mean to intimate that a state could not provide transportation only to children attending public schools,[38] we must be careful, in protecting the citizens of New Jersey against state-established churches, to be sure that we do not inadvertently prohibit New Jersey from extending its general state law benefits to all its citizens without regard to their religious belief.

---

[38] Editor's Note: The New Jersey statute in question authorized reimbursement to parents for the transportation of children to and from schools—including payment for transportation of some children to Catholic parochial schools.

Measured by these standards, we cannot say that the First Amendment prohibits New Jersey from spending tax-raised funds to pay the bus fares of parochial school pupils as a part of a general program under which it pays the fares of pupils attending public and other schools. It is undoubtedly true that children are helped to get to church schools. There is even a possibility that some of the children might not be sent to the church schools if the parents were compelled to pay their children's bus fares out of their own pockets when transportation to a public school would have been paid for by the State. The same possibility exists where the state requires a local transit company to provide reduced fares to school children including those attending parochial schools, or where a municipally owned transportation system undertakes to carry all school children free of charge. Moreover, state-paid policemen, detailed to protect children going to and from church schools from the very real hazards of traffic, would serve much the same purpose and accomplish much the same result as state provisions intended to guarantee free transportation of a kind which the state deems to be best for the school children's welfare. And parents might refuse to risk their children to the serious danger of traffic accidents going to and from parochial schools, the approaches to which were not protected by policemen. Similarly, parents might be reluctant to permit their children to attend schools which the state had cut off from such general government services as ordinary police and fire protection, connections for sewage disposal, public highways and sidewalks. Of course, cutting off church schools from these services, so separate and so indisputably marked off from the religious function, would make it far more difficult for the schools to operate. But such is obviously not the purpose of the First Amendment. That Amendment requires the state to be a neutral in its relations with groups of religious believers and non-believers; it does not require the state to be their adversary. State power is no more to be used so as to handicap religion than it is to favor them.

This Court has said that parents may, in the discharge of their duty under state compulsory education laws, send their children to a religious rather than a public school if the school meets the secular educational requirements which the state has power to impose. See *Pierce v. Society of Sisters,* 268 U.S. 510. It appears that these parochial schools meet New Jersey's requirements. The State contributes no money to the schools. It does not support them. Its legislation, as applied, does no more than provide a general program to help parents get their children, regardless of their religion, safely and expeditiously to and from accredited schools.

The First Amendment has erected a wall between church and state. That wall must be kept high and impregnable. We could not approve the slightest breach. New Jersey has not breached it here.

Mr. Justice Jackson, Dissenting:

It is no exaggeration to say that the whole historic conflict in temporal policy between the Catholic Church and non-Catholics comes to a focus in their respective school policies. The Roman Catholic Church, counseled by experience in many ages and many lands and with all sorts and conditions of men, takes what, from the viewpoint of its own progress and the success of its mission, is a wise estimate of the importance of education to religion. It does not leave the individual to pick up religion by chance. It relies on early and indelible indoctrination in the faith and order of the Church by the word and example of persons consecrated to the task.

Our public school, if not a product of Protestantism, at least is more consistent with it than with the Catholic culture and scheme of values. It is a relatively recent development dating from about 1840. It is organized on the premise that secular education can be isolated from all religious teaching so that the school can inculcate all needed temporal knowledge and also maintain a strict and lofty neutrality as to religion. The assumption is that after the individual has been instructed in worldly wisdom he will be better fitted to choose his religion. Whether such a disjunction is possible, and if possible whether it is wise, are questions I need not try to answer.

I should be surprised if any Catholic would deny that the parochial school is a vital, if not the most vital, part of the Roman Catholic Church. If put to the choice, that venerable institution, I should expect, would forego its whole service for mature persons before it would give up education of the young, and it would be a wise choice. Its growth and cohesion, discipline and loyalty, spring from its schools. Catholic education is the rock on which the whole structure rests, and to render tax aid to its Church school is indistinguishable to me from rendering the same aid to the Church itself. . . .

I agree that this Court has left, and always should leave to each state, great latitude in deciding for itself, in the light of its own conditions, what shall be public purposes in its scheme of things. It may socialize utilities and economic enterprises and make taxpayers' business out of what conventionally had been private business. It may make public business of individual welfare, health, education, entertainment or security. But it cannot make public business of religious worship or instruction, or of attendance at religious institutions of any character. There is no answer to the proposition . . . that the effect of the religious freedom Amendment to our Constitution was to take every form of propagation of religion out of the realm of things which could directly or indirectly be made public business and thereby be supported in whole or in part at taxpayers' expense. That is a difference which the Constitution sets up between religion and almost every other subject matter of legislation, a difference which goes to the very root of religious freedom and which the Court is overlooking today. This freedom was first in the Bill of Rights because it was first in the forefathers' minds; it was set forth in absolute terms, and its strength is its rigidity. It was intended not only to keep the states' hands out of religion, but to keep religion's hands off the state, and, above all, to keep bitter religious controversy out of public life by denying to every denomination any advantage from getting control of public policy or the public purse. Those great ends I cannot but think are immeasurably compromised by today's decision.

This policy of our Federal Constitution has never been wholly pleasing to most religious groups. They all are quick to invoke its protections; they all are irked when they feel its restraints. . . .

But we cannot have it both ways. Religious teaching cannot be a private affair when the state seeks to impose regulations which infringe on it indirectly, and a public affair when it comes to taxing citizens of one faith to aid another, or those of no faith to aid all.

If these principles seem harsh in prohibiting aid to Catholic education, it must not be forgotten that it is the same Constitution that alone assures Catholics the right to maintain these schools at all when predominant local sentiment would forbid them. *Pierce v. Society of Sisters,* 268 U.S. 510. Nor should I think that those who have done so well without this aid would want to see this separation between Church and State broken down. If the state may aid these religious schools, it may therefore regulate them. Many groups have sought aid from tax funds only to find that it carried political controls with it. Indeed this Court has declared that "It is hardly lack of due process for the Government to regulate that which it subsidizes." *Wickard v. Filburn,* 317 U.S. 111, 131.

3.12. SECTARIAN RELIGION MAY NOT BE TAUGHT ON PUBLIC SCHOOL PREMISES [39]

Hugo L. Black and Others

In 1940 interested members of the Jewish, Roman Catholic, and a few of the Protestant faiths formed a voluntary association called the Champaign Council on Religious Education. They obtained permission from the Board of Education to offer classes in religious instruction to public-school pupils in grades four to nine inclusive. Classes were made up of pupils whose parents signed printed cards requesting that their children be permitted to attend; they were held weekly, thirty minutes for the lower grades, forty-five minutes for the higher. The council employed the religious teachers at no expense to the school authorities, but the instructors were subject to the approval and supervision of the superintendent of schools. The classes were taught in three separate religious groups by Protestant teachers, Catholic priests, and a Jewish rabbi, although for the past several years there have apparently been no classes instructed in the Jewish religion. Classes were conducted in the regular classrooms of the school building. Students who did not choose to take the religious instruction were not released from public school duties; they were required to leave their classrooms and go to some other

[39] Hugo L. Black, majority opinion (8-1 decision), *McCollum v. Board of Education,* 333 U.S. 203 (1948). Footnotes omitted from these excerpts.

place in the school building for pursuit of their secular studies. On the other hand, students who were released from secular study for the religious instructions were required to be present at the religious classes. Reports of their presence or absence were to be made to their secular teachers.

The foregoing facts, without reference to others that appear in the record, show the use of tax-supported property for religious instruction and the close cooperation between the school authorities and the religious council in promoting religious education. The operation of the State's compulsory education system thus assists and is integrated with the program of religious instruction carried on by separate religious sects. Pupils compelled by law to go to school for secular education are released in part from their legal duty upon the condition that they attend the religious classes. This is beyond all question a utilization of the tax-established and tax-supported public school system to aid religious groups to spread their faith. And it falls squarely under the ban of the First Amendment. . . .

To hold that a state cannot consistently with the First and Fourteenth Amendments utilize its public-school system to aid any or all religious faiths or sects in the dissemination of their doctrines and ideals does not, as counsel urge, manifest a governmental hostility to religion or religious teachings. A manifestation of such hostility would be at war with our national tradition as embodied in the First Amendment's guaranty of the free exercise of religion. For the First Amendment rests upon the premise that both religion and government can best work to achieve their lofty aims if each is left free from the other within its respective sphere. Or, as we said in the *Everson* case, the First Amendment has erected a wall between Church and State which must be kept high and impregnable.

Here not only are the State's tax-supported public-school buildings used for the dissemination of religious doctrines. The State also affords sectarian groups an invaluable aid in that it helps to provide pupils for their religious classes through use of the State's compulsory public-school machinery. This is not separation of Church and State. . . .

Mr. Justice Frankfurter, Concurring:

The Champaign arrangement . . . presents powerful elements of inherent pressure by the school system in the interest of religious sects. The fact that this power has not been used to discriminate is beside the point. Separation is a requirement to abstain from fusing functions of Government and of religious sects, not merely to treat them all equally. That a child is offered an alternative may reduce the constraint; it does not eliminate the operation of influence by the school in matters sacred to conscience and outside the school's domain. The law of imitation operates, and non-conformity is not an outstanding characteristic of children. The result is an obvious pressure upon children to attend. Again, while the Champaign school population represents only a fraction of the more than two hundred and fifty sects of the nation, not even all the practicing sects in Champaign are willing or able to provide religious instruction. The children belonging to these non-participating sects will thus have inculcated in them a feeling of separatism when the school should be the training ground for habits of community, or they will have religious instruction in a faith which is not that of their parents. As a result, the public school system of Champaign actively furthers inculcation in the religious tenets of some faiths, and in the process sharpens the consciousness of religious differences at least among some of the children committed to its care. . . .

Separation means separation, not something less. Jefferson's metaphor in describing the relation between Church and State speaks of a "wall of separation," not of a fine line easily overstepped. The public school is at once the symbol of our democracy and the most pervasive means for promoting our common destiny. In no activity of the State is it more vital to keep out divisive forces than in its schools, to avoid confusing, not to say fusing, what the Constitution sought to keep strictly apart. "The great American principle of eternal separation"—Elihu Root's phrase bears repetition—is one of the vital reliances of our Constitutional system for assuring unities among our people stronger than our diversities. . . .

Mr. Justice Reed, Dissenting:

The phrase "an establishment of religion" may have been intended by Congress to be aimed only at a state church. . . .

Mr. Jefferson, as one of the founders of the University of Virginia, a school which from its establishment in 1819 has been wholly governed, managed and controlled by the State of Virginia, was faced with the same problem that is before this Court today: the question of the constitutional limitation upon religious education in public schools. In his annual report as Rector, to the President and Directors of the Literary Fund, dated October 7, 1822, approved by the Visitors of the University of whom Mr. Madison was one, Mr. Jefferson set forth his views at some length. These suggestions of Mr. Jefferson were adopted and Ch. II, § 1, of the Regulations of the University of October 4, 1824, provided that:

> Should the religious sects of this State, or any of them, according to the invitation held out to them, establish within, or adjacent to, the precincts of the University, schools for instruction in the religion of their sect, the students of the University will be free, and expected to attend religious worship at the establishment of their respective sects, in the morning, and in time to meet their school in the University at its stated hour.

Thus, the "wall of separation between church and State" that Mr. Jefferson built at the University which he founded did not exclude religious education from that school. The difference between the generality of his statements on the separation of church and state and the specificity of his conclusions on education are considerable. A rule of law should not be drawn from a figure of speech. . . .

3.13. PUBLIC SCHOOLS MAY ALLOW "RELEASED TIME" FOR SECTARIAN RELIGIOUS INSTRUCTION, PROVIDED SUCH RELIGIOUS EDUCATION IS NEITHER COERCED NOR CONDUCTED ON PUBLIC SCHOOL PROPERTY, NOR SUPPORTED BY PUBLIC TAX MONEY [40]

William O. Douglas and Others

New York City has a program which permits its public schools to release students during the school day so that they may leave

---

[40] William O. Douglas, majority (6-3) opinion, *Zorach v. Clauson*, 343 U.S. 306 (1951). Footnotes and bibliography not included in these excerpts.

the school buildings and school grounds and go to religious centers for religious instruction or devotional exercises. A student is released on written request of his parents. Those not released stay in the classrooms. The churches make weekly reports to the schools, sending a list of children who have been released from public school but who have not reported for religious instruction.

This "released time" program involves neither religious instruction in public-school classrooms nor the expenditure of public funds. All costs, including the application blanks, are paid by the religious organizations. The case is therefore unlike *McCollum v. Board of Education*, 333 U.S. 203, which involved a "released time" program from Illinois. In that case the classrooms were turned over to religious instructors. We accordingly held that the program violated the First Amendment which (by reason of the Fourteenth Amendment) prohibits the states from establishing religion or prohibiting its free exercise.

Appellants, who are taxpayers and residents of New York City and whose children attend its public schools, challenge the present law, contending it is in essence not different from the one involved in the *McCollum* case. Their argument, stated elaborately in various ways, reduces itself to this: the weight and influence of the school is put behind a program for religious instruction; public-school teachers police it, keeping tab on students who are released; the classroom activities come to a halt while the students who are released for religious instruction are on leave; the school is a crutch on which the churches are leaning for support in their religious training; without the cooperation of the schools this "released-time" program, like the one in the *McCollum* case, would be futile and ineffective. . . .

There is a suggestion that the system involves the use of coercion to get public-school students into religious classrooms. There is no evidence in the record before us that supports that conclusion. (Nor is there any indication that the public schools enforce attendance at religious schools by punishing absentees from the released-time programs for truancy.) The present record indeed tells us that the school authorities are neutral in this regard and do no more than release students whose parents so request. If in fact coercion were used, if it were established that any one or more teachers were using their office to persuade or force students to take the religious instruction, a wholly different case would be presented. (Appellants contend that they should have been allowed to prove that the system is in fact administered in a coercive manner. The New York Court of Appeals declined to grant a trial on this issue, noting, *inter alia*, that appellants had not properly raised their claim in the manner required by state practice.) . . . Hence we put aside that claim of coercion. . . .

There cannot be the slightest doubt that the First Amendment reflects the philosophy that Church and State should be separated. And so far as interference with the "free exercise" of religion and an "establishment" of religion are concerned, the separation must be complete and unequivocal. The First Amendment within the scope of its coverage permits no exception; the prohibition is absolute. The First Amendment, however, does not say that in every and all respects there shall be a separation of Church and State. Rather, it studiously defines the manner, the specific ways, in which there shall be no concert or union or dependency one on the other. That is the common sense of the matter. Otherwise the state and religion would be aliens to each other—hostile, suspicious, and even unfriendly. Churches could not be required to pay even property taxes. Municipalities would not be permitted to render police or fire protection to religious groups. Policemen who helped parishioners into their places of worship would violate the Constitution. Prayers in our legislative halls; the appeals to the Almighty in the messages of the Chief Executive; the proclamations making Thanksgiving Day a holiday; "so help me God" in our courtroom oaths—these and all other references to the Almighty that run through our laws, our public rituals, our ceremonies would be flouting the First Amendment. A fastidious atheist or agnostic could even object to the supplication with which the Court opens each session: "God save the United States and this Honorable Court."

We would have to press the concept of separation of Church and State to these extremes to condemn the present law on constitutional grounds. The nullification of this law would have wide and profound effects. A Catholic student applies to his teacher for permission to leave the school during hours on a Holy Day of Obligation to attend a mass. A Jewish student asks his teacher for permission to be excused for Yom Kippur. A Protestant wants the afternoon off for a family baptismal ceremony. In each case the teacher requires parental consent in writing. In each case the teacher, in order to make sure the student is not a truant, goes further and requires a report from the priest, the rabbi, or the minister. The teacher in other words cooperates in a religious program to the extent of making it possible for her students to participate in it. Whether she does it occasionally for a few students, regularly for one, or pursuant to a systematized program designed to further the religious needs of all the students does not alter the character of the act.

We are a religious people whose institutions presuppose a Supreme Being. We guarantee the freedom to worship as one chooses. We make room for as wide a variety of beliefs and creeds as the spiritual needs of man deem necessary. We sponsor an attitude on the part of government that shows no partiality to any one group and that lets each flourish according to the zeal of its adherents and the appeal of its dogma. When the state encourages religious instruction or cooperates with religious authorities by adjusting the schedule of public events to sectarian needs, it follows the best of our traditions. For it then respects the religious nature of our people and accommodates the public service to their spiritual needs. To hold that it may not would be to find in the Constitution a requirement that the government show a callous indifference to religious groups. That would be preferring those who believe in no religion over those who do believe. Government may not finance religious groups nor undertake religious instruction nor blend secular and sectarian education nor use secular institutions to force one or some religion on any person. But we find no constitutional requirement which makes it necessary for government to be hostile to religion and to throw its weight against efforts to widen the effective scope of religious influence. The government must be neutral when it comes to competition between sects. It may not thrust any sect on any person. It may not make a religious observance compulsory. It may not coerce anyone to attend church, to observe a religious holiday, or to take religious instruction. But it can close its doors or suspend its operations as to those who want to repair to their religious sanctuary for worship or instruction. No more than that is undertaken here. . . .

In the *McCollum* case the classrooms were used for religious instruction and the force of the public school was used to promote that instruction. Here, as we have said, the public schools do no more than accommodate their schedules to a program of outside religious instruction. We follow the *McCollum* case. But we cannot expand it to cover the present released-time program unless separation of Church and State means that public institutions can make no adjustments of their schedules to accommodate the religious needs of the people. We cannot read into the Bill of Rights such a philosophy of hostility to religion.

Mr. Justice Black, Dissenting:

. . . the sole question is whether New York can use its compulsory education laws to help religious sects get attendance presumably too unenthusiastic to go unless moved to do so by the pressure of this state machinery. That this is the plan, purpose, design and consequence of the New York program cannot be denied. The state thus makes religious sects beneficiaries of its power to compel children to attend secular schools. Any use of such coercive power by the state to help or hinder some religious sects or to prefer all religious sects over nonbelievers or vice versa is just what I think the First Amendment forbids. In considering whether a state has entered this forbidden field the question is not whether it has entered too far but whether it has entered at all. New York is manipulating its compulsory education laws to help religious sects get pupils. This is not separation but combination of Church and State.

The Court's validation of the New York system rests in part on its statement that Americans are "a religious people whose institutions presuppose a Supreme Being." This was at least as true when the First Amendment was adopted; and it was just as true when eight Justices of this Court invalidated the released-time system in *McCollum* on the premise that a state can no more "aid all religions" than it can aid one. It was precisely because eighteenth-century Americans were a religious people divided into many fighting sects that we were given the constitutional mandate to keep Church and State completely separate. Colonial history had already shown that, here as elsewhere, zealous sectarians entrusted with governmental power to further their causes would sometimes torture, maim and kill those they branded "heretics," "atheists" or "agnostics." The First Amendment was therefore to insure that no one powerful sect or combination of sects could use political or governmental power to punish dissenters whom they could not convert to their faith. Now as then, it is only by wholly isolating the state from the religious sphere and compelling it to be completely neutral, that the freedom of each and every denomination and of all nonbelievers can be maintained. It is this neutrality the Court abandons today when it treats New York's coercive system as a program which *merely* "encourages religious instruction or cooperates with religious authorities." The abandonment is all the more dangerous to liberty because of the Court's legal exaltation of the orthodox and its derogation of unbelievers.

Under our system of religious freedom, people have gone to their religious sanctuaries not because they feared the law but because they loved their God. The choice of all has been as free as the choice of those who answered the call to worship moved only by the music of the old Sunday morning church bells. The spiritual mind of man has thus been free to believe, disbelieve, or doubt, without repression, great or small, by the heavy hand of government. Statutes authorizing such repression have been stricken. Before today, our judicial opinions have refrained from drawing invidious distinctions between those who believe in no religion and those who do believe. The First Amendment has lost much if the religious follower and the atheist are no longer to be judicially regarded as entitled to equal justice under law.

State help to religion injects political and party prejudices into a holy field. It too often substitutes force for prayer, hate for love, and persecution for persuasion. Government should not be allowed, under cover of the soft euphemism of "cooperation," to steal into the sacred area of religious choice.

Mr. Justice Frankfurter, Dissenting:

The deeply divisive controversy aroused by the attempts to secure public-school pupils for sectarian instruction would promptly end if the advocates of such instruction were content to have the school "close its doors or suspend its operations"—that is, dismiss classes in their entirety, without discrimination—instead of seeking to use the public schools as the instrument for securing attendance at denominational classes. The unwillingness of the promoters of this movement to dispense with such use of the public schools betrays a surprising want of confidence in the inherent power of the various faiths to draw children to outside sectarian classes—an attitude that hardly reflects the faith of the greatest religious spirits.

Mr. Justice Jackson, Dissenting:

As one whose children, as a matter of free choice, have been sent to privately supported Church schools, I may challenge the Court's suggestion that opposition to this plan can only be antireligious, atheistic, or agnostic. My evangelistic brethren confuse an objection to compulsion with an objection to religion. It is possible to hold a faith with enough confidence to believe that what should be rendered to God does not need to be decided and collected by Caesar.

The day that this country ceases to be free for irreligion it will cease to be free for religion—except for the sect that can win political power. The same epithetical jurisprudence used by the Court today to beat down those who oppose pressuring children into some religion can devise as good epithets tomorrow against those who object to pressuring them into a favored religion. And, after all, if we concede to the State power and wisdom to single out "duly constituted religious" bodies as exclusive alternatives for compulsory secular instruction, it would be logical to also uphold the power and wisdom to choose the true faith among those "duly constituted." We start down a rough road when we begin to mix compulsory public education with compulsory godliness.

Section D: Questions and Readings for Study and Discussion

3.14. American Traditions of Church and State

Section C summarized three recent court decisions relative to religion and education. Name some other important historic decisions and traditions.

Bettenson, Henry, *Documents of the Christian Church,* New York: Oxford, 1947. (European backgrounds: primary sources.)

Blau, Joseph, *Cornerstones of Religious Freedom in America,* Boston: Beacon, 1949. (Historical American documents.)

Brickman, William W., "Religious Education," *School and Society* 76: 262-267, Oct. 25, 1952; 71: 273-282, May 6, 1950; 67: 245-253, March 27, 1948. (Annotated bibliographies of recent writings.)

Butts, R. Freeman, *The American Tradition in Religion and Education,* Boston: Beacon, 1950.

* Commager, Henry Steele, ed., *Living Ideas in America,* New York: Harper, 1951. (Chapter 10, "Church and State.")

Commonweal (periodical), *Catholicism in America,* New York: Harcourt, 1954 (Recent articles by William P. Clancy and other Catholic lay writers.)

Dawson, J. M., *America's Way in Church, State and Society,* New York: Macmillan, 1953. (A Protestant viewpoint.)

Flynn, Frederick E., "Clericalism, Anti-Clericalism," *Commonweal* 58: 43-47, April 17, 1953. (Explains the association of liberalism with anti-clericalism.)

* Howe, Mark DeWolfe, *Cases on Church and State in the United States,* Cambridge, Mass.: Harvard University Press, 1952. (Chapter 5, "Education.")

*Johnson, Alvin W., *Legal Status of Church-State Relationships in the United States,* Minneapolis: University of Minnesota Press, 1934.

Johnson, F. Ernest, ed., *American Education and Religion: The Problem of Religion in the Schools,* New York: Harper, 1952.

3.15. Religious Pluralism

What is meant by "religious pluralism"? "religious tolerance"? "separation of church and state"?

Black, Algernon D., "The Church and Religious Freedom," *The Standard,* New York: American Ethical Union, Vol. 36, No. 3, December 1949.

Childs, John L., "The Democratic Resolution of Conflicts," Chapter 10 in H. Gordon Hullfish, ed., *Educational Freedom in an Age of Anxiety,* Twelfth Yearbook, John Dewey Society, New York: Harper, 1953.

* Coker, Francis W., "Some Present-Day Critics of Liberalism," *American Political Science Review* 47: 1-27, March 1953.

Forster, E. M., *Two Cheers for Democracy,* New York: Harcourt, 1951 (pages 44-76).

Goodenough, Erwin R., *The Church in the Roman Empire,* New York: Holt, 1931 (Chapter 2). (A lively description of the beginnings of the European tradition of an established Christian church.)

*MacIver, Robert M., *The Ramparts We Guard,* New York: Macmillan, 1950 (Chapter 13).

MacIver, Robert M., *The Web of Government,* New York: Macmillan, 1948 (pp. 421-430, "The Multi-Group Society").

* Maritain, Jacques, *Man and the State,* Chicago: University of Chicago Press, 1951. (Chapter 6, "Church and State.")

* Nixon, Charles R., "Freedom *vs.* Unity: A Problem in the Theory of Civil Liberty," *Political Science Quarterly* 68: 70-88, March 1953.

Raup, R. Bruce, "Moral Authority and Religious Sanction," *Teachers College Record* 54: 299-306, March 1953.

Weigel, Gustave, "The Church and the Democratic State," *Thought: Fordham University Quarterly* 27: 165-184, Summer 1952.

Weigel, Gustave, "Religious Toleration in a World Society," *America* 90: 375-376, Jan. 9, 1954; revised, with other authors, in pamphlet form as "Pope Pius XII and World Community," New York: America Press, 1954.

Williams, J. Paul, *What Americans Believe and How They Worship,* New York: Harper, 1952. (Brief descriptions of many church groups.)

3.16. Freedom for Atheists and Agnostics

Are people who belong to no organized "church" necessarily lacking in religion? Do such people come under the protection of the First Amendment?

Boorstin, Daniel J., "Our Unspoken National Faith: Why America Needs No Ideology," *Commentary* 15: 327-337, April 1953.

Fairchild, Hoxie N., "Religious Faith and Loyalty," *New Republic* 131: 11-13, October 11, 1954.

* Fromm, Erich, *Psychoanalysis and Religion,* New Haven, Conn.: Yale University Press, 1950 (pages 25-26, 118-119).

Huxley, Julian, *Religion Without Revelation,* New York: Harper, 1927.

Lamont, Corliss, *Humanism as a Philosophy,* New York: Philosophical Library, 1949 (Chapter 1).

Morain, Lloyd and Mary, *Humanism as the Next Step,* Boston: Beacon, 1954 (p. 30 f).

Otto, Max Carl, *The Human Enterprise,* New York: Crofts, 1940 (Chapters 10 and 11).

Potter, Charles F., *Humanism: A New Religion,* New York: Simon and Schuster, 1930 (Chapter 3).

* Sibley, Mulford Q., and Jacob, Philip E., *Conscription of Conscience: The American State and the Conscientious Objector, 1940-1947,* Ithaca, N. Y.: Cornell University Press, 1952 (pages 429-431).

Smith, T. V., "Our Issue With Russia," *Vital Speeches* 19: 301-305, March 1, 1953.

* Stokes, Anson Phelps, *Church and State in the United States,* 3 Vols., New York: Harper, 1950 (III: 550-552).

White, Edward A., *Science and Religion in American Thought: The Impact of Naturalism,* Stanford, Calif.: Stanford University Press, 1952. (Choose any one of the several famous names discussed.)

3.17. Bible Reading in Public Schools

Should Bible reading be allowed in public schools? Should it be required?

Butts, R. Freeman, *The American Tradition in Religion and Education,* Boston: Beacon, 1950. (Numerous references. Consult index.)

* Kilpatrick, William Heard, "The Gideons Bible Case," *Nation* 176: front inside cover, June 13, 1953. (See also *Time* 62: 29, Dec. 14, 1953.)

Johnson, Alvin W., *Legal Status of Church-State Relationships in the United States,* Minneapolis: University of Minnesota Press, 1934 (Chapter 3).

* Pfeffer, Leo, *Church, State and Freedom,* Boston: Beacon, 1953 (Chapter 11).

Wills, George, *Alice in Bibleland,* New York: Philosophical Library, 1953.

3.18. Religious Dogma and Scientific Objectivity

Can a person have deep religious convictions without becoming narrow-minded? Can a person be completely open-minded without being empty-minded? Can teachers be truly liberal if committed to a religious creed or dogma?

* Bode, Boyd H., "Pragmatism in Education," *New Republic* 121: 15-18, Oct. 17, 1949.

Burkhardt, Frederick, ed., *The Cleavage in Our Culture: Studies in Scientific Humanism in Honor of Max Otto,* Boston: Beacon, 1952.

Casserley, J. V. Langmead, *The Retreat from Christianity in the Modern World,* New York: Longmans, 1952.

* Ducasse, Curt J., *A Philosophical Scrutiny of Religion,* New York: Ronald, 1953 (Chapter 9: "Religion, Faith and Truth").

Frank, Philipp G., and others, "The Variety of Reasons for the Acceptance of Scientific Theories," *Scientific Monthly* 79: 139-152, September 1954.

Gilson, Etienne, "Dogmatism and Tolerance: An Address" (Pamphlet), New Brunswick, N. J.: Rutgers University Press, 1952.

Jaspers, Karl, "Premises and Possibilities of a New Humanism," pp. 65-98 in *Existentialism and Humanism: Three Essays by Karl Jaspers,* ed. by H. E. Fischer, New York: Moore, 1952.

* Moberly, Sir Walter, *The Crisis in the University,* London: Student Christian Movement Press, 1949 (Chapters 10 and 11).

Moulton, Phillips P., "Education: Christian and Liberal," *Christian Century* 71: 488-489, April 21, 1954.

Organ, Troy Wilson, "The Chapel in a Liberal Arts College," *American Association of University Professors Bulletin* 38: 90-95, Spring 1952.

Planck, Max, *The Philosophy of Physics,* London: Allen & Unwin, 1936 (Chapter 4).

Rader, Melvin, "Crisis and the Spirit of Community," Presidential Address to the Western Division of the American Philosophical Association, *Proceedings and Addresses* 27: 40-58, November 1954, Yellow Springs, Ohio: Antioch Press, 1954.

* Rasmusson, H. Richard, "The Preacher Talks to the Man of Science," *Scientific Monthly* 79: 392-395, December 1954.

Reiser, Oliver L., *Nature, Man and God,* Pittsburgh, Pa.: University of Pittsburgh Press, 1951 (pages 59-60).

Shuster, George N., "Academic Freedom," *Commonweal* 58: 11-13, April 10, 1953.

Van Steenberghen, Fernand, *Epistemology,* New York: Wagner, 1949 (pages 258-260).

Withey, Raymond A., Jr., "The Role of Religion in Higher Education," *School and Society* 76: 257-261, October 25, 1952.

3.19. State Money for Parochial Schools

In 1929 Pope Pius XI wrote: "The so-called 'neutral' or 'lay' school—from which religion is excluded—is contrary to the fundamental principles of education." (Pope Pius XI, *Rappresentanti in Terra,* "On the Christian Education of Youth," Dec. 31, 1929.)

If Roman Catholics (and some Protestants and Jews) believe this, does their freedom of religious belief entitle them to public money for parochial schools? (Several aspects of this problem were considered in Section C on "Separation of Church and State: Some Recent Court Decisions." The following references may add further light [and heat!] to this problem.)

Blanshard, Paul, *American Freedom and Catholic Power,* Boston: Beacon 1949. (Compare O'Neill below, and Weigel in 3.15 above.)

Conant, James B., "Unity and Diversity in Secondary Education," reprinted in *American Association of School Administrators Official Report, 1952,* pp. 235-243, Washington, D. C.: National Education Association, 1952; in *Vital Speeches* 18: 463-465, May 15, 1952; and amplified in Conant's book, *Education and Liberty,* Cambridge, Mass.: Harvard University Press, 1953 (pp 77-87, 140-152). Also reprinted under title, "Education: Engine of Democracy," with replies by Archbishop Richard J. Cushing ("The Case for Religious Schools"), and Allan V. Heely ("A Call for Diversity"), *Saturday Review* 35: 11-15 f, May 3, 1952.

Cornell, Francis G., "Federal Aid Is a Religious Issue," *School Executive* 72: 47-49, June 1953 (bibliography); comment by R. H. Schenk, S.J., *ibid.* 72: 13, August 1953.

* Cunneen, Joseph E., "Catholics and Education," *Commonweal* 58: 437-441, 461-464, Aug. 7-14, 1953. (Viewpoint of a Catholic layman.)

Dunne, George Harold, *Religion and American Democracy: A Reply to Paul Blanshard's American Freedom and Catholic Power,* New York: America Press, 1949.

Katz, Wilber G., "The Freedom to Believe," *Atlantic* 192: 66-69, October 1953. (A Protestant lawyer gives partial support to the Catholic position.)

McManus, William E., "Agnes Meyer on Parochial Schools," *Catholic World* 178: 346-351, February 1954.

Meyer, Agnes E., "Clerical Challenge to the Schools," *Atlantic* 189: 42-46, March 1952.

O'Neill, James M., *Catholicism and American Freedom,* New York: Harper, 1952. (Compare Blanshard and Oxnam.)

Oxnam, [Methodist] Bishop G. Bromley, "Church, State and Schools," *Nation* 168: 67-70, January 15, 1949.

Sheerin, John B., "Conant and Catholic Schools," *Catholic World* 175: 161-165, June 1952.

Thayer, Vivian T., *The Attack Upon the American Secular School,* Boston: Beacon, 1951 (Chapter 5).

3.20. Moral and Spiritual Values

Should moral and spiritual values be taught in nonsectarian schools? Can they be taught well without appealing to religious teachings? without favoring one religion over another?

* Bower, William C., *Moral and Spiritual Values in Education*, Lexington, Ky.: University of Kentucky Press, 1952 (especially Chapter 7).

Caswell, Hollis L., "Are the Public Schools Irreligious?" *Teachers College Record* 54: 357-365, April 1953; also in *Vital Speeches* 19: 399-402, April 15, 1953.

Caswell, Hollis L., "Moral and Religious Teaching in the Public Schools," *School Executive* 73: 19-21, October 1953.

Brown, Kenneth I., *Not Minds Alone: Some Frontiers of Christian Education*, New York: Harper, 1954. (Protestant view.)

* Educational Policies Commission, *Moral and Spiritual Values in the Public Schools*, Washington, D. C.: National Education Association, 1951.

Hallowell, John H., *The Moral Foundation of Democracy*, Chicago: University of Chicago Press, 1954.

Lotz, Philip H., ed., *Orientation in Religious Education*, Nashville, Tenn.: Abingdon-Cokesbury, 1950. (A Protestant view.)

Thayer, Vivian T., *The Attack Upon the American Secular School*, Boston: Beacon, 1951 (Chapters 10 and 11).

Van Dusen, Henry P., *God in Education*, New York: Scribner's, 1951 (pages 99-120).

* Weigle, Luther A., "The Crisis of Religion in Education," *Vital Speeches* 20: 147-149, Dec. 15, 1953.

4. RACIAL SEGREGATION IN EDUCATION

Section A: The Sociological Backgrounds

4.1. INTRODUCTION: RACIAL SEGREGATION IN THE SCHOOLS

Within the memory of some people still alive, there was a time when human beings were bought and sold as chattel property, when men honestly affirmed that dark-skinned people had neither souls nor intellects, and that Negroes were incapable of rational, moral action or of intellectual achievement. Today most educated people would consider such attitudes both irrational and undemocratic. Tremendous changes in fact and in attitude have occurred within the past century.

These changing attitudes are as genuine in the South as in the North. In 1950 the Southern Regional Council affirmed that the best way to attain equality between the races is for the Negro to have a voice in the policy-making which determines the quality of education children are to receive—not "arithmetical equality," not "paternalism," but "true equality." The Southern Regional Council recommended that Negroes be named to membership in all policy-making bodies that administer laws and govern public services, especially school boards, both elective and appointive. Such Southern leaders believe that the time is rapidly running out when postponement and token approaches to equalization will suffice. The Negro is fully aware of the long record of evasion and inaction.

Of fifteen million U. S. Negroes about ten million live in the South. Northern migrations will probably continue, but in diminishing quantity, so that the proportion of Negroes will continue to be somewhat as it now is for many generations. Differences in tradition and in race-proportion lead to different situations. It is one thing to speak of treating Negro citizens fairly in Minnesota, where less than 15,000 of the population are Negroes, or about one out of every 200 inhabitants. It is quite a different matter in Mississippi, where there are nearly a million Negroes, or about 90 out of every 200 inhabitants. It is easy for Northerners who happen to be removed from concrete racial problems to argue that the Ten Commandments and the Golden Rule know no state boundaries. But it is doctrinaire to suggest that their interpretation and application must be precisely alike in all situations. For this reason, Southern leaders generally resent outside imposition, and prefer to accept local responsibility for wiping out differentials.[1]

It may be noted that segregation occurs in the North as well as in the South, and that some of the worst recent racial problems have occurred in the North. In Chicago over 90 per cent of the Negroes live in areas predominantly Negro. Segregation distinguishes Negro housing from slum housing in general. People trapped behind such "ghetto walls" generally live in neighborhoods characterized by poverty, filth and vice, and find it difficult to live according to the social and ethical standards of the larger community, or to assimilate the prevailing cultural standards. "The distortion of social values in the Negro neighborhood is manifest in higher crime rates, and in relatively greater expense to the community in required police, fire and health services. In Chicago's Black Belt, for example, the rate of juvenile delinquency is eight times and the death rate almost twice that in the rest of the city." [2]

---

[1] Henry H. Hill, "The South is the Nation's Laboratory," *National Education Association Proceedings* 71-78, January 1953; Rufus E. Clement, "America and Education at the Crossroads," *Association of American Colleges Bulletin* 39: 249-253, May 1953.

[2] David M. Helfeld and Isaac N. Groner, "Race Discrimination in Housing," 57 *Yale Law Journal* 426 (1948); cited, p. 995 f, by Thomas I. Emerson and David Haber, *Political and Civil Rights in the United States*, Buffalo, N. Y.:

Throughout the United States Negroes are generally engaged in occupations which denote the lowest economic and social status. If the Southern Negro enjoys less education than the Negro in the North and West, it is partly because the South generally has a lower standard of income. Southern educational facilities are certainly behind those of the North and West. But in recent years the *proportion* of money spent on education is higher in the South than in the nation as a whole; and there has been a gradual but definite reduction of the differential between Negro and white schools.

The general disparity between white and Negro schools has its counterpart in the inequalities between urban and rural schools in the South. In every [Southern] state there are counties in which the best white school by any standard of comparison is inferior to the worst Negro schools in the larger cities.[3]

A few states have a very marked differential: Mississippi spends about $117 per white pupil as compared with $35 per Negro. But over the South as a whole the differential has been reduced to about fifteen per cent in 1952.

Economically and socially the past few decades have witnessed many impressive changes in the New South: ". . . the gradual redistribution of the Negro minority both nationally and within the Southern states; the growth of educational facilities nationally and regionally; the number of white-faced Herefords now grazing on Southern acres once devoted to cotton; the remarkable shift of cotton production to the Southwest and California and its rapid mechanization; the industrialization and urbanization of the South; the increased mobility of population that has come with a revolution in transportation; the stabilization of agricultural prices, including that of cotton; the spread of rural electrification and soil conservation, and the impact of the T.V.A."[4]

There are over a million Negroes in labor unions that used to bar them. The Army's last all-Negro outfit was said to be "inte-

---

Dennis, 1952, p. 995 f (Chapter 9 on "Discrimination" is an excellent over-all summary of many legal and sociological aspects of the subject.)

[3] Harry S. Ashmore, *The Negro and the Schools,* Chapel Hill, N. C.: University of North Carolina Press, 1954, p. 110. By permission.

[4] Carey McWilliams, "Climax of an Era," *Nation* 178: 453-456, May 29, 1954. By permission.

grated" racially in June 1954. The Air Force and Navy are gradually extending a nonsegregation policy in all units. All schools on military posts were to have been nonsegregated by September 1954, under a presidential decree.

Discrimination or segregation in streetcars, busses, hotels, theaters, restaurants, public parks, swimming pools and housing districts continues, but is gradually decreasing in most areas. All-white primaries are outlawed by Supreme Court decision, and Southern States now have over a million registered Negro voters, compared with less than 300,000 in 1938.

Segregation continues in the South in day coaches, though it is almost gone in chair cars, Pullman cars, dining cars and airplanes. Negroes can now stay in most hotels in Washington, D. C.—a change that has taken place within the past decade.

Walter White, Secretary of the National Association for the Advancement of Colored People, summarized the prevailing view when he said:

> We don't claim as yet to have a perfect democracy in the United States, but it is a system of society where through constitutional means we can wipe out existing evil. We are doing that in America—not at the speed that some of us would like, but nevertheless we are steadily making progress, and we are doing it through democratic means, which would never be permitted under Communism or any other form of totalitarian government.[5]

4.2. THE NEGRO IN THE UNITED STATES [6]

Edward C. McDonagh and Eugene S. Richards

The Negro in the South

At the present time it is impossible to refer to the status of *"the Negro"* in the United States. The fact is he has many statuses. These

---

[5] Walter White, copyrighted interview, *U. S. News & World Report* 36: 56, May 28, 1954. By permission.

[6] Edward C. McDonagh and Eugene S. Richards, *Ethnic Relations in the United States*, New York: Appleton-Century-Crofts, Inc., 1953 (excerpts from Chapters 5 and 6; charts and footnotes omitted). By permission. Mr. McDonagh

statuses vary in keeping with the different regions, the many states, and even within any one state in the United States. . . . However, it seems as if there is a high correlation between points of concentration and low status. Where the concentration is most intense the status of the Negro is lowest. On the other hand, in the areas where they are few in number Negroes appear to be accorded a higher status. . . .

With the development of slavery in the South, there was established a vertical stratification of whites and Negroes according to which all whites were considered superior to all Negroes. In keeping with this stratification Negroes were forced to accept always an inferior status in all contacts between whites and Negroes. The extent to which the inferior status of the Negro was recognized is illustrated by the majority opinion of the United States Supreme Court in the Dred Scott Case [1859], when it was declared that the Negro had no rights which the white man was bound to respect. Since slavery continued in the South for about two hundred years, this superior-inferior pattern of race contacts became so deeply entrenched that more than eighty years of Negro freedom have not been able to remove it, and in some areas have not modified it to any considerable extent. . . .

Social Status

The social status of the Negro in the South will be determined by the nature of the attitudes and opinions of whites in the South toward Negroes. In an attempt to point out the attitudes and opinions of whites in the South toward Negroes, many studies have been made by students of ethnic relations in the United States. Five of these studies have been reviewed for the purpose of determining the predominant attitudes of whites in the South toward Negroes.[7] . . .

is Professor of Sociology, University of Southern California. Mr. Richards is Chairman, Division of Social Sciences, Texas Southern University.

Compare: Howard University Bureau of Educational Research, *Relative Status of the Negro in the United States,* Washington: Howard University Press, 1954.

[7] Editor's Note: Studies by Powdermaker (1939), Dollard (1940), Johnson (1943), Odum (1943) and Myrdal (1944). Full references and charts are in the original text. Read also: Gordon W. Allport and others, *The Nature of Prejudice,* 2 vols., Cambridge, Mass.: Addison-Wesley, 1954; Gerhart Saenger, *The Social Psychology of Prejudice,* New York: Harper, 1953.

The following six attitudes were reported in all five of the studies reviewed as attitudes of whites toward Negroes: (1) Negroes are mentally inferior, (2) social equality is impractical if not impossible, (3) Negroes are lazy and shiftless, (4) Negroes are incapable of self-discipline, (5) segregation is necessary, and (6) Negroes are criminally inclined. The following eight attitudes were reported in four of the five studies reviewed: (1) Negroes are all right in their place, (2) intermarriage should be prohibited, (3) Negroes possess a low moral standard, (4) are happy-go-lucky and carefree, (5) are not capable of assuming responsibility and leadership, (6) are highly sexual, (7) will lie, and (8) are satisfied with their present status.

A study of the attitudes . . . reveals that whites in the South assign the Negro to a very low social status for at least four reasons. In the first place, the Negro is considered as inferior from a mental and moral standpoint. In the second place, the Negro is believed to possess several traits that denote a low social status in the American social order, such as being lazy and shiftless, criminally inclined, happy-go-lucky and carefree, highly sexual, and very untruthful. In the third place, since he is not capable of assuming responsibility and leadership and is incapable of self-discipline, social equality is impractical if not impossible. Therefore, segregation is necessary, and intermarriage should be prohibited. In the fourth place, the Negro is all right in his place, which the preceding attitudes indicate is a very low place, and is satisfied with his present status. In summary, whites in the South assign Negroes to a very low social status because they believe that they have certain inferior characteristics, possess several traits that denote a low social status, are not capable of full participation in the American social order, and are satisfied with their present low social status. . . .

An evaluation of the attitudes of whites in the South toward Negroes will show that these attitudes include some of the stereotypes that are commonly held concerning Negroes. Many of these stereotypes are traditional in nature, and represent a carry-over from the period of slavery in the United States. As stereotypes these attitudes have been handed down from generation to generation without much reflection or evaluation. It is therefore valid to assume that many of these attitudes are fallacious concerning

Negroes at the present time. *Whether these attitudes are fallacious or valid, the social status of the Negro will be determined by these attitudes as long as they are held by whites in the South.* Thus, until efforts are exercised in an attempt to change the present attitudes of whites in the South toward Negroes, the Negro will continue to be assigned a low social status in the South. . . .

Legal Status

Since the ratification of the Thirteenth Amendment, which abolished slavery; the Fourteenth Amendment, which guaranteed to the Negro citizenship and certain other personal rights; and the Fifteenth Amendment, which protects the Negro in his right to vote, the Negro has had the same legal status as other citizens according to the Constitution of the United States. . . . *In other words, if the legal status as stated or implied by federal laws were recognized, there would be very little, if any, difference between the legal status of Negroes and that of whites in the South.* However, the principles included in some federal laws are written in such general terms that it is possible for many interpretations to be given to them. Even the United States Supreme Court at different times has given varied interpretations to the principles of the Federal Constitution. The many interpretations of federal laws have provided states with opportunities to enact state laws that are in keeping with these interpretations, but contrary to what many authorities consider the fundamental principles of federal laws. . . .

Although the Negro is accorded by federal laws the same legal status as other citizens, this sameness fades when attention is directed to the laws of the states in the South. Many laws exist that provide for the separation of Negroes and whites. These laws range from the possible separation of the races in telephone booths in Oklahoma, to laws prescribing separation in the most intimate of all social relations—that of marriage—in all of the states of the South. As with marriage, all of the states of the South have required separation of the races in public schools, in colleges, and in institutions for juvenile delinquents. The following are areas where separation is required by law in most of the states in the South; on railways, in penal institutions, in mental institutions, on busses, on streetcars, in waiting-rooms, and in institutions for physical defectives. Some of the other areas of activity in which separation is required in the South are: in places of amusement, in institutions for tubercular patients, in homes for orphans and the aged, in hospitals, in libraries, and in the use of textbooks. . . .

Areas where separation is practiced but not required legally, in many instances, include employment, hotels, tourist camps, cafes and restaurants, churches, Christian Associations, boys' and girls' clubs, residences, social clubs, professional and occupational organizations, and many other activities where social contacts are involved. On the other hand, most economic enterprises in the South, in which profit is the major motive, will deal with the Negro on a basis of equality. A Negro can go into most stores and other economic enterprises with the expectation of receiving equal attention, and in most instances he will not be disappointed. *In other words, functional democracy is frequently practiced more in private economic enterprises than in social, religious, or governmental agencies.* . . .

Educational Status

Educational Facilities. Although the public school facilities available for Negroes in the South have increased at a rapid rate since 1930, they were still inferior to those for whites in all of the states in the South in 1945. . . . In Arkansas only two Negro schools were accredited by the regional accrediting agency, while seventy white schools were accredited by this agency. In Georgia the value of school property per pupil enrolled was $35.00 for Negro schools and $160.00 for white schools. In Louisiana there was one white teacher to every thirty pupils registered and only one Negro teacher to every fifty-one pupils. In Mississippi 2,015 (61.2 per cent) of the Negro schools were one-teacher schools, while only 105 (less than 5 per cent) of the white schools were one-teacher schools. In North Carolina 45.58 per cent of the white pupils were transported to and from school, while 17.76 per cent of the Negro pupils were transported. In South Carolina the expenditure per pupil enrolled was $37.00 for Negro pupils, but $113.00 for white pupils.[8] Although

---

[8] Editor's Note: In 1951, South Carolina, under the leadership of Governor Byrnes, launched a huge educational budget, about 69 per cent of which went to Negro schools. (H. S. Ashmore, *op. cit.* p. 51)

the Negro school population in Texas was 15.3 per cent of the total school population, Negro schools received only 5.7 per cent of the appropriations for facilities and special instructional programs in 1945. These illustrations should be sufficient to warrant the conclusion that, from the standpoint of facilities, the status of Negro education in public schools is on a very low level, even much lower than the level for white education in the South.

If attention is directed to facilities for higher and professional education for Negroes in the South, the situation is much worse than it is in public schools. In the sixteen states included in the South in this study there was not a Negro institution that was qualified to offer work for the Doctor of Philosophy degree in 1948, and only two of the Negro universities that offered work leading to the Master's degree were on the approved list of the Association of American Universities. One medical school was recognized by the American Medical Association in the sixteen states in 1948, and one school of social work was recognized by the American Association of Schools of Social Work. On the other hand, not a single recognized school for Negroes existed in the professional areas of engineering and architecture. Although several universities in a few southern states have admitted Negroes to graduate and professional schools during the past few years, Negroes with the desire and ability to pursue professional training are still very restricted in their choice. . . . Further, the inferior educational facilities that are available for Negroes on the lower levels make it difficult, if not impossible, for many of them to qualify for admission to the graduate and professional universities to which they are now eligible for admission. . . .

Years of School Completed. The educational status of the Negro, as reflected by the number of school years completed by persons twenty-five years old and over, is very low for the Negro in the South. The percentages for no school years completed ranged around 11 per cent for Negroes and 3 per cent for whites in 1940. Percentages for both groups decreased by 1950, but the percentages for Negroes were still much larger than those for whites. As examples, the rates in South Carolina for 1950 were 10.5 per cent for nonwhites and 2.6 per cent for whites. In Arkansas the rates were 7.8 per cent for nonwhites and 1.7 per cent for whites. The aver-

age for all states in the South was around 9 per cent for nonwhites
and 2 per cent for whites.

On the higher levels the educational status of the Negro is much
lower than that of whites in the South. In 1940 the rates for four
years of high school were approximately 13 per cent for whites and
3.0 per cent for nonwhites. In 1950 the rates in Arkansas were
15.5 per cent for whites and 3.2 per cent for nonwhites, and in
South Carolina they were 10.9 per cent for whites and 1.7 per cent
for nonwhites. A similar picture was evident in 1950 for four years
or more of college completed. In Arkansas the rates were 3.6 per
cent for whites and 1.2 per cent for nonwhites, and in South Carolina they were 7.2 per cent for whites and 1.7 per cent for nonwhites. These figures indicate that the educational status of the
Negro in the South is much lower than that of whites as far as
years of school completed are concerned.

The median number of school years completed is also much
lower for Negroes than for whites in the South. In 1940 the range
for Negroes was from 2.8 years in Louisiana to 6 years in Oklahoma,
while it ranged from 6.3 years in Louisiana to 8.1 years in Mississippi for whites. In 1950 the median number of school years completed in Arkansas was 8.7 years for whites and 5.6 years for nonwhites, and in South Carolina it was 9.0 years for whites and 4.8
years for nonwhites. On the average, whites in the South have
completed between three and four more years of formal schooling
than Negroes.

Professional Training. The educational status of the Negro in
the South is also low if judged by the proportion of the trained
professional personnel to the total Negro population. As illustrations, there is one Negro physician and surgeon to about every
5,000 Negroes, but one white physician and surgeon to about every
800 whites. There is one Negro dentist for about every 12,000
Negroes, but one white dentist for about every 2,500 whites. There
is one Negro lawyer for about every 25,000 Negroes, but one white
lawyer for about every 700 whites. The number of lay persons
for Negro professionals is five times or more the number for white
professionals. . . .

Economic Status

On the one hand, facilities for training and experience are not available for Negroes in the occupations that make possible a high economic status. On the other hand, Negro youth is often discouraged from training for higher occupations. He is told that there is no place for him in higher occupational activities and, therefore, he resigns himself to occupations that are on a low economic level. . . .

For nonwhites in the South 43.9 per cent of the family incomes were below $1,000 [in 1949], while for the South 24.2 per cent were below this sum. . . . The median income for nonwhite families in the South was $1,168, for the South it was $2,248, and for the United States it was $3,068. . . . [The Negro in the South] owns very little property, and that which he owns is valued much lower than that of whites. However, it is true that the Negro's economic status has advanced and is advancing. . . .

Summary

The Negro's social status is low because whites have accepted many attitudes and opinions that are degrading to the Negro, and that tend to make him socially unacceptable to whites. There are many laws that serve to restrict the advancement of the Negro in the South, and to relegate him to a position much lower than that of whites. Educationally, he is segregated in schools, and the schools and facilities provided for him are far inferior to those provided for whites. Also, he has acquired a much lower educational status than whites, as measured by the years of school completed. Economically, he is on the lowest level in the South, but the trend is in the direction of upward mobility.

The Negro in the North and West

Social Status

In the North and the West attitudes and opinions toward the Negro differ in several ways from those in the South. It is recognized that basically there is much similarity in the attitudes and opinions toward the Negro in all sections of the United States. Yet . . . three conditions serve to modify these attitudes and opinions to an important degree in the North and West: (1) limited contacts of whites and Negroes resulting from a scattered Negro population, (2) the urban concentration of the Negro population, and (3) the presence of other minority ethnic groups in these regions. These conditions make for somewhat superficial Negro-white relations, since in many instances these relations are based on vicarious experience instead of actual contacts.

Nevertheless, it has been pointed out that several attitudes and opinions are well fixed in the North and West. Among these attitudes and opinions accepted by whites are: (1) residential segregation is necessary and should be continued, (2) social equality is impractical if not impossible, (3) Negroes should be segregated in close social relations, (4) Negroes are best fitted for unskilled labor and domestic work and should be denied white-collar jobs, (5) close personal contacts with Negroes should be avoided, and (6) interracial marriages are taboo and should be avoided. . . .

Educational Status

In theory the facilities available to whites for higher and professional education are also available to Negroes in all of the states in the North and West with the exception of Missouri. However, if the study conducted in the state of New York is representative, Negroes are discriminated against for many reasons when they apply for admission to colleges and universities. In this study, 16 of the 39 high schools (41 per cent) having some Negroes in their student bodies reported that Negro graduates had encountered some form of discrimination in seeking admission to the colleges and universities in the state of New York. Although they were not denied admission, many excuses were offered in discouraging Negro high-school graduates from entering many colleges and universities in New York. Among the most common excuses were: (1) social life for Negro students is negligible, (2) parents object to Negro students, (3) the institution is not interested in Negro students, (4) the situation might not be happy for Negro students, and (5) scholarship or work aids are not available. To these reasons might be added the following: (6) most Negroes lack the economic resources necessary to attend many of these schools, (7) Negro youth receive little encouragement from their elders, and (8) many schools are not ready to admit Negroes into their dormitories. Thus, although Negroes are not denied admission to many of the colleges and universities in the North and West, they are confronted with many discouragements when they seek it. This means that only the courageous will follow through and many capable students who can be misled or discouraged will drop by the wayside. As a result, Negroes in the North and West are not able to make the best use of the facilities for higher and professional education that are available to them. . . .

The educational status of the Negro in the North and West is far above that of the Negro in the South; it approaches that of whites in the South; but it is far below that of whites in the North and West. The general conclusions that these facts will support are that the educational status of the Negro in the North is above that of foreign-born whites, but below that of native whites; in the West the educational status of the Negro is above that of several minority ethnic groups, but, again, below that of native whites.

Economic Status

In the North and West, as in the South, Negro workers are engaged in occupations that require the least training, pay the lowest income, are the least desirable, and are accorded the lowest social status. . . . Occupations engaged in by Negro workers pay an income much smaller than that required to maintain a minimum standard of living; they provide little economic security; and they offer few chances for occupational advancement. . . .

Summary

In general, the status of the Negro is low in the North and West when compared with that of native whites. Although the laws in many of these states prohibit differential treatment between ethnic groups, the fact remains that differences are made. The source of these differences seems to be the attitudes and opinions that are common among members of the majority ethnic group. These attitudes and opinions relegate the Negro to a low social status, and this low social status predominates in all other areas of group life. *This fact strongly suggests the conclusion that attitudes and opinions are more important than laws in determining the general status of an ethnic group.* Therefore, if ethnic relations in the United States are to be improved, it is essential that constructive programs and procedures be established that will modify attitudes and opinions. These programs and procedures should be so planned that they will serve to modify the many fallacious attitudes and opinions that are accepted, and to reinforce the democratic attitudes and opinions that science and logic have been able to prove valid.

Section B: The Present Situation

4.3. INTRODUCTION

Many Americans accept "majority rule" as an adequate definition of democracy. But when we ask "Whose majority?" we realize that all of us are members, not of one society, but of many. For example, a Roman Catholic in upper New York may be part of the majority of his local school district or township; a minority in his state and nation; a majority in a Pan-American conference; a minority in the world. A laboring man may belong to the majority union of his company, which union may be a minority group in the AFL, which AFL may be affiliated with the political party in power representing the majority of the state or nation. An Alabama Negro may belong to the "colored" majority in his local town or county; to the minority in his state and nation; and to the majority in the world.

So far as the Negro is concerned, most white men, in the North as well as in the South, accept it as a matter of fact and as a matter of habit that the "white man" should rule. This attitude causes relatively few problems where there are relatively few Negroes. But in the deep South, the number of Negroes approaches a majority, and in many local areas is a majority, so that the granting of full equality would clearly involve major shifts of political, social and racial power. Prejudices, habits and traditions being as they are, it should be obvious that it will take more than an

Emancipation Proclamation before the Negro gains his full freedom.

But laws are important, and the 1954 Supreme Court decision means that the "separate but equal" doctrine of the majority of the Supreme Court in the Plessy case (1896) is overthrown. The 1954 court, in a unanimous opinion, vindicated the dissenting opinion of Mr. Justice John Marshall Harlan who in 1896 said the effect of the Plessy decision was "to permit the seeds of race hate to be planted under the sanction of the law," and who affirmed that "our Constitution is colorblind, and neither knows nor tolerates classes among citizens."

The significance of the new court ruling has been evaluated by Harry S. Ashmore as follows:

> In the long sweep of history the public-school cases before the Supreme Court may be written down as the point at which the South cleared the last turning in the road to reunion—the point at which finally, and under protest, the region gave up its peculiar institutions and accepted the prevailing standards of the nation at large as the legal basis for its relationship with its minority race. This would not in itself bring about any great shift in Southern attitudes, nor even any far-reaching immediate changes in the pattern of bi-racial education. But it would redefine the goal the Southern people, white and Negro, are committed to seek in the way of democracy.[9]

The two selections that follow consist of the recent Supreme Court decision, and an evaluation of its possible consequences by members of the Southern Regional Council.

4.4. IN THE FIELD OF PUBLIC EDUCATION THE DOCTRINE OF "SEPARATE BUT EQUAL" HAS NO PLACE [10]

Earl Warren

These cases come to us from the States of Kansas, South Carolina, Virginia, and Delaware. They are premised on different facts and

---

[9] Harry S. Ashmore, *The Negro and the Schools,* Chapel Hill, N. C.: University of North Carolina Press, 1954, p. 139. By permission.

[10] Chief Justice Earl Warren (speaking for a unanimous court), *Brown v. Board of Education,* 347 U.S. 483 (1954). Most footnotes here omitted.

different local conditions, but a common legal question justifies their consideration together in this consolidated opinion.

In each of the cases, minors of the Negro race, through their legal representatives, seek the aid of the courts in obtaining admission to the public schools of their community on a non-segregated basis. In each instance, they had been denied admission to schools attended by white children under laws requiring or permitting segregation according to race. This segregation was alleged to deprive the plaintiffs of the equal protection of the laws under the Fourteenth Amendment. In each of the cases other than the Delaware case, a three-judge federal district court denied relief to the plaintiffs on the so-called "separate but equal" doctrine announced by this Court in *Plessy v. Ferguson,* 163 U.S. 537.[11] Under that doctrine, equality of treatment is accorded when the races are provided substantially equal facilities, even though these facilities be separate. In the Delaware case, the Supreme Court of Delaware adhered to that doctrine, but ordered that the plaintiffs be admitted to the white schools because of their superiority to the Negro schools.

The plaintiffs contend that segregated public schools are not "equal" and cannot be made "equal," and that hence they are deprived of the equal protection of the laws. Because of the obvious importance of the question presented, the Court took jurisdiction. Argument was heard in the 1952 Term, and reargument was heard this Term on certain questions propounded by the Court.

Reargument was largely devoted to the circumstances surrounding the adoption of the Fourteenth Amendment in 1868. It covered exhaustively consideration of the Amendment in Congress, ratification by the states, then existing practices in racial segregation, and the views of proponents and opponents of the Amendment. This discussion and our own investigation convince us that,

---

[11] Editor's Note: "The object of the (Thirteenth) Amendment was undoubtedly to enforce the absolute equality of the two races before the law, but in the nature of things it could not have been intended to abolish distinctions based upon color, or to enforce social, as distinguished from political equality, or a commingling of the two races on terms satisfactory to either. Laws permitting, or even requiring, their separation in places where they are liable to be brought into contact do not necessarily imply the inferiority of either race to the other. . . ."—*Plessy v. Ferguson,* 163 U.S. 537 (1895).

although these sources cast some light, it is not enough to resolve the problem with which we are faced. At best, they are inconclusive. The most avid proponents of the post-war Amendments undoubtedly intended them to remove all legal distinctions among "all persons born or naturalized in the United States." Their opponents, just as certainly, were antagonistic to both the letter and the spirit of the Amendments and wished them to have the most limited effect. What others in Congress and the state legislatures had in mind cannot be determined with any degree of certainty.

An additional reason for the inconclusive nature of the Amendment's history, with respect to segregated schools, is the status of public education at that time. In the South, the movement toward free common schools, supported by general taxation, had not yet taken hold. Education of white children was largely in the hands of private groups. Education of Negroes was almost nonexistent, and practically all of the race were illiterate. In fact, any education of Negroes was forbidden by law in some states. Today, in contrast, many Negroes have achieved outstanding success in the arts and sciences as well as in the business and professional world. It is true that public-school education at the time of the Amendment had advanced further in the North, but the effect of the Amendment on Northern States was generally ignored in the congressional debates. Even in the North, the conditions of public education did not approximate those existing today. The curriculum was usually rudimentary; ungraded schools were common in rural areas; the school term was but three months a year in many states; and compulsory school attendance was virtually unknown. As a consequence, it is not surprising that there should be so little in the history of the Fourteenth Amendment relating to its intended effect on public education.

In the first cases in this Court construing the Fourteenth Amendment, decided shortly after its adoption, the Court interpreted it as proscribing all state-imposed discriminations against the Negro race.[12] The doctrine of "separate but equal" did not make its

---

[12] *Slaughter-House Cases,* 16 Wall. 36, 67-72 (1873); *Strauder v. West Virginia,* 100 U.S. 303, 307-308, (1880):

"It ordains that no State shall deprive any person of life, liberty, or property, without due process of law, or deny to any person within its jurisdiction the

appearance in this Court until 1896 in the case of *Plessy v. Ferguson, supra,* involving not education but transportation. American courts have since labored with the doctrine for over half a century. In this Court there have been six cases involving the "separate but equal" doctrine in the field of public education. In *Cumming v. County Board of Education,* 175 U.S. 528, and *Gong Lum v. Rice,* 275 U.S. 78, the validity of the doctrine itself was not challenged. In more recent cases, all on the graduate-school level, inequality was found in that specific benefits enjoyed by white students were denied to Negro students of the same educational qualifications. *Missouri ex rel. Gaines v. Canada,* 305, U.S. 337; *Sipuel v. Oklahoma,* 332 U.S. 631; *Sweatt v. Painter,* 339 U.S. 629; *McLaurin v. Oklahoma State Regents,* 339 U.S. 637. In none of these cases was it necessary to re-examine the doctrine to grant relief to the Negro plaintiff. And in *Sweatt v. Painter, supra,* the Court expressly reserved decision on the question whether *Plessy v. Ferguson* should be held inapplicable to public education.

In the instant cases, that question is directly presented. Here, unlike *Sweatt v. Painter,* there are findings below that the Negro and white schools involved have been equalized, or are being equalized, with respect to buildings, curricula, qualifications and salaries of teachers, and other "tangible" factors. Our decision, therefore, cannot turn on merely a comparison of these tangible factors in the Negro and white schools involved in each of the cases. We must look instead to the effect of segregation itself on public education.

In approaching this problem, we cannot turn the clock back to

---

equal protection of the laws. What is this but declaring that the law in the States shall be the same for the black as for the white; that all persons, whether colored or white, shall stand equal before the laws of the States, and, in regard to the colored race, for whose protection the amendment was primarily designed, that no discrimination shall be made against them by law because of their color? The words of the amendment, it is true, are prohibitory, but they contain a necessary implication of a positive immunity, or right, most valuable to the colored race,—the right to exemption from unfriendly legislation against them distinctively as colored,—exemption from legal discriminations, implying inferiority in civil society, lessening the security of their enjoyment of the rights which others enjoy, and discriminations which are steps towards reducing them to the condition of a subject race."

See also *Virginia v. Rives,* 100 U.S. 313, 318 (1880); *Ex parte Virginia,* 100 U.S. 339, 344-345 (1880).

1868 when the Amendment was adopted, or even to 1896 when *Plessy v. Ferguson* was written. We must consider public education in the light of its full development and its present place in American life throughout the nation. Only in this way can it be determined if segregation in public schools deprives these plaintiffs of the equal protection of the laws.

Today, education is perhaps the most important function of state and local governments. Compulsory school attendance laws and the great expenditures for education both demonstrate our recognition of the importance of education to our democratic society. It is required in the performance of our most basic public responsibilities, even service in the armed forces. It is the very foundation of good citizenship. Today it is a principal instrument in awakening the child to cultural values, in preparing him for later professional training, and in helping him to adjust normally to his environment. In these days, it is doubtful that any child may reasonably be expected to succeed in life if he is denied the opportunity of an education. Such an opportunity, where the state has undertaken to provide it, is a right which must be made available to all on equal terms.

We come then to the question presented: Does segregation of children in public schools solely on the basis of race, even though the physical facilities and other "tangible" factors may be equal, deprive the children of the minority group of equal educational opportunities? We believe that it does.

In *Sweatt v. Painter, supra,* in finding that a segregated law school for Negroes could not provide them equal educational opportunities, this Court relied in large part on "those qualities which are incapable of objective measurement but which make for greatness in a law school." In *McLaurin v. Oklahoma State Regents, supra,* the Court, in requiring that a Negro admitted to a white graduate school be treated like all other students, again resorted to intangible considerations: ". . . his ability to study, to engage in discussions and exchange views with other students, and, in general, to learn his profession." Such considerations apply with added force to children in grade and high schools. To separate them from others of similar age and qualifications solely because of their race generates a feeling of inferiority as to their status in the community that may affect their hearts and minds in a way unlikely ever to be undone. The effect of this separation on their educational opportunities was well stated by a finding in the Kansas case by a court which nevertheless felt compelled to rule against the Negro plaintiffs:

> Segregation of white and colored children in public schools has a detrimental effect upon the colored children. The impact is greater when it has the sanction of the law; for the policy of separating the races is usually interpreted as denoting the inferiority of the Negro group. A sense of inferiority affects the motivation of a child to learn. Segregation with the sanction of law, therefore, has a tendency to retard the educational and mental development of Negro children and to deprive them of some of the benefits they would receive in a racially integrated school system.

Whatever may have been the extent of psychological knowledge at the time of *Plessy v. Ferguson,* this finding is amply supported by modern authority. Any language in *Plessy v. Ferguson* contrary to this finding is rejected.

We conclude that in the field of public education the doctrine of "separate but equal" has no place. Separate educational facilities are inherently unequal. Therefore, we hold that the plaintiffs and others similarly situated for whom the actions have been brought are, by reason of the segregation complained of, deprived of the equal protection of the laws guaranteed by the Fourteenth Amendment. This disposition makes unnecessary any discussion whether such segregation also violates the Due Process Clause of the Fourteenth Amendment.

Because these are class actions, because of the wide applicability of this decision, and because of the great variety of local conditions, the formulation of decrees in these cases presents problems of considerable complexity. On reargument, the consideration of appropriate relief was necessarily subordinated to the primary question— the constitutionality of segregation in public education. We have now announced that such segregation is a denial of the equal protection of the laws. In order that we may have the full assistance of the parties in formulating decrees, the cases will be restored to the docket, and the parties are requested to present further argument on Questions 4 and 5 previously propounded by the Court for the reargument this Term. The Attorney General of the United States is again invited to participate. The Attorneys General of the states requiring or permitting segregation in public education will also be permitted to appear as *amici curiae* upon request to do so by September 15, 1954, and submission of briefs by October 1, 1954.[13]

It is so ordered.

4.5. THE SCHOOLS AND THE COURTS: QUESTIONS AND ANSWERS [14]

Southern Regional Council (1953)

Q. *What are the main arguments that have been made for segregation?*

A. That the Supreme Court's 1896 decision upholding the "separate-but-equal" doctrine [was, until the 1954 decision quoted above] . . . still the law of the land.

That a state has the same right to separate school children by race as it has to separate them by age or sex or any other standards.

That the public-school systems are state-supported, and therefore the state legislatures are the proper bodies to say how they shall be run.

That a court ruling against school segregation would create bitterness, strife, and even violence in the South.

---

[13] Editor's Note: "Questions 4 and 5 provided for future hearings before the Court in order better to implement the new doctrine. On November 24, 1954, the United States Attorney General submitted to the Supreme Court a 30-page brief which recognized that problems involved in school segregation will vary from area to area, suggested that there be no immediate deadline for state compliance with the Supreme Court's decision, and recommended that the lower courts supervise racial integration by requiring periodic progress reports from school officials."—*New York Times*, Nov. 25, 1954, p. 1.

[14] George S. Mitchell and others, "The Schools and the Courts" (Pamphlet), Atlanta, Ga.: Southern Regional Council, 1953. The concluding four questions and answers are from a more recent pamphlet, "Answers for Action: Schools in the South," which was prepared and published *after* the 1954 Supreme Court decision. By permission.

That an end to segregation would virtually destroy public education, since the public would not support revenue measures for "mixed schools."

Q. *What are the main arguments that have been made against segregation?*

A.   That recent Supreme Court decisions have clearly repudiated the "separate-but-equal" doctrine.

That, under the Constitution, race is not a proper basis for classifying school children—that it is unlawful to single children out for separate treatment solely on account of their race.

That segregation has always bred inequality—"separate-but-equal" has meant separate, but almost never equal.

That setting Negro children apart in segregated schools handicaps them psychologically, promotes feelings of inferiority, interferes with healthy emotional development, and retards their ability to learn.

That the Supreme Court "has always asserted the Federal rights to which citizens are entitled, regardless of state statutes and constitutions."

That segregation in the public schools is inconsistent with democracy and gravely weakens the United States' position as the leader of the free world.

Q. *If the Court rules against segregation, can separate schools be continued by turning them over to private groups?*

A.   Governor Byrnes of South Carolina and Governor Talmadge of Georgia have threatened to do so. But neither of them has explained in detail how such a plan could be carried out.

Many questions have been raised. For example, could tax funds legally be spent to support private segregated schools? If not, how could they be supported? What assurance would there be that children from poorer families would get an even break? Would good teachers be attracted to positions that lacked public safeguards? What guarantees would parents have that their children would get a sound education, on a par with that of other children? These and many other objections to the private-school plan have gone unanswered.[15]

---

[15] Editor's Note: Other questions: "How can uniform standards of education be maintained without the authority of state law? How could all children be re-

In 1952, South Carolinians were asked to approve an amendment removing from their constitution the requirement that a public-school system be maintained. The amendment was passed. But in the process many responsible citizens spoke their minds on the dangers of such action. State Representative William H. Nicholson, Jr., of Greenwood, had this to say:

> If it comes to a question of abandoning the public school system, I tell you frankly that the crisis would have to be serious indeed before I could approve of that action. The public school has served the state well in educating thousands of poor girls and boys who otherwise would not have been educated. It has been the bulwark of democracy in destroying old lingering prejudices among our white citizens. Private or church schools would only bring about a return of social snobbery and religious bigotry, not to speak of the almost inevitable result that a number of white children, as well as Negro children, would be left in the shuffle, without an education.

In November of 1954, Georgians will vote on a proposed constitutional amendment authorizing "private" operation of the state school system.[16] . . .

_____

quired to attend school without a compulsory state law? Would separation of church and state be jeopardized? How could teachers' salaries, qualifications, pension rights, and working conditions be regulated? How could public-school property be turned over to private ownership?"—*Answers for Action,* Atlanta: Southern Regional Council, 1954, p. 8.

[16] Editor's Note: In 1951 Governor James Byrnes declared, "Should the Supreme Court decide this case against our position, we will face a serious problem. Of only one thing can we be certain. South Carolina will not, now or for some years to come, mix white and colored children in our schools.

"If the Court changes what is now the law of the land, we will, if it is possible, live within the law, preserve the public-school system, and at the same time maintain segregation. If this is not possible, we will abandon the public-school system. To do this would be choosing the lesser of two evils."—Quoted in *U. S. News* 35: 41-42, Dec. 18, 1953. (Compare Harry S. Ashmore, *op. cit.,* pp. 51-52, 96, 109, 131-132. For a defense of private schools, and the abolition of public schools, as a move away from federal "autocracy" and "absolutism," read Frank Chodorov, "A Solution of Our Public School Problem," *Human Events,* Vol. 11, No. 20, May 19, 1954.)

In 1954, after the Supreme Court decision was announced, Governor Byrnes said, "I earnestly urge all of our people, white and colored, to exercise restraint and preserve order."

About the same time a Mississippi Negro leader declared, "So far as changing

Q. *If the Court outlaws segregation, will the public-school systems be transformed overnight?*

A. No. . . . Most educational authorities in the Southern states have talked in terms of ten or more years. . . . There are several reasons why this is so:

First, the Court's decisions will have an immediate effect only in those areas where the suits were brought. Further suits will be necessary to get decisions affecting other places. That is a slow process.[17]

Second, a court ruling against segregation would not mean that the two races would have to be equally represented in every school. It would simply mean that children must be admitted, without regard to race, to the schools serving their district. Under the segregated housing arrangements found in most Southern cities, few schools would be greatly affected.[18] Rather, integration would grow in the schools along with increased integration in the community as a whole.

---

the pattern of life, I don't think the decision will have much effect. But the decision puts a tremendous responsibility on the white man. Any violent reaction to the decision by whites would solidify the Negroes toward breaking down the segregation barriers."—*U. S. News* 36: 14, 21-25, May 28, 1954.

[17] Editor's Note: The recent Supreme Court decision will apply only to the five cases before it: Clarendon County, South Carolina; Prince Edward County, Virginia; Topeka, Kansas; and the one case in Delaware (and Washington, D. C.). Some localities will move immediately toward desegregation, as some states have done in the case of higher education; but others may have to be ordered to do so by the courts.

[18] Editor's Note: In rural areas, there are no such well-defined residential areas, so that "gerrymandering" would be almost impossible. However, Mississippi now has a law which reads: "In making assignments of children to schools or attendance centers . . . the board of trustees shall take into consideration the emotional needs and welfare of the child involved, the welfare and best interest of the pupils attending the school or schools involved . . . and all other factors which the board of trustees may consider pertinent, relevant or material in their effect on the welfare and best interest of the school district and the particular school or schools involved. All such assignments shall be on an individual basis as to the particular child involved and, in making such assignment, the board of trustees shall not be limited or circumscribed by the boundaries of any attendance areas which may have been established by such board of trustees."—Regular Mississippi Legislative Session, 1954. House Bill No. 45, Section 2. Approved March 10, 1954.

If such "pupil assignments" are declared legal, Negro and white pupils could be segregated without mention of the word "segregation," and the present pattern might continue for years to come.

Third, Court decisions alone do not produce change. Only the people, through their state and local governments, can translate a decision into everyday practice. The great danger is not over-hasty change, but too great a lag between law and practice.[19]

Q. *If the Court rules against segregation, will Negro teachers lose their jobs?*

A. This argument was put forward by some of the defense lawyers in the public-school cases. For several reasons, however, it seems most unlikely that there would be any mass discharge of Negro teachers.

For one thing, it is hard to see how they would be replaced. According to the latest figures available (1949-50), there were 71,362 Negroes teaching in the segregated public schools of seventeen states and the District of Columbia. Furthermore, there was a shortage of both white and Negro elementary teachers, and only a small surplus of high school teachers. It is difficult to believe that these school systems would try to get along with 70,000 fewer teachers than they now have.

These figures are doubly important in view of the fact that the number of school children is steadily growing and, according to the population experts, will continue to grow. So the demand for elementary teachers is likely to become even more acute.

Forty-three per cent of the Negro teachers are protected against arbitrary dismissal by state tenure laws. As the effort to abolish school segregation applies to teachers as well as pupils, these tenure rights would undoubtedly be defended in the courts, if necessary.

In those places outside the South where school segregation has recently been abandoned, Negro teachers for the most part have kept their positions.

---

[19] "In many parts of the South, Negro parents will move very cautiously. . . . Proof for this view is seen in the case of interstate travel. Although a goodly number of Negroes ride across state lines unsegregated, the vast majority of Negroes ride segregated across state lines. It will be this way for a while in the public schools even after segregation has been declared unconstitutional."— Benjamin E. Mays, "We Are Unnecessarily Excited," *New South*, Vol. 9, No. 2, February 1954.

Q. *Is the whole South opposed to any change in the present pattern of segregated schools?*

A.   No.   In those parts of the South where the Negro population is small, there appears to be a growing feeling that separate schools are prohibitively costly and difficult to maintain.[20] . . .

Q. *Why do Negroes want mixed schools? Wouldn't Negro children be happier in schools of their own?*

A.   Dr. Benjamin E. Mays, noted Negro churchman and educator of Atlanta, has put it this way: "To argue that the suit makes an attack on segregation because the initiators of the suit want Negro children to go to school with white children is to miss the point entirely. Mixed schools are not the heart of the suit. Negroes opposed the curtain and the partition on the dining cars not because they wanted to eat with white people, but because the curtain and the partition were embarrassing to Negroes and because they set Negroes off as inferior persons. This the Negro resented. Eating with white people on the diner was not the issue. . . .

"The motive behind the (school segregation) suit represents the growing conviction, rightly or wrongly, among Negroes everywhere that there can be no equality under segregation—the growing belief that the 'separate but equal' theory is a myth. . . . The Negroes who believe this way may be in error, but there is one thing that sustains their belief. The history of segregation is a history of inequality. History seems to be against the idea of 'separate but equal.' " [21] . . .

[20] Editor's Note: But "In areas where the Negro population is high, often 50 per cent and more, and where economic and social forces are strongly propped by prevailing racial customs, the controlling group may want segregation at any cost, even if it means flouting the law and eliminating public schools."—John N. Papham, *The Chattanooga Times*, May 23, 1954.

[21] Editor's Note: "Few Negroes advocate segregated education. Those who do give the following reasons for supporting separate schools: (1) Mixed schools are concerned only with the needs of the white group; (2) the social discrimination which Negro children face in mixed schools has detrimental personality effects; (3) segregated schools provide an increased number of administrative and teaching positions for Negroes; and (4) segregated schools, completely controlled by Negroes, are better than mixed schools in which Negroes have no influence at all. . . .

"Most Negroes fight segregation if there is any chance of success. Even among those who are seemingly resigned to the force of race prejudice, there is strong

Q. *What about the argument that mixed schools will lead to violence?*

A.   In the words of Dr. Guy B. Johnson of the University of North Carolina, "Anyone who thinks that the transition from segregation to racial co-education can be made without problems, tensions, and even personal tragedies is a fool. Anyone who thinks that the transition means the end of civilization is also a fool. The operation may be serious, but the patient will recover. And when he recovers and looks back over his experience, he may say, 'Well, it wasn't half as bad as I thought it would be.' " . . .

The prophets of violence were wrong . . . when the Court gave Negroes the right to vote in Democratic primaries, when segregation in railroad dining cars was outlawed, when Southern graduate schools were opened to qualified Negroes. There was no widespread public disorder when public-school segregation was abandoned in such border states as New Mexico and Delaware or in parts of New Jersey, Illinois and Arizona with a long-standing tradition of segregation.

Predictions are risky. But past experience argues strongly against the likelihood of violence. Most Southern newspapers have urged that whatever decision the Supreme Court renders be accepted with calmness and restraint. If political leaders and law-enforcement authorities prove equally responsible, there is every reason to expect the people of the South to react as responsible, law-abiding citizens.

·   ·   ·   ·

Q. *Can children adjust to integrated schools?*

A.   There is much truth in the saying that if school integration were left to the children there would be no problem. Children are born without prejudice and only acquire it through constant exposure to the attitudes of grownups. As all previous experience indicates, children of different races adjust to each other

resentment against segregation and discrimination. The principle grounds for opposing segregation are that (1) separate schools invariably mean inferior schools for Negroes, and (2) Negroes cannot participate fully in American life as long as they are compelled to live separately."—George E. Simpson and John M. Yinger, *Racial and Cultural Minorities*, New York: Harper, 1953, pp. 562-563. By permission.

quickly and naturally when given half a chance. Most Southern-
ers can find confirmation of this in their own childhood, when
they accepted playmates of the other race without a thought.

However, adults—particularly parents and teachers—often
transmit their feelings to children without even realizing it. In
this sense, then, the largest part of the adjustment will have to
be made not by the children, but by their elders.

Q. *Does school planning reflect the views of the whole community?*

A.   No one thing can contribute more to harmonious adjustment
to the decision than full participation by Negroes in the planning and administration of local school systems. As Dr. Benjamin E. Mays has said, "If one racial group makes all the laws
and administers them, holds all the power and administers it,
and has all the public money and distributes it, it is too much
to expect that group to deal as fairly with the weak, minority,
non-participating group as it deals with its own." In the case of
schools, able Negro representation on boards of education is a
long step toward agreement and mutual confidence between the
races. . . .

Q. *What is the role of discussion groups?*

A.   Joint discussion, fact-finding, and planning by local people of
both races are the hallmarks of healthy community change in the
South. Discussion groups for these purposes, which have already
demonstrated their effectiveness in many Southern communities,
are now needed more than ever.

The first objective of such a group should be frank exchange
of opinions. There must be ample opportunity for the members
of the group to gain a sympathetic understanding of their respective points of view.

Once attitudes and views have been shared, the group can
address itself to the facts about the local school system. For example, what are the local effects of state laws and policies? Which
schools will likely be affected by the terms of the Supreme Court
decision? How many pupils, teachers, and classrooms are involved? How are school-district lines drawn? How is the matter
of integration related to such broader educational questions as
school financing, transportation, overcrowding, teacher training
and supply, curricula, textbooks, and so on?

Armed with the facts, the discussion group is equipped to work constructively with its school superintendent and board of education. Since most people feel strongly about the schools their children attend, education authorities are particularly sensitive to public opinion. So it is especially important for right-thinking citizens to express their interest in the problems and progress of their school system. Most school officials will welcome positive criticism, suggestions, and support by people who understand the practical problems faced by the policy-maker and administrator.

Clearly local discussion groups that have reached informed agreement between people of both races can make a most valuable contribution in this time of challenge and adjustment.

Q. *Are there other things we can do in our communities?*

A. As church members, we can recognize the special obligation of religious groups to create sound parental attitudes toward school integration. The churches can do more than any other institution to spread awareness that children must not be made to suffer the effects of adult prejudice.

As citizens, we can work for impartial and effective law enforcement in the event of racial tension in the community.

As members of civic groups, service clubs, labor organizations, and the like, we can support enlightened action by public officials and help foster a healthy climate of opinion.

As parents, we can urge that our school systems be reshaped to provide the most and the best education to every child, irrespective of race.

Section C: Questions and Readings for Study and Discussion

4.6. Civil Rights and Civil Liberties

To promote a better understanding of its aims and purposes, The American Civil Liberties Union (170 Fifth Avenue, New York 10) supplies *gratis* copies of "Twenty Questions on Civil Liberties." Secure copies of these for each class member; then discuss the questions pertaining to racial equality.

4.7. The Meaning of "Race"

What is "race"? What are the major races of mankind? Are they clearly distinguishable?

*Ashley-Montague, M. F., *Statement on Race,* New York: Schuman, 1951.

Benedict, Ruth, *Race: Science and Politics,* New York: Viking, 1947.

Beals, Ralph L., and Hoijer, Harry, *An Introduction to Anthropology,* New York: Macmillan, 1953 (Chapter 6, "Racial Types Among Modern Men") (bibliography).

Boas, Franz, *Race, Language and Culture,* New York: Macmillan, 1940 (pages 3-17, 76-81, 191-195).

* Krogman, Wilton M., "The Concept of Race," pp. 38-62, in *The Science of Man in the World Crisis,* ed. by Ralph Linton, New York: Columbia University Press, 1945.

Shannon, Alexander Harvey, *Racial Integrity of the American Negro,* New York: Public Affairs Press, 1953. (This is the only book here listed which defends the so-called racialist school, a school which has few adherents among contemporary anthropologists.)

4.8. Other Racial Minority Groups

While the Negro population constitutes the major problem in race relations in the South, other smaller minority groups, such as the American Indians, Chinese, Japanese-Americans, Mexicans and Puerto Ricans are the subject of considerable attention in other areas of the country. Which racial minority is a "problem" in your community?

The references below present a general treatment of American minority groups. More specific local information may be had through specialized books, news stories, local interviews, etc.

Brown, Frances J., and Roucek, Joseph S., eds., *One America: The History, Contributions and Present Problems of Our Racial and National Minorities,* 3rd ed., New York: Prentice-Hall, 1952.

McDonagh, Edward C., and Richards, Eugene S., *Ethnic Relations in the United States*, New York: Appleton-Century-Crofts, 1953.

McWilliams, Carey, *Brothers Under the Skin*, rev. ed., Boston: Little, 1951.

President's Committee on Civil Rights, *To Secure These Rights*, New York: Simon and Schuster, 1947 (Chapter II).

Rose, Arnold M., ed., *Race Prejudice and Discrimination*, New York: Knopf, 1951.

Simpson, George E., and Yinger, John M., *Racial and Cultural Minorities*, New York: Harper, 1953.

4.9. Social Reform and Social Revolution

To what extent, if any, are the struggles of minority groups for racial equality a part of the "Communist conspiracy"? The viewpoint under consideration is illustrated by the following brief quotation: "Readers of *Common Sense* will be shocked to learn that the recent decision of the Supreme Court outlawing segregation in schools actually carried out a 1921 Resolution of the Communist International!"—*Common Sense*, 530 Chestnut Street, Union, New Jersey, July 1, 1954, page 1.

Bunche, Ralph J., "The Barriers of Race Can be Surmounted," *Vital Speeches* 15: 572-574, July 1, 1949.

Cox, Oliver C., *Caste, Class, and Race*, New York: Doubleday, 1948 (Chapters 16-20, 25).

Davis, Jerome, *Character Assassination*, New York: Philosophical Library, 1950 (Chapter V).

Logan, Spencer, *A Negro's Faith in America*, New York: Macmillan, 1946.

Record, Wilson, *The Negro and the Communist Party*, Chapel Hill, N. C.: University of North Carolina Press, 1951.

Ruchames, Louis, *Race, Jobs and Politics: The Story of FEPC*, New York: Columbia University Press, 1953.

4.10. The Contemporary Situation

References included in this chapter do not go beyond November 1954, the beginning of the first school year following the Supreme Court's decision banning "separate but equal" education for Negroes. Consult the *Reader's Guide to Periodical Literature,* the *Education Index* and other sources for current literature on the subject. What are some of the major problems encountered in the actual implementation of the program of racial integration in the schools?

Allport, Gordon, and others, "The Effect of Segregation and the Consequences of Desegregation: A Social Science Statement," 37 *Minnesota Law Review* 427-439, May 1953.

Downey, Clifford, "A Southerner Looks at the Supreme Court," *Saturday Review* 37: 9 f, Oct. 9, 1954; Reply by Fred Rodell, *ibid.* 37: 9 f, Oct. 16, 1954; Discussion by Howard P. Wile, *ibid.* 37: 26, Oct. 30, 1954.

MacIver, Robert M., *The More Perfect Union: A Program for the Control of Inter-Group Discrimination in the United States,* New York: Macmillan, 1948 (Chapter 10, "Conclusions") .

Morse, Arthur D., "When Negroes Entered a Texas School," *Harper's* 209: 47-49, September 1954.

Phillips, Cabell, "What Happens When Segregation Ends?" *New York Times Magazine,* May 30, 1954, p 7 f.

Sutherland, Arthur E., "The Supreme Court and the Public School," *Harvard Educational Review* 24: 71-85, Spring 1954.

"Will South End Negro Schools?" *U. S. News* 36: 21-24, May 28, 1954.

Williams, Robert M., Jr., and Ryan, Margaret W., *Schools in Transition,* Chapel Hill, N. C.: University of North Carolina Press, 1954.

5. CLASSROOM METHODS AND MATERIALS

Section A: Contemporary Education Under Criticism

5.1. INTRODUCTION

Let us begin this discussion with two facts. First, more than a million *additional* students will enter our public schools *each year* for the next several years. Unless a lot of money is spent soon, crowded classrooms and burdensome teaching loads—already commonplace—will become a national catastrophe. On this point the United States Commission of Education declared in 1954: "We need 340,000 classrooms at an estimated cost of nine to twelve billion dollars. . . . It is now time to get the public to support long-range programs that would relieve teacher shortages and classroom crowding." [1]

The second fact is this: Although the great majority of Americans gladly support their public schools, there are elements in our society who do not believe in public education at all, or who believe it should terminate at the 8th or 10th grade level. These elements

---

[1] Dr. Samuel M. Brownell, Address to a Conference of School Superintendents, Teachers College, Columbia University, July 9, 1954, *New York Times,* July 10, 1954, p. 15.

Compare: Samuel M. Brownell, "The People's Schools," *School Life* 37: 1 f, October 1954; Emery M. Foster and Carol Joy Hobson, "Vital Statistics of American Education: 1954-1960," *School Life* 37: 6 f, October 1954; Earl J. McGrath, "Crucial National Problems in Education," *School Life* 35: 99-101 f, April 1953; Ray C. Maul, various articles, including "High School Teacher Shortage Impends," *American School Board Journal* 128: 37-38, February 1954.

constitute such a small minority that they dare not openly oppose education (and taxes for education). But they can obstruct and confuse and delay by raising a great hue and cry over false issues.

Not all criticisms of education are of this type, as our selections indicate. But many of them are undoubtedly smoke screens to conceal the fact that the critics do not wish to spend money for public schools. Consider some of the question-begging titles that grace the pamphlets now circulating our nation: "How Red is the Little Red Schoolhouse?" "Should American Professors be Pro-American?" "Reducators at Harvard." Liberally sprinkled through such books are smear-words such as "betrayal," "collectivist dupes," "godless," "secularists," "wanton spenders"—and the broad term "Progressives." If a new high school brings into a single unit children from what were formerly separate "Mexican" and "white" districts, nothing is openly said about the racial issue: the critics attack "Progressive Education." If better teaching requires better teachers and fewer pupils per teacher, nothing is said about how to finance the added costs; instead a smear campaign is conducted against "Progressive Education." If our schools attempt to develop diversity of student talent through courses in art, music, shop, or physical education, we hear a great demand for the elimination of "fads and frills" and "the 3 P's of Progressive Education—Painting, Pasting and Puttering!"

There are many who believe that some of the extremist groups now condemning the public schools are reactionary and even fascistic at heart, and opposed to a whole democratic philosophy of life and of education. John Eklund, President of the American Federation of Teachers, has written:

> . . . Until the advent of John Dewey and the development of a truly democratic philosophy of education, much of the public schools' program was based on three social concepts: (1) that there was a privileged class to whom special concessions and benefits should go; (2) that the aggrandizement of big business and monopoly was synonymous with free enterprise, and (3) that property rights were top priority in society, frequently to the disadvantage of human rights.
>
> Eventually these concepts and the schools in which they prevailed were weighed and found wanting. . . .

The groups which are assailing the public schools want a return to the days of special privilege for the few; unorganized, timid and cheap labor; the supremacy of property rights. They want a constricted social and economic system. And they view the schools as the first target if they are to achieve their program. . . .

The motives of these hostile groups are to reduce the average American to serfdom, to enslave the workers again, to discredit progress.

If the ultimate powers of democracy are to be left to the people themselves, as they should be, labor and education must fight back.[2]

There can be little doubt but that the extremist type of criticism has intimidated a good many teachers.[3] But free men are not easily scared, and the majority of educators have learned to accept such criticism as part of the give-and-take of a democratic society. They know that self-preservation is a basic instinct, and that it is natural for each individual to approach any problem with the question, "How does this affect *me?*" From the standpoint of making profits, a business man will generally look upon labor organizers as "dangerous," while the laboring man looks upon the National Association of Manufacturers as "dangerous" to his personal quest for higher wages and shorter working hours. Hence any school teacher who deals with labor-management problems soon finds himself caught in the cross fire of these competing interests. Such conflicts are an accepted part of our society. Since each individual, group or party is primarily concerned with its own interests, it will generally try to repress opposing groups whose views seem "dangerous." But it should be obvious that what is "dangerous" (from a partisan viewpoint) need not be "subversive" (from a national viewpoint).

[2] John Eklund, "We Must Fight Back," *The American Federationist* 59: 14-15, January 1952. By permission. Quoted at greater length by C. Winfield Scott and Clyde M. Hill, *Public Education Under Criticism*, New York: Prentice-Hall, 1954, pp. 350-353.

[3] Read "The Timid Ones," *Time* 63: 46, April 5, 1954; Robert M. Hutchins, "Are Our Teachers Afraid to Teach?" *Look* 18: 27-29, March 9, 1954.

However, some opinion polls indicate that nearly 90 per cent of the American public are reasonably well satisfied with their schools. Several of these surveys are cited by Scott and Hill, *op. cit.,* p. 208 f.

"What I dislike (personally)" cannot be equated with "what is un-American."

Since this problem was the major topic of Chapter 1, we need not give it detailed consideration here. However, the article by J. C. Peel on "Education to the Right and to the Left" shows a measure of caution not always manifest in the educational writings of the past generation.

But caution is not the road to progress, and in a period of rapid social change it is imperative that educators experiment with new ideas. We cannot return to the 19th century, when only one-tenth of the youngsters of high-school age were in school; when the scientific study of psychology and educational methods had scarcely begun; and when education was almost entirely vocational (but for only four vocations—medicine, law, teaching and the ministry).

Fifty years ago teachers emphasized memorization and rigid adherence to textbooks and courses of study. Now we have better textbooks, but teachers place greater emphasis on problem-solving, the use of reference books, learning by doing, good health, good sportsmanship, and all-round growth.[4] If there are some who claim that the only good school is the old-fashioned school, we should remember that "What we're not up on, we're generally down on." Not only should parents learn what the teachers are doing, but parents and teachers should join together in what is obviously their common task. Not only should parents learn about schools as passive spectators; they should take an active part in the formation of basic educational policies.

In conclusion, insofar as recent criticisms of our schools have increased public interest and understanding, insofar as school and community have thereafter joined together in the establishment of basic educational policies—to that extent the bitter antagonisms of

---

[4] For contrasts between the old and the new in education, read: William H. Kilpatrick, "American Education and American Life," *New Republic* 122: 12-16, March 20, 1950; J. B. Edmonsen, "Then and Now," *National Education Association Journal* 42: 49, January 1953; Clark Robinson, "Order Through Controlled Freedom," *National Education Association Journal* 43: 543-545, December 1954. For a summary of thousands of books and articles which attempt to give objective answers to educational problems, read Walter Scott Monroe, ed., *Encyclopedia of Educational Research,* New York: Macmillan, 1950.

recent years will automatically disappear. In the words of Robert
A. Skaife:

> There is only one good way to combat "The Sound and the Fury,"
> and that is to keep citizens informed of what the schools are
> doing. This is a program which must be carried on at all times,
> not merely when local pressures are at white heat. Resistance to
> such pressures against the schools is automatic when the schools
> and the community are thought of as inseparable. The attack on
> the schools is then considered, as it should be, an attack on the
> community.[5]

The article by Henry Steele Commager shows that for over a
hundred years our public schools have shared in the problems of
American society. The selection by Maurice Ahrens presents some
specific suggestions whereby contemporary educators may develop
better cooperation between school and community.

5.2. EDUCATION TO THE LEFT AND TO THE RIGHT [6]

J. C. Peel

A recent interest in our changing educational program has
brought question as to whither it is tending, and as to what effect
it will have on the American way of life. How progressive has our
education become? Has it gone too far? Dewey, Bode, Childs, and
others have expressed concern about Progressive Education. Childs,
latest of the progressive critics of Progressive Education, says that

> . . . if our schools are to serve as agencies for the maintenance of
> a free society, they must be concerned with "society" as well as

---

[5] Robert A. Skaife, "The Sound and the Fury," *Phi Delta Kappan* 34: 357-362,
June 1953 (also entire June 1953 issue, pages 353-432) ; Robert A. Skaife, "The
Conflict Continues: Current Attacks on Education Introduce Some Different
Names and Some New Strategies," *Nation's Schools* 53: 44-49, March 1954. (Both
of Skaife's articles list specific attacking groups, with samples of their lines of
attack.)

[6] James C. Peel, "Education to the Left and to the Right," *Educational Forum*
17: 195-198, January 1953. Copyright article, reprinted by permission.

Mr. Peel is Dean, Florida State College.

Compare Eduard C. Lindeman, "John Dewey on the Doctrine of the Golden
Mean," *Progressive Education* 30: 8-10, October 1952; Paul Woodring, *Let's Talk
Sense About Our Schools,* New York: McGraw-Hill, 1953, pp. 173-178, 207-213.

with the "child," with "subject-matter" as well as with "method," with "product" as well as with "process," with human "responsibilities" as well as with human "freedoms," and with social and moral "ends" as well as with classroom "procedures" and educational "means." [7]

In this statement, Childs has taken a position which he hopes will "bring the individual and social aspects of education into organic unity." [8] This would do much to correct the weaknesses of extreme types of Progressivism and at the same time likely save our schools from an overdose of traditionalism.

In the present period of confusion in education many would like to find some means of working out their educational philosophy on some sane, sound ground in an attempt to arrive at some degree of certainty and intellectual satisfaction.

Since statisticians have found that approximately five degrees of quality may be observed subjectively with fair accuracy, it is proposed to subsume educational attitudes and practices under five categories: reactionary, traditional, golden mean, Progressive (capital P) education, and "lunatic fringe." [9]

The reactionary would like to go back to the simplicity of the "Little Red Schoolhouse" of our forefathers, believing it better suited to the needs of our day than any new-fangled ideas cooked up by modern pedagogues.

The traditional type likes to-day to label itself as essentialist, emphasizing the need of system and sequence in education and decrying its absence in the activity program.

The golden-mean type would combine the best values of traditional and progressive education in an evolutionary fashion, rather than as Bode has suggested "throw the baby out with the bath."

The Progressive credo puts its emphasis on experience getting, on "learning by doing," on the Child Centered School, on individual growth, and on pupil freedom.

---

[7] John L. Childs, *Education and Morals*, New York: Appleton-Century-Crofts, 1950, p. ix.

[8] *Ibid.*, p. x.

[9] This term was borrowed from John A. Sexson, *The Phi Delta Kappan*, 20: 209, March 1938.

The lunatic fringe is willing to change all the features of our educational structure, and would also change the features of our social order through educational processes, whenever and wherever it is possible.

This classification needs to be qualified with the statement that it is an oversimplification, and likely colored by personal experience and prejudice. The "name calling" device has admittedly been used to express prejudice against certain extreme practices. Hence, the reader should be aware of this propaganda technique as he seeks to make up his mind.

Aims of Education

Reactionary: Transmission of the social heritage, unchanged and unchanging.

Traditional: Adjustment of the individual to the established institutions of society.

Golden Mean: Both the needs of the child and the nature of the social order should determine education's goal. Happy and effective living in a democratic social order. Proper balance between education of the individual and education of the citizen.

Progressive: Education should take all its cues from the nature and needs of the child.

Lunatic Fringe: The immediate interests of the child furnish the aims of education.

Curriculum

Reactionary: The 3 R's. Fads and frills should be omitted.

Traditional: School work should be organized by subjects which should be "covered" systematically. The method should be repetitive drill. The curriculum should be determined by experts. Textbooks are education's most important tools.

Golden Mean: Both activities and subjects should be included. The curriculum should be enriched far beyond the 3 R's. Education should be developed both as psychological process and as social policy.

Progressive: Teaching by subjects is passé. The activity program should be adopted *in toto*. The Curriculum should be in a constant state of revision ("curriculum confusion," traditionalists deride). The curriculum should be developed by the teacher in the light of the child's needs.

Lunatic Fringe: The "emerging curriculum." [10] No advance planning by the teacher. Pupils and teacher plan the curriculum "on the spot."

Administration-Supervision

Reactionary: Line of staff organization. Go over the head of any line officer at your own peril. Intelligence and orders come from above downward.

Traditional: A benevolent despotism is the most efficient type of organization.

Golden Mean: Cooperative management under the leadership of professional principals, supervisors, and superintendents.

Progressive: The cooperative type with the initiative in the hands of the teachers.

Lunatic Fringe: Schools are to be democratized by having them operated by faculty committees. Such committees are to take their cues from pupil desires. Superintendents and principals are executive secretaries for teachers; teachers have as their main functions carrying out of pupil desires.

Discipline

Reactionary: "Spare the rod and spoil the child."

Traditional: Emphasis on respect for the teacher. As to the children: "Theirs not to reason why."

Golden Mean: Emphasizes responsibilities as well as freedoms. A flexible modicum of restraint in an atmosphere of freedom.

Progressive: No punishments. Discipline should come from deep interest in the work which children undertake voluntarily.

Lunatic Fringe: The pupils are free; this makes the teachers their slaves.

---

[10] Hollis L. Caswell and A. Wesley Foshay, *Education in the Elementary School,* New York: American Book Company, 1950, pp. 243-246.

Relation to the Social Order

Reactionary: The chief function of the school should be transmission of the social heritage. So far as possible, it should take us back to "the good old days."

Traditional: Maintenance of the status quo should be primary.

Golden Mean: The school should educate in and for a democratic social order. Socialistic and communistic trends should not be imposed on children of public-school age. The dynamic nature of the social order should be recognized and education should seek to produce flexibility of adjustment in children.

Progressive: Children should (through social studies units) be made especially critical of established institutions.

Lunatic Fringe: Elementary school children are to be propagandized in favor of a "better social order" (more socialized and collectivized, presumably). Through such teaching and by the seizing of power by the teachers, a new social order is to be created.

Academic Freedom

Reactionary: The eternal verities have already been fully discovered. These should be taught and accepted on the authority of the past. Doubt in regard to any of these is the unpardonable educational sin.

Traditional: The values of life have been determined by the experience of the race. These should be accepted by the young on the authority of history. Critical thinking by school children is suspect, especially with reference to foreign ideologies or strange isms.

Golden Mean: The child should not be exposed to ideas beyond the maturity of his experience. With this qualification, he should be permitted to examine both sides of controversial questions. Indoctrination is uneducative; this implies that the dice should never be loaded in favor of new ideas, as well as that the child should not be biased by authoritarian pronouncements in favor of established practices. Where the mental health of the individual is involved because of uncertainty, the teacher is justified in assisting him in working out his position.

Progressive: Controversial issues should form the core of the curriculum. Both sides of these issues should be examined. The child should be completely free to choose his own beliefs.

Lunatic Fringe: Because of the dynamic nature of society and the consequent necessity of new points of view, children should be propagandized in favor of radical notions. The impact of a conservative society should be offset by indoctrination toward radical views.

How far shall education swing to the right or to the left? This point of view assumes that a middle-of-the-road policy is likely to be best. Evolution should be given preference over revolution in affairs educational as well as elsewhere. Many radical practices have been worked out, frequently emphasizing only the negative side of education. In the name of progress there have been advocated such changes as no report card, no school marks, no classification by grades, no punishments, no advance planning by the teacher, no systematic development of a school subject, and finally no subjects. Insofar as any of these proposals has a sound social or psychological basis, it should be used; otherwise, it should be rejected; mere change is no proof of progress. Genuine common sense, critical thought, and a sound philosophy of education and of life are all needed to pass on any suggested educational change. It is now wise for educators to keep their ears to the ground listening to the rise and fall of public opinion so that they may decide wisely as to where they will next take their educational stance.

5.3. OUR SCHOOLS HAVE KEPT US FREE [11]

Henry Steele Commager

No other people ever demanded so much of schools and of education as have the American. None other was ever so well served by its schools and its educators.

From the very beginning of our national existence, education has had very special tasks to perform in America. Democracy could not work without an enlightened electorate. The States and sec-

---

[11] Henry Steele Commager, *Living Ideas in America,* New York: Harper, 1951, pp. 546-548; adapted from a longer article by same title in *Life* 29: 46-47, Oct. 16, 1950. By permission.

Mr. Commager is professor of history, Columbia University.

tions could not achieve unity without a sentiment of nationalism. The nation could not absorb tens of millions of immigrants from all parts of the globe without rapid and effective Americanization. Economic and social distinctions and privileges, severe enough to corrode democracy itself, had to be overcome. To schools went the momentous responsibility of doing these tasks—of inculcating democracy, nationalism, and equalitarianism.

The passion for education goes back to the beginnings of the Massachusetts Bay Colony; the Law of 1647, for all its inadequacy, set up the first even partially successful system of public education anywhere in the world. Only three universities in Britain ante-date those of America, and by the time of independence America boasted more colleges than did the mother country, while the State Universities of the early national period represented something new under the sun.

From the first, then, education was the American religion. It was—and is—in education that we put our faith; it is our schools and colleges that are the peculiar objects of public largess and private benefaction; even in architecture we proclaim our devotion, building schools like cathedrals.

Has this faith been justified? A case might be made out for justification on purely scholarly grounds, for after all the highest of our schools of higher learning are as high as any in the world. But this is a somewhat narrow test. Let us look rather to the specific historical tasks which were imposed upon our schools and which they have fulfilled. The first and most urgent task was to provide an enlightened citizenry in order that self-government might work. It is well to remember that democracy, which we take for granted, was an experiment—and largely an American experiment. It could not succeed with a people either corrupt or uninformed. People everywhere—as Jefferson and the spokesmen of the Age of Reason believed—were naturally good, but they were not naturally enlightened. To enlighten the people was the first duty of a democracy, and an enlightened people, in turn, saw to it that "schools and the means of education" were forever encouraged.

The second great task imposed upon education and on the schools was the creation of national unity. In 1789 no one could take for granted that the new nation, spread as it was over a continental domain, would hold together. Yet Americans did manage to create unity out of diversity. Powerful material forces sped this achievement: the westward movement, canals and railroads, a liberal land policy, immigration, and so forth. No less important were intellectual and emotional factors—what Lincoln called those "mystic chords of memory stretching from every battlefield and patriot grave to every living heart and hearthstone." These—the contributions of poets and novelists, naturalists and explorers, orators and painters—were transmitted to each generation anew through the schools.

The third task imposed on schools was that which we call Americanization. Each decade after 1840 saw from two to eight million immigrants pour into America. No other people had ever absorbed such large and varied racial stocks so rapidly or so successfully. It was the public school which proved itself the most efficacious of all agencies of Americanization—Americanization not only of the children but, through them, of the parents as well.

A fourth major service that the schools have rendered democracy is that of overcoming divisive forces in society and advancing understanding and equality. The most heterogeneous of modern societies —heterogeneous in race, language, color, religion, background— America might well have been a prey to ruinous class and religious divisions. The divisive forces did not, however, prevail, and one reason that they did not prevail is that the public school overcame them. In the classroom the nation's children learned and lived equality. On the playground and the athletic field the same code obtained, with rewards and applause going to achievements to which all could aspire equally, without regard to name, race, or wealth.

In spite of all the monumental services which schools have rendered American society, they have been, and are, under continuous pressure and attack. They are under pressure and attack from those who want to make them facile instruments to advance particular causes. They are attacked because they are too conservative and because they are not conservative enough; because they emphasize overmuch the old-fashioned disciplines and because they are overly progressive and fail to teach such things as spelling and geography; because they are too secular, and because they are not secular enough but permit some religious teachings. They are under attack because they cost too much money, or because they teach children to think for themselves, or because their teams do not win games, or because they do not maintain sufficiently high standards; or for a hundred and one other reasons. In one sense the controversy over education is a healthy thing—especially if we remember that men have been disputing about the nature and contents of education since the days of Plato and Aristotle. In another sense, however, it is a dangerous and even a sinister thing. It is a dangerous thing if it leads to demands that schools adapt themselves to a single pattern, if it crushes initiative and experimentalism in teachers and administrators. And it is a very dangerous thing indeed if it takes the form of pressure and intimidation—of pressure for the inculcation of some special form of Americanism or for the teaching of some special kind of economics or of history.

5.4. THE SCHOOLS BELONG TO THE PEOPLE [12]

Maurice Ahrens

•   •   •   •   •

While the schools belong to all the people, they have accorded the teaching profession many rights, prerogatives and privileges since the beginning of public education in America. Among these are the right to plan the curriculum for the boys and girls in our schools and the responsibility of choosing textbooks and other teaching aids for use in the classrooms. These and other rights and responsibilities have been given teachers only as they have earned them. And how have they earned them? Through steady improvement in professional stature and capacity and through continuous demonstration of the highest type of honesty and integrity. Since all of the people have delegated these rights and responsibilities to teachers, we must be certain that if they are withdrawn, it is the will of all the people that it be done.

[12] Maurice Ahrens, "Freedom to Learn: Censorship and Learning Materials," *Social Education* 17: 165-170, April 1953. By permission.

Mr. Ahrens is director of curriculum of schools in Corpus Christi, Texas.

Compare Frederick C. McLaughlin, "Control of Education in Public Schools," *Teachers College Record* 55: 293-300, March 1954 (bibliography).

Sharing the Rights and Responsibilities

In recent years there has been a growing belief among educators that many of the rights and responsibilities which have been assumed almost wholly by the teaching profession should be assumed cooperatively by the teachers and the people. This is especially true in the improvement of the instructional program. In many schools and school systems today, we find teachers, parents and other laymen and often students working together toward a better educational program for our young people. This does not mean that the people have withdrawn this right from teachers and are dictating the program. It does mean that the democratic concepts of participation and cooperation have been put to work for the benefit of the younger generation. It recognizes the fact that laymen who are willing to study problems with us can contribute materially to the improvement of instruction in our schools.

An Analysis of the Present Situation

In a much smaller scale we find laymen participating in the selection of learning materials. Let us analyze for a moment the situation that exists at the present time regarding the selection of these materials.

First: The teaching profession has done a creditable job in the selection of learning materials. In any school system there is a tremendous amount of time and human energy expended in examining and evaluating materials for use in the classrooms. Committees of teachers working for weeks and months on the selection of textbooks, other committees studying audio-visual materials, librarians and teachers examining library and reference materials, and committees identifying resources in the community are commonly found at work in most school systems. The trend toward the use of a variety of materials has made the job a tremendous responsibility.

Second: There has been a continuous attempt to improve the methods of selecting materials. The most promising improvement is that of involving many individuals in the examination, evaluation and selection. Whereas it was the practice for a small committee to do the complete job of selecting textbooks in many school systems, teachers in every school now participate in setting up criteria for the selection of the materials and in the selection itself.

Third: The attempts made by individuals and groups have caused many teachers to be fearful of dealing with any problems or using any material of a controversial nature. The following statement found in the November 1952 issue of *Social Education* was made by a teacher who is withdrawing from the teaching profession:

> Frankly speaking, I'm leaving education because I can't teach. . . . Sure, you guessed it; I'm a social studies teacher. Yes, that's right, too; I'm thinking about school-community pressures and controversial issues when I say "I can't teach." . . . Certainly there is an atmosphere of fear hanging over the school system. Yet, for the most part, teachers are unaware of the increasing pressures placed upon them to conform to these extra-school dictates. . . . But, as I say, I'm not coming back this year. Oh, you won't miss *me,* so don't even bother to look. But think! Think about me, and think about the reasons for my absence! Will *you* be absent next year for similar reasons?

There is always a question in the minds of teachers as to whether the censorship demands are coming from a special interest group or whether they represent the thinking of all the people. The Conference of American Small Business Organizations is one special interest group which through its publication, *The Educational Reviewer,* has assumed responsibility for examining textbooks. The House Select Committee on Lobbying Activities, U. S. 81st Congress, 2nd Session, makes the following statement which is an excerpt from report No. 3232.

> We all agree, of course, that our textbooks should be American, that they should not be the vehicle for the propagation of obnoxious doctrines. Yet the review of textbooks by self-appointed experts, especially when undertaken under the aegis of an organization having a distinct legislative axe to grind, smacks too much of the book-burning orgies of Nuremberg to be accepted by thoughtful Americans without foreboding and alarm. It suggests, too, that the reviewers profoundly distrust the integrity, good faith, and plain common sense of the school boards and teachers

of the country. If these educators are so utterly naive and untrained as to need help from a lobbying organization in selecting proper classroom materials, then our educational system has decayed beyond all help. This proposition we cannot accept.

Fourth: Many national and local organizations and individuals have come to the defense of the schools. The American Library Association has developed a Library Bill of Rights. *McCall's Magazine* has published a series of articles designed to clarify the issues. The Educational Policies Commission of the National Education Association and AASA have published information to establish the position of education relating to the censorship of materials. There are numerous groups and individuals at the local level, such as the businessmen in Scarsdale, who have reaffirmed their belief in education's ability to provide opportunities to youth to consider the problems of our society and to use materials providing facts upon which varying points of view are based.

Fifth: There is little or no feeling in the teaching profession that all criticism is destructive and undesirable. For many years educators have welcomed constructive criticism. From it have come many significant improvements in our educational program. While constructive criticism is desirable and helpful, destructive and unwarranted criticism creates tensions and fears which are reflected in education of boys and girls. Analysis of statements made in attacks upon materials used in the school all too often reveal that they are based upon inadequate information.

Sixth: The situation relating to the censorship of materials varies greatly in communities. Reports from a great majority of the communities indicate that the people have continuing faith in the integrity of teachers in so far as the selection of learning materials is concerned. In many of these communities attempts have been made to involve representative groups of people in participating with teachers in setting up criteria for the selection of learning materials. The response is often made by laymen that the job is a technical one for which teachers have been prepared, and that the people have faith that the teaching profession has done and will do the job in a way that is acceptable.

In other communities there is a long history of cooperative effort in which representative groups of laymen participate with teachers, not only in developing criteria for selection of learning materials, but also in understanding the implications of censorship and in providing help in keeping the community informed.

Representing a very small minority of communities are those in which self-appointed, special interest groups and individuals are attempting to assume full responsibility for the selection and censorship of learning materials. Many of the criticisms and attacks are not based upon careful consideration and study of the factors and implications involved.

Desirable Practices

In conclusion, let us look briefly at some of the desirable practices, many of which are now in operation in many communities, and which seem to be effective and acceptable.

First: Since the schools belong to the people, and since the trend in education is to involve the people in cooperatively planning for the improvement of education, it appears to me that every effort should be made to involve representative groups of people in the selection of learning materials.

Second: Care should be exercised in the way in which the lay group is selected and in being sure that the group represents every facet of community life. Too frequently community committees are hand-picked and more frequently the community is not aware of what is going on. The community should feel that the committee represents all the people in a cooperative effort to improve education for youth.

Third: A debatable question is whether such a committee should serve in the actual examination and evaluation of learning materials in addition to setting up criteria for selection. It must be recognized that the job of determining criteria for selection involves hours and hours of time, of study, and discussion. We should also be aware of the fact that even after the criteria have been determined, the work of using the criteria in examining and evaluating the materials is a technical one involving skills which take considerable time and energy to develop. Whether laymen are willing to take the time to develop these skills is problematical. If they are, their services should prove valuable and helpful. Needless to say many teachers have developed these skills, through training and through many years of valuable experience in carrying on the activity.

Fourth: Another desirable practice which is gaining favor in many school systems is that of involving many teachers instead of a few in the selection of materials. A few years ago this responsibility was usually assumed by small committees of teachers. Today it is not uncommon to find all teachers who are concerned with a particular type of material participating. For instance where this procedure is used, a book on economics would be examined and evaluated by all social studies teachers. These appraisals should always be based on agreed upon criteria. In fact criteria are essential in the selection of any kind of learning material.

Fifth: The last practice which I should like to commend to you is that of keeping the people informed. Whatever method of selection is employed, the people should know about it; they should be aware of their responsibilities; they should understand the issues and implications; they should be familiar with the criteria for selection, and last but not least, they have a right to know the educational approach used in dealing with the problems of our society in the classroom. . . .

Section B: Liberal Education in an Age of Technology

5.5. INTRODUCTION

"Johnnie," said the discouraged teacher, "Isn't there *anything* you can do better than anyone else?" "Yes'm," replied the moronic pupil, "I can read my own handwriting." In this age of specialized knowledge, there are too many who can read their own handwriting, but who can read little else.

The selections to follow deal with problems arising out of technical, specialized vocational education. Like the ancient scribe, some modern critics are saying—

The wisdom of the learned cometh by opportunity of leisure. . . . How can he get wisdom that holdeth the plough, that glorieth in the goad, that driveth the oxen therewith, and is occupied in their labours, and whose talk is about the offspring of bulls? [13]

Speaking in terms of our democratic ideal of self-government, Robert Maynard Hutchins has stated the problem as follows:

A republic . . . can maintain justice, peace, freedom, and order only by the exercise of intelligence. When we speak of the consent of the governed, we mean, since men are not angels who seek the truth intuitively and do not have to learn it, that every act of assent on the part of the governed is a product of learning. A republic is really a common educational life in process. So Montesquieu said that, whereas the principle of a monarchy was honor, and the principle of a tyranny was fear, the principle of a republic was education.[14]

But "education" in this sense must include consideration of the larger problems of life and existence, and cannot be narrow or technical in scope. It must include "law for man" as well as "law for thing," as Ralph Waldo Emerson said:

There are two laws discrete,
Not reconciled—
Law for man, and law for thing;
The last builds town and fleet,
But it runs wild,
And doth the man unking.[15]

In an age of science and technology, our schools must advance scholarship in engineering, medicine and in all the physical and biological sciences that deal with man as rooted in the world of things. But schools must also keep open the lines of communica-

---

[13] *Ecclesiasticus* 38: 25 f (Douay Version).

[14] Robert Maynard Hutchins, *The Conflict in Education,* New York: Harper, 1953, pp. 75-76. By permission.

[15] Ralph Waldo Emerson, "Ode Inscribed to W. H. Channing."

tion with the "law for man," the great spiritual inheritance of religion, art and literature. A generation ago, John Duncan Spaeth posed the problem as a conflict between "science and humanism":

> Science is organized knowledge of the law for thing. Efficiency is the result of the use of this knowledge. Humanism is insight into the law for man; enrichment of life, enlargement of spirit is the fruit of this insight. Science advances by experiment; humanism builds on experience. We experiment with what happens outside ourselves; we experience what happens within. Science through controlled experiment builds the knowledge that is power; humanism through controlled experience creates the power that is character. Science as opposed to empiricism is controlled experiment; humanism as opposed to temperamentalism is controlled experience. Humanism builds up personality by enriching it with the experience of the past. This enrichment of personality by vicarious experience is culture.

> The conflict between the so-called cultural and the scientific type of higher education cuts to the very core of human nature, because man belongs to two worlds—the world of things and the world of experience, the world of fact and the world of faith, the world of matter and the world of mind, the world of sense and the world of spirit. The primary business of education is the unification of the two worlds in each individual.[16]

Admitting that science and technology have greatly altered our knowledge of the "law for thing," many critics of pragmatism and experimentalism believe that the "law for man" remains constant; and they urge a return to neo-orthodoxy in religion and/or a renewed study of the "great books" of European culture.

> . . . the cataclysmic changes of recent decades have not really altered the nature of our essential problems. They remain with us and require the virtues familiar of old, and as difficult to practice now as then. For our society collectively, and for each of us individually, a willingness to learn from past history and a proper

---

[16] John Duncan Spaeth, "Science and Humanism in University Education," an address delivered at the 69th Commencement of Washington University, June 10, 1930, St. Louis, Mo., Washington University Studies, n.s., 1930. By permission.

humility toward the experience of other peoples constitute . . .
the prerequisites of wisdom.[17]

At the opposite pole are the experimentalists and progressives
who believe that our spiritual as well as our scientific heritage
changes significantly with each passing generation.[18] As proof of
progress in the "law for man" they point to the fact that Aristotle,
St. Paul, St. Augustine and other great moralists of ancient and
medieval times accepted slavery. Progressives tend to look upon
traditionalists as men who display a conspicuous failure of nerve—
men who look upon man as a feeble creature whose chief virtue is
humble resignation before the inevitable.

Such an attitude may have been justified in the dark ages when
life was hard, hope scanty, and possibilities of improvement slight.
But the progressive believes that modern man should assert his
faith in a more positive manner. "The worship of God is not a
rule of safety," said Alfred North Whitehead, "it is an adventure
of the spirit, a flight after the unattainable. The death of religion
comes with the repression of the high hope of adventure." [19]
"Faith," wrote John Dewey, "is the power of intelligence to imagine
a future which is the projection of the desirable in the present, and

---

[17] J. Glen Gray, "Is Progressive Education a Failure?" *Commentary* 14: 107-
116, August 1952. By permission.

The following prayer by Rev. Peter Marshall, chaplain of the United States
Senate, for Sunday, July 4, 1948, illustrates the prevalent viewpoint, that the
ends of life remain constant, and that only the means change:

"O God our Father, we pray that the people of America, who have made such
progress in material things, may now seek to grow in spiritual understanding.

"For we have improved means, but not improved ends. . . .

"We need Thy help to do something about the world's true problems—the
problem of lying, which is called propaganda; the problem of selfishness, which
is called self-interest; the problem of greed, which is often called profit; the
problem of license, disguising itself as liberty; the problem of lust, masquerading
as love; the problem of materialism, the hook which is baited with security."
—*Time* 52: 59, July 12, 1948.

[18] Read George G. Simpson, "Man's Place in Nature," Chapter 15 in *The
Meaning of Evolution,* New Haven, Conn.: Yale University Press, 1949 (Chapter
9 in the paper-bound Mentor edition) ; Philip Frank, *Modern Science and Its
Philosophy,* Cambridge, Mass.: Harvard University Press, 1949, Chapters 15 and
16.

[19] Alfred North Whitehead, *Science and the Modern World,* New York: Macmillan, 1936, conclusion of chapter 12. Read also Whitehead's *Adventures in
Ideas,* New York: Macmillan, 1944, pages 125-126.

to invent the instrumentalities of its realization is our salvation." [20]
"Not fear and submission but love and the assertion of one's own
powers are the basis of the mystical experience," says Erich Fromm.
"God is not a symbol of power over man but of man's own
powers." [21] Such ideas are neither new nor heretical. While critics
of "pragmatism" and "relativism" are to be praised for their efforts
to join American thought onto the main stream of European
philosophy, such efforts have been largely misspent because they
have generally attempted to interpret the European tradition only
in terms of its static or Eleatic extreme. They forget the warning
of the ancient prophet, "Say not thou, 'What is the cause that
former days were better than these?'" [22] The future, says Raymond B. Fosdick, belongs to the irresistible power of things that
can grow:

> That is why democracy, rightly interpreted, is the last best hope
> of earth. It is rooted in the principle of growth; it is adapatable
> to new concepts of social justice. It is built, not on a fixed creed
> or on a system of regimented ideas, but on the sure knowledge
> that frontiers are never stationary, that the thrust of events is
> steadily forward, that there are no privileged ideas around which
> magic circles can be drawn to protect them from competition.
> It is only free men who dare to think, and it is only through free
> thought, freely expressed, that the soul of a people can be kept
> alive. [23]

Obstacles exist to be overcome, it is now believed, and therefore
they are overcome. New frontiers await discovery, it is believed,
and therefore new frontiers are discovered. When Daniel Boone's
frontier is gone, Thomas Edison's frontier comes on the scene. The
wider man's sphere of knowledge, the greater its contact with the
unknown; and if man will only hold firm in his faith in his own

---

[20] John Dewey, *Creative Intelligence*, New York: Holt, 1917, p. 17. Compare
Harry L. Hollingworth, *Psychology and Ethics*, New York: Ronald, 1949, p. 162.

[21] Erich Fromm, *Psychoanalysis and Religion*, New Haven, Conn.: Yale University Press, 1949, p. 49. Compare Rabbi Joshua Loth Liebman, *Peace of Mind*,
New York: Simon and Schuster, 1946, p. 172 f.

[22] *Ecclesiastes* 7: 10. Compare *Hebrews*, Chapters 11 and 12; I *Samuel* 4: 9.

[23] Raymond B. Fosdick, "We Must Not Be Afraid of Change," *New York
Times Magazine*, April 3, 1949; slightly revised to become Chapter 3 of *Within
Our Power* by Raymond B. Fosdick, New York: Longmans, 1952.

divine nature, the process knows no limit. Surely it is not "lack of faith" or "sin of pride" for men to believe that there are new worlds to conquer, new worlds to explore, and a future as bright (or as dim) as men through their cooperative intelligence win (or lose) for themselves.

Since the Renaissance, and certainly since the French Revolution, say the liberals, modern democracy has been a fervent social movement because its liberty, equality and fraternity have not been utopian and otherworldly, but have provided social and economic opportunities for larger and larger percentages of the population. Prior to the industrial revolution, economic productivity in terms of output per man-hour was low; consequently the total supply of economic goods was limited. But during the past few centuries, the Western democracies have been able to assume leadership among the peoples of the world because they have enjoyed the added strength that comes when more and more people develop their potentialities of intellect, personality and economic productivity. Men are free because they produce more; and they produce more because they are free.

But the traditionalists often speak with contempt of science and technology, and say modern machinery and mass production are reducing everything to a monotonous uniformity. Like a child with a new toy, they say, modern man is so taken up by gadgets and mechanical devices that he has de-emphasized some of his finest spiritual traditions. Appetites grow but aspirations perish. We know the price but not the value of things. We develop every kind of control except self-control. Our outer life is killing the inner. Pursued as he is by the telephone, phonograph, radio, the clamor of the factory, the uproar of the streets, modern man is reduced to the level of the newspaper, the movie, jazz. Vulcan has killed Apollo.

In answering this indictment, say the progressives, let us first admit that we cannot compare the average twentieth-century citizen with an Aristotle or a St. Francis; yet our modern geniuses compare very favorably with geniuses of former times, and the modern workingman generally lives on a plane far superior to that of the serfs and slaves of former ages.

The ancients declared it took five slaves to make one free man. Today machinery has taken the place of the slaves, but not of the free man. Three things, which seemed contradictory to one another, have materialized or are on the way of becoming realities through industrial progress; reduction in work hours, higher wage schedules, and lower costs. More and more we are realizing that the machine can be labor-serving as well as labor-saving; that steam, electric and atomic power can reduce physical fatigue; and that electronic robots can replace men in many of the more repetitive tasks.[24] Today power-driven machines do over 90 per cent of American physical labor, and the percentage is still rising.[25] Increased population somewhat offsets these advances.[26] Nevertheless the future holds possibilities of changes as great as have occurred during the past century. Unrest among the "backward" peoples occurs because these hungry, sick and desperate peoples now know that modern science and modern technology make their hunger and sickness unnecessary.[27]

Man has possessed writing and agriculture for eight or ten thousand years, and the traditions of aristocracy date back that far. But science in its modern form came into existence only about 300 years ago. Machine-power technology and mass production techniques are scarcely 150 years old. When we consider how recently these new developments have occurred, we realize that we are only at the very beginning of a new era.[28] The great issue today is

[24] Read Norbert Weiner: *The Human Use of Human Beings,* Boston: Houghton, 1949; *Scientific American* 187: 44-160 (1951), entire issue on "Automatic Controls."

[25] Read Sumner H. Slichter, "Productivity: Still Going Up," *Atlantic* 190: 64-68, July 1952; Summary of the 125th Anniversary of the "Journal of the Franklin Institute" and the 75th Anniversary of the American Chemical Society, *Chemical and Engineering News* 29: 3936-3984, Sept. 29, 1951; Fenton B. Turck, "The American Explosion," *Scientific Monthly* 75: 187-191, September 1952; Lyman Bryson, editor, *Facing the Future's Risks,* New York: Harper, 1953.

[26] Read A. V. Hill, "The Ethical Dilemma of Science," *Vital Speeches* 19: 110-114, Dec. 1, 1952; Warren Weaver, "People, Energy, and Food," *Scientific Monthly* 78: 359-364, June 1954; Harrison S. Brown, *The Challenge of Man's Future,* New York: Viking, 1954.

[27] Stringfellow Barr, *Let's Join the Human Race,* Chicago: University of Chicago Press, 1950.

[28] Not all changes have been for the better. In the transition from an agricultural civilization, many families of modest or low income lost their small farms and home crafts to large power-driven factories. In the rise of large scale capitalism, unemployment became a common hazard of family life, as tragic as the epidemics which swept our cities a hundred years ago. The livelihood of families could be cut off as quickly and unexpectedly as their lives once were cut off by typhus, yellow fever or cholera.

whether modern civilization can provide leisure, education and culture for all men as former societies provided for the aristocratic few.

And in this conclusion, the traditionalist and the progressive often join hands.

5.6. SOME PROBLEMS OF MODERN EDUCATION [29]

C. C. Trillingham

.   .   .   .   .

Educators face a terrific task in helping the general public understand the nature of today's pupil population and how it relates to today's school program.

According to figures compiled by the U. S. Office of Education in 1900, about 11 per cent of the nation's youngsters of high-school age were enrolled in high schools and academies; by 1910 the number increased to 15 per cent.

The school program in that day, and for almost 100 years prior to that date, was organized for boys who planned to go to college and to enter the professions. Hundreds of the relatively small handful of youngsters in high school who did not get along dropped out and

To meet such problems, the government has undertaken systematic provision for underwriting the basic minimum security and well-being of the unemployed, to the end that every family may have the goods and services necessary for a decent living, and receive these basic essentials in a manner that preserves self-respect.

Private industry has also met problems of poverty, unemployment and insecurity by a number of devices: decentralization, profit sharing, stock distribution, personnel relations, employee dividends, bonus systems, and rewards for outstanding services.

Read William Haber and Wilber J. Cohen, eds., *Readings in Social Security*, New York: Prentice-Hall, 1948; Elton Mayo, *The Social Problems of an Industrial Civilization*, Cambridge, Mass.: Harvard University Press, 1945.

[29] Clinton C. Trillingham, "What's *Right* with Public Education?" *School Executive* 70: 39-42, April 1951. By permission. Mr. Trillingham is Superintendent of Schools, Los Angeles County, California.

Compare: Leo A. Molinaro, "Progressive Education Charts Its Course at Mid-Century," *Progressive Education* 29: 38-42, November 1951; Willard B. Spaulding, "The Stereotype of Progressive Education in the Profession and in the Public," *Progressive Education* 29: 42-50, November 1951 (bibliography).

went to work. The high school was a selective institution catering primarily to the intellectually aristocratic. Scholastic standards were high. Everyone took the same courses. Youngsters who could not produce were automatically eliminated from school.

Pupil Population Increases

Since that day, because of our increasing technological development, the advent of organized labor, and compulsory attendance laws, each decade has found more youngsters attending school and remaining in school longer. By 1920, 32 per cent of the children of high-school age were in high school; by 1930, 51 per cent; by 1940, this figure had increased to 73 per cent. Today, in California, well over 90 per cent of the boys and girls of high-school age are in high school.

Today's public schools claim to be democratic institutions. They attempt to serve *all the children of all the people*. The philosophy has gradually changed from "get it or get out" to "keep the youngsters in school as long as they can profit from a good educational offering." Although not every teacher or every parent agrees with this point of view, we try to hold the youngsters in school today and serve them in accordance with their differing needs and capacities. Instead of one kind of program for youth with highly specialized interests, modern schools develop diversified programs to encompass the interests of all youth.

Teachers and laymen alike must be helped to realize that in a typical elementary classroom of 35 boys and girls, two of them will be near the moron in intellectual capacity, while on the other extreme, two will be highly gifted or near the genius class. Between these extremes exists every possible variety of potentiality with most of the group falling near the middle, or average.

Parents' Hopes Too High

When most parents expect their sons and daughters to qualify in the upper 10 per cent scholastically, while 90 per cent of the youngsters cannot possibly achieve this goal statistically, is it any wonder that the resulting frustrations lead to a high incidence of mental illness and juvenile delinquency? Is it false pride or just wishful thinking when 63 per cent of the parents surveyed by a city school system recently indicated their hopes that their youngsters would enter professions when it was obvious there would be such job opportunities available for not more than 8 per cent of them? . . .

Too many times the friends of public schools have supported us on the basis of faith and confidence in leadership rather than on the basis of genuine understanding. . . . [Today] Parents and teachers are discovering that the old-fashioned report card is a poor substitute for the two-way communication that should go on between home and school. They are finding out that boys and girls do not learn at the same rate; that it is normal for youngsters to differ widely; that all children of all abilities are important and each has a contribution to make; that learning is a growing-out rather than a pouring-in process; that schools and homes need to do more about making boys and girls secure with what they have instead of resentful of what they do not have; and that our world needs the barbers, bus drivers, clerks, and farmers as well as the doctors, architects and engineers.

What Is Progressive Education?

The critics say that the public schools are promoting "progressive education," leading the country toward socialism, ignoring fundamental skills, and fostering unrestricted pupil freedom. Let's try to clarify this nonsense about "progressive education."

The *first concept* of "progressive education" grew out of the work of the Progressive Education Association. This organization emphasized: (1) the individual differences existing among children; (2) the basic needs of all children; (3) learning as a process of growth and development; (4) the development of the whole child as a personality including his physical, emotional, and social well-being as well as his intellectual growth; and (5) learning by doing.

Much experimental work was done, particularly in well equipped, well staffed private schools. Generally classes were small and pupil groups were selected. This movement was psychologically well founded and made a genuine contribution to good education, but relatively few teachers were properly trained for the program. Attempts to be "progressive" resulted in confusion and error on the part of many teachers and serious misunderstanding on the part of parents.

It should be pointed out that the Progressive Education Association at its height had less than 15,000 paid members out of nearly a million public school teachers.

Everything Bad Is "Progressive"

The *second concept* of "progressive education" is the popular and misguided notion held by many lay persons and educators. This alleged brand of education is new-fangled. It is said to disregard the fundamentals and to permit unrestricted pupil freedom. The classroom is supposedly given over to busy work and pupil conduct is bad. Pupil personalities are unrepressed and pandemonium reigns. Pupils are never failed and satisfactory grades are given regardless of accomplishment. The main emphasis is upon play, self-expression, and general contentment.

This concept of education no doubt grew out of the efforts of many well-intentioned teachers who were untrained for conducting the program as conceived by the Progressive Education Association. All *bad* education became popularly known as "progressive education." Fifty years ago a poor teacher of reading was just a poor teacher of reading, but today a poor teacher of reading is a "progressive."

There is no group of educators today which advocates this second concept of "progressive education." Wherever this kind of education exists, it is poor education and we cannot tolerate it. In fact, we prefer to use the term "modern" rather than "progressive" because so many people have become allergic to the term "progressive."

Blending the Old and New

The *third concept* of "progressive education" holds that the modern school should be alert to new developments which prove themselves sound while utilizing methods of proven value from the past.

Modern education serves the needs of individual boys and girls and the needs of society. It emphasizes acquisition of fundamental learning tools, and the development of sound work habits. It makes use of vital, up-to-date curriculum content, builds proper attitudes, provides opportunities for a variety of learning experiences, and emphasizes democratic relationships between pupils, teachers, administrators, board members, and lay citizens.

Just as business, industry, and science do research to improve their products and their methods, so should education constantly seek to evaluate and to better itself. This is the kind of "progressive education" in which we believe. . . .

5.7. CONTEMPORARY EDUCATION AS SEEN BY A CLASSICIST [30]

Gilbert Highet

Now, in the Western world, there are three errors which help to account for the weaknesses of contemporary education.

The first is the mistaken idea that schools exist principally to train boys and girls to be sociable, "integrated with their group," "equipped with the skills of social living," "adjusted to family and community cooperation," and so forth. Obviously that is *one* of the aims of schooling, sometimes neglected in the past though usually emerging as a by-product. It was a necessary and valuable function of school and college at the most recent stage in American history to create a more or less uniform pattern of culture for the new middle class, and a stable social order in which the children of the unparalleled flood of immigrants who reached the country between 1880 and 1920 could find their place as Americans. But another aim of education, equally important or more important, is to train the individual mind as intensely and to encourage it as variously as possible—since much of our better and our more essential life is lived by us as individuals, and since (in the advancing age of mass-culture) it is vital for us to maintain personal independence.

The second of these three errors is the belief that education is a closed-end process, which stops completely as soon as adult life begins. During the war a friend of mine was in a unit (it might have been in any of the Western armies) where no one was illiter-

---

[30] Gilbert Highet, *Man's Unconquerable Mind*, New York: Columbia University Press, 1954, pages 75-78, 94, 128. By permission.

Mr. Highet is Anthon Professor of the Latin Language and Literature at Columbia University, and author of *The Art of Teaching*, New York: Knopf, 1950.

ate, but no one ever opened a book. He bought paper-backed novels and collections of essays to read in the long hours of boredom which are inseparable from military life. As he turned page after page and went through book after book, the others watched him with bewilderment. Finally, as he threw away the fifteenth volume and opened the sixteenth, one of his buddies came up and said "Studyin' all the time, don't you never get tired?" This fellow could not imagine that reading a book could possibly be anything but work—hard, exhausting work. Just in the same way many of the young people who graduate from schools and colleges in Europe, in North and South America, in Australia and elsewhere, immediately drop their languages, forget their science (unless they move into a scientific job), abandon their economic and political thinking, and fail to relate their four or eight years of intellectual training to the rest of their lifetime. It is like learning music for nearly a decade, and then never going to a concert or playing a single note. Here the schools, colleges, and teachers are surely to blame. Too many teachers (especially in college) seem to limit the interest of their students by implying that their own true and central aim is to train professional scholars, and that amateur interest in their subject is to be deprecated.

The third error which limits the use of knowledge in the Western world is the notion that learning and teaching always ought to have immediate results, show a profit, lead to success. Now, it is true that education is intended to benefit the entire personality. But it is not possible, not even desirable, to show that many of the most important subjects which are taught as part of education will make the learner rich, fit him for social life, or find him a job. Some values must be postulated. Poetry is better than pinball. The man who does not know anything about biology is in that respect inferior to the man who does, even although he may be richer in pocket. A training in philosophy makes few men wealthy, but it satisfies an instinct in them which cries for fulfillment as hungrily as the drives to survive and to reproduce, and which is less easily sated. People who know no history always learn wrong history, and can never understand the passing moment as it changes into history. Yet sometimes it is difficult to convince young people of this, difficult even to explain it to parents and to school supervisors. The result is that important and long-fruitful subjects tend to be squeezed out of education, neglected, even ignored and deformed. For instance, English literature is one of the finest literatures in the entire world: a thing to be proud of and to enjoy. To be brought up speaking and reading English is to be presented with the key to a massive and incorruptible treasure. Our literature from Chaucer to Eliot contains enough to make a man happy, thoughtful, and eloquent through an entire lifetime. And yet many unfortunate boys and girls in the English-speaking countries are being denied that opportunity. Their teachers tell their parents that language is a "tool"; and instead of showing them how to read and appreciate the best fifty of those miraculous books, they instruct them in a dreary pastiche sometimes called "language arts," which is to literature as finger painting is to the National Gallery. Year by year, more youngsters go to high school and to college. Year by year, standards go down and down—and not because there is an inevitable degradation in admitting large crowds into our educational system, but simply because we are recklessly ready to waste both the minds of the young and the rich inheritance of the past. . . .

Dante . . . made Ulysses say to his sailors, as they shrank from the horror of the unknown,

Consider well the seed from which you grew:
you were not formed to live like animals
but rather to pursue virtue and knowledge.

There, in a single sentence, is the faith of the Western universities. . . .

[Dedication to such faith means] . . . to forget one's own petty self, to revere the ardors and efforts of the great thinkers and teachers who have helped to make our world, and to feel, like the majestic roll of some vast river, the urgent march of the mind, imperfect but marvelous, unique in every individual and yet superpersonal, the mysterious power which has brought us out of bestial savagery toward civilization and wisdom, and will take us further still. It is to dedicate oneself again to the purpose of the university, which is to acquire and to extend knowledge for the service of all mankind.

5.8. THE "GREAT BOOKS" OF
LITERATURE AND OF HISTORY [31]

Albert Guérard

. . . books do not grow in a vacuum, and books do not grow purely out of other books. At all times, the essential relation is not between book and book, but between book and life. A revolution in literature is part of a general revolution in thought, itself inseparable from a change in social conditions. The great spirit of confidence, energy, adventure, which is the true glory of the Renaissance, and which was so admirably expressed by Rabelais, did not originate in the flight of a few grammarians from Constantinople: it is the same spirit that stirred in discoverers, conquistadors, reformers. Classicism, the Enlightenment, Romanticism, Realism, were not mere literary fashions. Even esoteric movements, the Symbolist and Decadent schools of the Yellow Nineties, the Ecclesiastes mood of the sophisticates after the First World War, were odd manifestations of a universal *malaise*. Political history, social history, economic history, literary history, are constantly fed from the common reservoir which we must call vaguely "the spirit of the time."

These considerations should throw some light on the problem of the "Great Books." That we should read "great books" rather than poor ones is a venerable truism; that we should make them the core of a liberal education is not quite so obvious. My attitude toward the plan so successfully carried out at St. John's College and Chicago will be called by some of my friends ambiguous, or perhaps—since the word is now in fashion—"ambivalent." It is definitely friendly; and, because criticism is my rule of life, it is no less definitely critical.

In the first place, it is evident that the whole of life is not covered by a hundred books. Erasmus and Rabelais are splendid mani-

---

[31] Albert Guérard, *The Education of a Humanist,* Cambridge, Mass.: Harvard University Press, 1949, pages 128-135. Footnotes omitted. By permission.

Albert Guérard, professor emeritus of general and comparative literature at Stanford University, is author of eighteen books, including *Bottle in the Sea,* Cambridge, Mass.: Harvard University Press, 1954.

Compare Dwight McDonald, "Book-of-the-Millenium Club," *New Yorker* 28: 171 f, Nov. 29, 1952; F. R. Leavis, "Great Books and a Liberal Education," *Commentary* 16: 224-232, September 1953.

festations of the Renaissance: they are not the whole Renaissance. Luther is greater than anything he wrote, and the Reformation is immeasurably greater than Luther. Certain immense changes, of the utmost importance to mankind, never were recorded in commensurate books. The Industrial Revolution had incalculable consequences; but even if James Watt had happened to write a book, it might very well not have deserved to be considered a world classic. And in the mounting tide of socialism for the last century and a half, no single book, however mighty, can be treated even as an adequate symbol.

One of the boasted advantages of the proposed method is to go back directly to the source, pure and uncontaminated: not books about books, but the original works themselves. Yet if we want fully to understand any one of these masterpieces, we have to study not its bare text alone but the antecedents and concomitants that explain it. Most of the books on the proposed list are termed "great" because they were moments in history: we cannot pick up *Das Kapital* as though it had appeared this morning. I defy any one to read Marx intelligently unless he also reads about Marx and his times.

To isolate a few books out of millions, and to assume that they and they alone are necessary and sufficient, is to transfer to the world of books the Carlylean delusion of hero-worship. It is not true that all we see in history is but the prolonged shadow of a few great men, be their instrument the pen or the sword. . . .

I am no scientist; but I have heard scientists question the wisdom of teaching science through the works of the past. The very nature of science is to disregard tradition and courteously to rule out individual authority. Nothing is true simply because Euclid, Ptolemy, Kepler, Newton, or Einstein said so. The ascertained, classified, organized facts accumulate; the method grows more exacting, more searching; the actual work of any particular scientist is incorporated in the general body of science. The gropings of a genius have a personal, not a scientific, interest. As the merest layman, I have no right to speak about, say, Lyell's *Elements of Geology* or Darwin's *Origin of Species,* both epochmaking books. But I happened . . . to grow professionally interested in Malthus. The problem of population is of the utmost importance to mankind; it might well become the all-absorbing one if the time comes when even standing room can no longer be found upon this earth. Malthus had the merit of focusing the problem so sharply that his name remains inseparable from it. Moreover, he started a rebellion against the fundamental optimism of the Christians ("God's in His heaven"), of Rousseau ("Man is good"), even of Adam Smith ("the guiding hand"). Long before Unamuno, and in the dreariest prose, he too had a tragic sentiment of life. No history of thought would be adequate without at least a paragraph devoted to that formidable question mark in the garb of a country parson. Political scientists may well desire, periodically, to re-examine the pregnant *Essay* itself. But is there any reason why our young people should have to wade through hundreds of pages of antiquated, inaccurate, ill-digested facts? For a man's general education, a good textbook on "Theories of Population" would be much more to the point.

As the "Great Books" idea weakens the connection between the author and his times, it loosens also the chain between an author, his predecessors, and his successors. There are no Melchizedeks in science: every idea has a history and a pre-history. Malthus himself was rather surprised to find that his "discovery" had been anticipated, or at least adumbrated. Only the unwary will entertain the idea that artificial languages were "invented" by Dr. Zamenhof, or flying machines by the Wright Brothers. And ulterior development is an essential factor in the fame, that is to say, in the importance, of a man. A pioneer whose thought disappears altogether does not belong to history. Imagine Jesus without disciples! Marx is important because of Marxism; and Marxism is not a single formula but the whole Marxist movement. Scientific research could proceed without formal history, starting from our present knowledge and with our present equipment. But if we do study the history of science, it must be scientific, not sensational; it must trace the long and complex growth, not focus our attention exclusively upon isolated peaks. If we are told that, in Introductions, Notes, Aids to Study, Lectures, and the like, all these elements will receive proper treatment, then we shall have Histories of Science, of Philosophy, of Politics, and so forth, with selected texts as illustrations. Which is exactly what has been done, often indifferently, but at times very well, for several generations.

The chief weakness of the "Great Books" idea is that, in spite of the rare intellectual quality of its promoters, no clear criterion of "greatness" is revealed by their choice. Their list represents a vague consensus, a composite image of many compromises. There is of course no single authoritative collection of "Great Books" as—with a twilight zone of Apocrypha—there is a Canon of Holy Scripture. The best that can be said of any such list—Sir John Lubbock's, for instance—is that it is "as good as the rest." There will always be omissions to be deplored, admissions that will rouse mild astonishment. The bulk of the list is composed of "safe" names, about which there is polite if at times unenthusiastic agreement, a convention not outrageous enough to call for a challenge. It is simply not true that all these "Books That Every Child Ought to Know" are indispensable to culture. Many intelligent men, past and present, have read most of them "by title only," and have derived greater sustenance from works not on the approved syllabus.

A great temptation in drawing up such a canon is the distributive, the encyclopedic method. There must be samples of everything: this introduces a standard very different from that of intrinsic value. Inferior works have to be brought in so as to preserve the balance between kinds, countries, periods. For the sake of completeness, the collection is stuffed with books which are admirably suitable to the composite statistical Man, but which do not appeal to this or that individual reader. Upon all such series lies heavily the curse of the ready-made: it is good, it is practical, it is cheap, it does not quite fit any one.

But the chief ambiguity in selecting the Hundred Best Books results from the effort to combine two criteria, the intrinsic (artistic or scientific) and the social: books that live because of their beauty and truth, books which once were events in the history of mankind. When the two criteria happen to be in agreement, it is little short of a miracle. The most miraculous case of all is that of Plato. St. Paul, in rare passages, reaches supreme heights of spiritual and literary power; Jean Jacques Rousseau was not merely a portent, but, once in a while, a poet. But as a rule, the scales are not the same. It cannot be denied that the poetry of Emily Dickinson, of Keats, of Blake, failed to deflect the course of human events, while Thomas Paine with his *Crisis,* or Harriet Beecher Stowe with

Uncle Tom's Cabin, appreciably did. If *Hamlet* had never been written, mankind would have been deprived of a jewel; but, because Luther nailed his ninety-five theses on the church door at Wittenberg, the lives of millions were transformed. There is an abyss between a classic and a document.

Many years ago, a British publisher asked me whether I would write for him "The Fifteen Decisive Books of the World." The scheme was obviously inspired by *The Fifteen Decisive Battles,* by Sir Edward Shepherd Creasy, a hardy perennial in the book trade. I do not remember why the deal fell through, unregretted. But I had given the subject some thought. I wanted to work out the problem on a definite instance. In connection with French civilization, I had had to look into the population problem, with Malthus looming vaguely in the background. I tackled the *Essay on the Principle of Population as it affects the Future Improvement of Society,* with all the biographical and critical data thereunto appertaining. I watched an epoch-making book in the act of making an epoch. It was a good experiment: the work was important enough to be worth observing, the influence narrow enough to be observable. It taught me a few things which could be applied to more obvious and mightier books. Above all, it left me puzzled: do we mean anything definite when we say that *The Prince,* or *The Origin of Species,* or *Das Kapital* are decisive books?

For some twenty years, I had a series of symposia on the subject with my advanced students. We did not solve the riddle, but we had some good mental exercise in the attempt: it was a twentieth-century equivalent of "How many angels can stand on the point of a needle?" We derived some enlightenment from the "List of the Twenty-Five Volumes three noted scholars, John Dewey, Edward Weeks, and Charles A. Beard, considered to have had the most influence on thought and action during the last half-century" (1936). We came to the safe conclusion that if one noted scholar could be muddled, the combined efforts of three noted scholars were confusion in the third power. Good pragmatists, they mentioned, haphazard, those works that had been most talked about, those titles which had crashed the front page. People discuss books they neither enjoy nor believe in, not seldom books they have not read and do not intend to read, books that are an annoyance rather than a force. Notoriety and influence are not identical.

Although the Three Noted Scholars defined their problem a little more closely than other list-concocters, they made no clear distinction between *great, good, successful, influential, decisive. . . .*

We must revert, therefore, to our fundamental distinction between art and history. Art does not seek influence—which is another way of asserting that it exists on its own ground and for its own sake only. History, on the contrary, is a concatenation of influences: the soil and the dead, as Barrès put it, mass psychology and its unaccountable chain-reactions, facts of the most material kind, and, mingling with the facts, legends all the more potent for being vast and vague. I do not deny that among these innumerable factors, certain books have their place. But that place has very little relation with their aesthetic worth, and it is small at best in the warp and woof of history.

5.9. THE REAL PROBLEM OF THE LIBERAL ARTS [32]

Norman Cousins

For many years the complaint has been heard that young people going into the sciences were being incompletely educated. It was said that they were being prepared for a compartmentalized and specialized world but not for a full life in a large and complex world.

These complaints have generally come from the liberal arts. Educators were troubled not only by the limitations of the sciences but by the fact that the humanities were being relegated to a secondary position in terms of public recognition and support. Yet in their own way the men of the liberal arts suffer just as seriously from compartmenalization and overspecialization. Indeed, the competition between the humanities and the sciences today tends to obscure basic weaknesses within the humanities.

[32] Norman Cousins, "The Real Problem of the Liberal Arts," *Saturday Review of Literature* 36: 20, June 6, 1953. By permission. Mr. Cousins is editor, *The Saturday Review of Literature*. Compare National Education Association Personal Growth Leaflet No. 186, "Interdependence Reader," Washington 6, D. C.: National Education Association, 1954.

At its largest, the failure of the liberal arts today is one that can be measured in its own terms: the liberal arts are inadequately meeting the needs of the whole man in whose name they claim their reason for being. The average liberal arts graduate is educated for an enclosure labeled "Western Civilization" and not for a world that has become a single geographic unit. He is prepared to understand the smaller part of a complex whole. Yet the smaller part can understand itself only if it also understands the whole. In fact, failure to know the whole is unpreparedness at its worst at a time when preparedness has become something of a national watchword.

This is not merely a matter that can be easily corrected by a slight shift in college curriculum. It goes to the core of our training and attitudes in history and philosophy—and scholarship in general. We have allowed such terms as "Western Civilization" or "Christendom" to become stock phrases or slogans—without any real comprehension of the fact that what is finest in the "Western tradition" is universal and not geographic. We write books or articles about the "uniqueness" of our Western values with little acknowledgment of the cross-fertilization of ideas and cultures between East and West. We blandly assume that when we refer to Western values everyone knows *precisely* what it is we are talking about.

It may be argued that these values are addressed to and built around individual man or around philosophical affirmation. Even here a proper answer might be that the natural rights of man have never been more finely espoused than under Confucianism. Or if it is argued that a large part of the East is under totalitarian control and that this automatically defines the basic differences between East and West, a countering argument would be that Communism, Nazism, and Fascism came out of the West. In fact, it was the political and philosophical corruption of Platonism that led in a direct line to authoritarianism in the modern world. Nor ought we ever to forget that Christianity originated in the East, or the fact that there is an organic connection between the Koran and the Old and New Testaments.

A real danger represented by the compartmentalization of the liberal arts, so far as Western civilization is concerned, is that it often produces the symptoms of a superiority complex. The reaction of other peoples to such symptoms is exactly what one would expect. If we are anxious to keep the majority of the world's peoples from going under and over to a global authoritarian system, a good thing to avoid is sloganeering largely devoid of content.

Certainly our civilization has values. But we diminish these values the moment we seem to arrogate them to ourselves. The values we prize most highly are human values. They were born in men's minds and can be born again anywhere—so long as there are propitious conditions for their birth. If we seem to give these values special geographical significance or sanction, they may lose their luster and eventually their meaning. Our philosophers and scholars and educators should be among the first to recognize that in a crisis of ideas the biggest ideas are the universal ones.

A moment ago we ventured the opinion that the failure of the liberal arts is not something that can be easily fixed merely by tinkering around with the curriculum. What is needed is not merely an extra survey course or two on comparative cultures, philosophies, or religions. What is needed is fundamental recognition that, although the world may be split politically, mankind does not exist in compartments. The human race is the new frame of reference, not geographical or cultural groupings—however great their old historical validity. And if our philosophers want to summon us to great deeds, let them do it in the name of the institution of man.

Section C: Questions and Readings for Study and Discussion

5.10. INTRODUCTION

Sections A and B of this chapter dealt with three major criticisms of modern education: (1) that educators should exercise a greater measure of caution and moderation (J. C. Peel); (2) that greater community understanding and participation in public education be developed (Maurice Ahrens); and (3) that a better balance should be established between (a) the immediate, practical, pragmatic, vocational, realistic and (b) the classic, perennial, general, aesthetic, idealistic. Four other major criticisms were the subject matter of Chapters 1, 2, 3 and 4.

But these are not the only criticisms, even though they are among the more important ones. The questions and readings to follow enumerate several others. Some of these, such as juvenile delinquency, concern the family, church and law enforcement agencies as well as the schools. Others arise from social and cultural changes (e.g., federal aid) or from the impact of science and technology (e.g., vocational education). They are not so much "issues" as "problems to be solved."

But the "issues" should also be considered as problems to be solved. In order to point up an issue, it is necessary to emphasize opposition and conflict. But to solve an issue, or to resolve a conflict, it is best to focus attention on elements of *agreement* rather than on elements of difference. Above all, in trying to reduce existing tensions, we should avoid an either-or, all-none approach. For example, a biologist might ask "Does heredity *or* environment cause certain characteristics?" But the question "How do specific hereditary factors interact with a particular environment?" would probably lead to more fruitful results. Similarly, the problem of "the individual *versus* society" might be changed to "How can the needs of this particular individual best be realized in our society?" Such an approach will generally de-emphasize conflict, allay anxieties, and result in a more fruitful inquiry.

The task of our schools is to keep before the student and society the variegated approaches to the ventures and issues of life. Mutual aid is significant only because the abilities and perspectives of individuals are *not* alike. But the insights of any individual or group are of value only to the extent that they can be shared and supplemented by equally valid perspectives of others.

5.11. Vocational versus Cultural Education

How can the dual needs of vocational and of general education best be met in an age of specialization?

Austin, David B., "Potential of the Comprehensive High School," *National Association of Secondary-School Principals Bulletin* 37: 74-81, December 1953.

Beck, Robert N., "Let Us Liberalize Liberal Education," *School and Society* 77: 3-4, Jan. 3, 1953.

Benjamin, Harold, *The Saber-Tooth Curriculum,* New York: McGraw-Hill, 1939.

Butler, Judson R., "Certain Characteristics of General Education," *Journal of Higher Education* 24: 425-431 f, November 1953.

Chamberlain, Lawrence H., and Buchler, Justus, "Specialization or General Education?" *School and Society* 75: 273-276, May 3, 1952.

Cole, Charles W., "Impact of the Expansion of Knowledge," *Educational Record* 34: 231-236, July 1953.

Cunningham, William F., *General Education and the Liberal College,* St. Louis: Herder, 1953.

* De Zafra, Carlos, Jr., "General Education: Where It Stands Today," *Clearing House* 28: 387-393, March 1954; same condensed, *Education Digest* 19: 16-18, May 1954 (bibliography) .

Fortune Survey, "Should a Businessman Be Educated?" *Fortune* 47: 113-114, April 1953.

Henry, Nelson B., ed., Forty-second Yearbook, National Society for the Study of Education, Part I, *Vocational Education,* Chicago: University of Chicago Press, 1943.

Henry, Nelson B., ed., Fifty-first Yearbook, National Society for the Study of Education, Part I, *General Education,* Chicago: University of Chicago Press, 1952.

* Hook, Sidney, *Education for Modern Man,* New York: Dial, 1946 (Chapter 5.

* Hutchins, Robert M., *The University of Utopia,* Chicago: University of Chicago Press, 1953.

Mays, Arthur B., *Principles and Practices of Vocational Education,* New York: McGraw-Hill, 1948 (Chapter 6) .

* Oliva, Peter F., "Which General Education?" *Educational Forum* 18: 235-238, January 1954 (bibliography) .

Selden, William K., *versus* Stoke, Harold W., "What is Happening to Liberal Arts?" *National Education Association Journal* 42: 498-499, November 1953.

Van Doren, Mark, *Liberal Education,* New York: Holt, 1943 (pages 166-168.)

Walters, Raymond, Jr., ed., "Industry and the Liberal Arts," *Saturday Review* 36: 31-46, Nov. 21, 1953.

5.12. "The Three R's" versus "Fads and Frills"

We sometimes hear such phrases as "Back to the Three R's" or "Get rid of the fads and frills in education." Make a list of subjects taught in schools you have attended or observed, and try to decide which might be classified as "3 R's" (i.e., as essentials or fundamentals) and which as "fads and frills" (i.e., as extra-curricular or non-essential.)

Are the fundamentals being taught as well as in former generations? To what extent is criticism of modern education based on a misunderstanding of what is happening in the schools? For example: If history and geography are incorporated into "units" such as "The United Nations," or if reading and writing are joined together into a "core curriculum," does this imply that "history," "geography," "reading," and "writing" are "not being taught"?

Do comics and television discourage good reading habits? Have comics any place in the classroom, other than the wastebasket?

Benjamin, Harold R. W., "Whose Fundamentals?" *Phi Delta Kappan* 33: 87-89, October 1951.

Brady, Margaret E., "Comics—to Read or not to Read," *Wilson Library Bulletin* 24: 662-667, May 1950 (bibliography).

* Cremin, Lawrence A., "The Curriculum Maker and His Critics: A Persistent American Problem," *Teachers College Record* 54: 234-245, February 1953.

Cunningham, Robert M., Jr., "By Their Fruits . . . ," *National Education Association Journal* 41: 143-144, March 1952.

Dunham, Franklin, "Effect of Television on School Achievement of Children," *School Life* 34: 88 f, March 1952 (bibliography).

Elicker, Paul E., "How Good Are Our Schools?" *Collier's* 133: 78-83, June 11, 1954.

* Gray, William S., "Summary of Reading Investigations," *Journal of Educational Research* 44: 401-441, February 1951; 45: 401-437, February 1952; 46: 401-437, February 1953; 47: 401-439, February 1954 (lengthy bibliographies).

Harding, Lowry W., "How Well Are Schools Now Teaching the Basic Skills?" *Progressive Education* 29: 7-14, 32, October 1951 (bibliography).

* Haverstick, John, "The ABC's of the Battle Over the Three R's," *Saturday Review* 37: 14-19, September 11, 1954.

Hersey, John, "Why Do Students Bog Down on the First R?" *Life* 36: 136-150, May 24, 1954.

* Lynd, Albert, *Quackery in the Public Schools,* Boston: Little, 1953. For briefer statements by the same author and replies by other educators, read: *Atlantic* 185: 33-38, March 1950; 185: 57-60, June 1950; 191: 29-34, April 1953; 191: 59-62, May 1953.

Makey, Herman O., "Comic Books—A Challenge," *English Journal* 41: 547-549, December 1952.

Murrell, Jesse L., D.D., "Annual Rating of Comic Magazines," *Parents' Magazine* 27: 48 f, November 1952; 28: 54-55, October 1953.

Newsom, Carroll V., ed., *A Television Policy for Education,* Washington, D. C.: American Council on Education, National Education Association, 1952 (bibliography).

Shayon, Robert Lewis, "Television and Children's Reading," *Horn Book* 29: 91-100, April 1953.

Whitman, Howard, "Progressive Education—Which Way is Forward?" *Collier's* 133: 32-36, May 14, 1954.

* Witty, Paul A., "Are Children Learning to Read?" *School and Society* 75: 289-294, May 10, 1952: "How Well Do Modern Schools Teach Reading?" *Today's Health* 30: 22-24, 54-56, November 1952 (good bibliographies).

5.13. The Gifted Child

What should our schools do for the gifted child—the occasional pupil whose intelligence is far above the average? Should he be given extra activities, such as membership in clubs or special reading assignments? Should he be permitted to use his extra energy serving as teacher's errand boy? Should he be segregated into special classes? If so, for the entire day? or for only one or two hours a day?

Is there such a thing as the gifted child? whose distinctive abilities are recognizable in *advance,* and *before* they are developed?

Is the education of gifted children a more difficult problem in an age of specialized knowledge than it was in pre-scientific days? If so, why?

*Andree, Robert G., and Meister, Morris, "What are Some Promising Programs for Gifted Children?" *National Association of Secondary School Principals Bulletin* 38: 314-323, April 1954 (bibliography).

Baker, Harry J., *Introduction to Exceptional Children,* rev. ed., New York: Macmillan, 1953.

Cutts, Norma E., and Moseley, Nicholas, *Bright Children: A Guide for Parents,* New York: Putnam, 1953.

Hech, Arch O., *The Education of Exceptional Children,* New York: McGraw-Hill, 1953.

Hildreth, G. H., *Educating Gifted Children,* New York: Harper, 1952.

Justman, Joseph, and Wrightstone, J. Wayne, "The Opinions of Junior High-School Principals Concerning the Organization of Special Classes for Gifted Children," *Educational Administration and Supervision* 37: 396-404, November 1951.

Liebman, Malvina, "Our Best Minds Were Running Errands," *National Education Association Journal* 43: 35-36, January 1954.

Marshall, Max S., "The Case of the 'Gifted' Child," *Educational Administration and Supervision* 40: 155-162, March 1954.

Meister, Morris, and Odell, Harold A., "What Provisions for the Education of Gifted Children?" *National Association of Secondary School Principals Bulletin* 35: 30-46, April 1951.

* Scharer, Norman B., and Alpern, Hymen, "How Can the School Meet the Needs of Gifted and Superior Students," *National Association of Secondary School Principals Bulletin* 36: 99-117, March 1952 (bibliography).

White, Lynn, Jr., "The School Library and the Gifted Child," *Library Journal* 78: 1480-1483, Sept. 15, 1953.

* Witty, Paul, and Bloom, Samuel W., "Education of the Gifted," *School and Society* 78: 113-119, Oct. 17, 1953; *ibid.* 78: 177-191, Sept. 20, 1952 (bibliographies).

Witty, Paul, ed., *The Gifted Child,* Boston: Heath, 1951.

5.14. Juvenile Delinquency

More than half the inmates of our prisons for adults were once juvenile delinquents. Given proper treatment when they were still young, these men and women might have become responsible citizens, able to contribute their share to society. **It is quite certain that the number of juvenile delinquents will increase by half within the coming decade. What can be done about this problem?**

Is it a task for the local community? the state? the nation? Should it be handled by parents? by policemen and judges? or by the school? Should it be a joint effort of every agency available?

So far as the schools are concerned, is juvenile delinquency a result of "secularism"? of "soft discipline"? of "poor teacher training"? Is it caused by maladjustment to rigid courses of studies? by harshness and lack of understanding? by large classes and lack of personal guidance and individual attention? What can the schools do to alleviate the situation?

Brickman, William W., "Causes and Cures of Juvenile Delinquency," *School and Society* 75: 405-411, June 28, 1952; 68: 305-311, Oct. 30, 1948 (annotated bibliographies).

Carr, Lowell J., *Delinquency Control,* rev. ed., New York: Harper, 1950.

* Eliot, Martha M., "Some Facts About Juvenile Delinquency" (Pamphlet), Children's Bureau Publication No. 340, Washington, D. C.: United States Department of Health, Education and Welfare, 1953 (bibliography).

* Hill, Arthur S., Miller, Leonard M., and Gabbard, Hazel F., "Schools Face the Delinquency Problem," *National Association of Secondary School Principals Bulletin* 37: 181-221, December 1953. (Excellent article; outstanding bibliography).

* Larson, John F., and others, "Congress Studies the Problem of Juvenile Delinquency . . . Pro and Con," *Congressional Digest* 33: 289-314, December 1954.

Meyer, Agnes E., "Schoolboy Racketeers," *Atlantic* 193: 35-39, March 1954.

New York City, "Report of the Superintendent's Committee on Delinquency in the Secondary Schools," *High Points* 36: 5-40, April 1954.

Powers, Edwin, and Witmer, Helen L., *Experiment in the Prevention of Delinquency,* New York: Columbia University Press, 1951.

Smith, Philip M., "The Schools and Juvenile Delinquency," *Sociology and Social Research* 37: 85-91, November-December 1952 (bibliography).

* Strang, Ruth, "Facts About Juvenile Delinquency," Life Adjustment Booklet, Chicago: Science Research Associates, 1952.

Whitman, Howard, "The New Way in School Discipline: Be Firm But Fair," *Collier's* 134: 58-61, Aug. 6, 1954.

5.15. Teachers' Unions

Is teaching a trade or a profession? Is the NEA (a professional organization) so dominated by administrators that ordinary teachers should join the AFT (a branch of the AFL) in order to gain increased salaries and better working conditions? Does affiliation with the AFL disqualify teachers in a society where schools should be neutral toward capital-labor disputes? Do teachers ever have a right to strike? **In short, should we encourage teachers' unions? If so, what kind?**

Brameld, Theodore B. H., *Ends and Means in Education: A Midcentury Appraisal,* New York: Harper, 1950 (Chapter 11, pp. 95-106).

* Eby, Kermit, *versus* Kilpatrick, William Heard, "Teachers' Unions? Yes! No!" *Progressive Education* 20: 260-263 f, October 1943.

Emerson, Thomas I., and Haber, David, *Political and Civil Rights in the United States*, Buffalo, N. Y.: Dennis, 1952 (pp. 910-912).

Garber, Lee O., "The Legal Status of Teachers' Unions," *Nation's Schools* 49: 78-80, April 1952.

Hullfish, Gordon, "Educators, Education, and Teachers' Unions," *School and Society* 59: 81-83, Feb. 5, 1944.

Levitan, Star A., "Professional Organization of Teachers in Higher Education," *Journal of Higher Education* 22: 123-128, March 1951.

Martin, Theodore D., and others, "Compulsory Membership?—A Symposium," *Phi Delta Kappan* 33: 56-61, September 1951.

Rosen, Samuel R., and Rogers, Charles M., "I Like Local Associations," *National Education Association Journal* 41: 590-591, December 1952.

Wakeham, G. *versus* Cohen, J. W., "Should College Teachers Join the AFT?" *School and Society* 54: 441-443; November 15, 1941; 55: 190-193, February 14, 1942.

Yabroff, Bernard, and David, Lily Mary, "Collective Bargaining and Work Stoppages Involving Teachers," *Monthly Labor Review* 76: 475-479, May 1953.

5.16. Federal Aid to Education

Fifty years ago about three-fourths of every tax dollar went to state and local governments, only one-fourth to the federal government. Today, the federal government receives approximately three-fourths of all taxes collected. During this same period costs have increased and school enrollments have skyrocketed. The United States Commissioner of Education estimates that the public schools currently need 340,000 additional classrooms, at a cost of over ten billion dollars. Many cities and states seem unable to bear such heavy expenditures.

This raises the issue of federal aid to education. **Should the federal government assist the states, or should the states continue to handle the problem alone?** Will federal aid mean federal control? If federal aid is granted, should it be only for public schools? or should private and parochial schools also receive a share?

Allen, Hollis P., "Basic Answer to Federal Control," *Nation's Schools* 47: 34-36, March 1951.

Brown, F. J., "Current Issues in National Legislation for Education," *Junior College Journal* 24: 520-530, May 1954.

Brownell, Samuel M., and others, "The Question of Federal Funds for Public School Construction . . . Pro and Con," *Congressional Digest* 33: 257-288, November 1954.

* Cornell, Francis G., "Federal Aid is a Religious Issue," *School Executive* 72: 47-49, June 1953 (bibliography); reply by R. H. Schenck, S.J., *ibid.* 72: 13, August 1953.

* Hearings on S. 246 and H. R. 4634, 81st Congress, 1st Session, Hearings of May 17-26, June 1-6, 1949, Washington, D. C., U. S. Government Printing Office, 1949. (This is still the best reference for pros and cons on all the major issues involved.)

McGrath, Earl J. (former U. S. Commissioner of Education), "Crucial National Problems in Education," *School Life* 35: 99-101, 106-111, April 1953.

National Commission on Teacher Education and Professional Standards, *Nationwide Survey of Teacher Supply and Demand for Academic Year 1953-1954*, Washington 6, D. C.: National Education Association, March 1954.

Rozzell, Forrest, "Why I Believe in Federal Aid," *National Education Association Journal* 39: 502-503, October 1950.

Senior Scholastic Editors, "Taxes for Tuition? A Pro and Con Discussion," *Senior Scholastic* 60: 5-6, April 30, 1952.

Stanley, Charles J., "Organized Interests and Federal Aid to Education," *School and Society* 73: 1-4, Jan. 6, 1951.

West, Paul D., "Federal Aid to Education—Lost Cause or Live Issue?" *National Education Association Journal* 43: 296-297, May 1954.

5.17. Sex Education as Human Relations

It has been urged that modern education should include "the fourth R," namely, "Right Relations," or "Human Relations." Does this include a study of the relations between the sexes? Or should such problems be left to the home and church?

Ashley-Montague, Montague F., *The Natural Superiority of Women,* New York: Macmillan, 1953 (annotated bibliography on the emancipation of women).

* Brickman, William W., "Sex Instruction: Educational Literature Review," *School and Society* 68: 138-143, Aug. 28, 1948 (annotated bibliography).

Fay, Ruth H., "I'll Take Care of Teaching Sex!" *Better Homes and Gardens* 29: 6 f, October 1950; same, condensed as "Leave My Child Alone!" *Reader's Digest* 57: 122-124, November 1950.

Jessine, Sister Mary, "Our Children Need Sex Education," *America* 85: 376-378, July 14, 1951.

Kane, John J., *Marriage and the Family: A Catholic Approach,* New York: Dryden, 1952 (Chapters 13, 14 and 15).

Kirkendall, Lester A., *Sex Education as Human Relations,* New York: Inor, 1950 (good bibliography).

* Landis, Paul H., "Sex Education: The Facts about Two Generations." *Clearing House* 24: 451-455, April 1950 (bibliography); same condensed, *Education Digest* 16: 46-48, October 1950.

Sweeney, Esther E., "Partners in Sex Education," *Journal of Social Hygiene* 38: 49-55, February 1952.

Tuller, Josephine V., "Progress and Trends in Sex Education in the United States," *Journal of Social Hygiene* 38: 68-83, February 1952 (bibliography).

* Weaver, Warren, "People, Energy, and Food," *Scientific Monthly* 78: 359-364, June 1954. (A good introduction to problems of over-population in relation to the world's food supply; bibliography.)

5.18. Approaches to Sex Education for Adolescents

If sex education is included in the school curriculum, should it be conducted as a separate course? Should it consist of occasional special lectures by outside speakers? Should it be integrated into various elementary and secondary courses in health education, physical education, biology, general science, social science, home economics, and health education?

Is "sex education" one problem? Or is it a general term containing several more specific problems? Discuss these questions in the light of the following 1952 surveys:

. . . most of their respondents considered the following areas as important and appropriate for high-school students: (1) boy and girl relationships; (2) love, courtship, and choosing a mate; (3) marriage, parenthood, human reproduction; (4) sex behavior and conduct; (5) biological facts of sex including human reproduction; (6) menstruation; and (7) venereal disease education. A substantial majority of their respondents did not consider birth-control methods, sexual techniques, sexual perversions, and methods of VD prophylaxis appropriate topics for high-school students.[33]

Chicago Museum of Science and Industry and the University of Illinois. *The Miracle of Growth* (illustrated), Urbana: University of Illinois Press, 1950.

"Christopher Sex Talks: Recordings," *Newsweek* 38: 80, July 16, 1951; cited at length by Edward B. Lyman, "Let's Tell the Whole Story about Sex," *Journal of Social Hygiene* 37: 8-37, January 1951.

* Force, Elizabeth, "What Teen-agers Want to Know About Sex and Marriage," *Reader's Digest* 62: 69-71, April 1953; from *American Magazine* 155: 34-35 f, January 1953.

Gruenberg, Mrs. Benjamin C., *Wonderful Story of How You Were Born* (illustrated), New York: Doubleday, 1952.

Kirkendall, Lester A., "Sex Education," *National Education Association Journal* 40: 633-634, December 1951.

* Kirkendall, Lester A., and Hamilton, Archie, "Current Thinking and Practices in Sex Education," *High School Journal* 37: 143-148, February 1954; same condensed, *Education Digest* 19: 37-39, April 1954.

Levine, Milton I., and Seligman, Jean H., *The Wonder of Life* (illustrated), New York: Simon and Schuster, 1952.

* New Jersey Dept. of Education, "Approach in Schools to Education for Personal and Family Living," *Journal of Social Hygiene* 38: 56-67, February 1952.

Reid, Helen, "Handbook on Sex Education of Children," *Parent's Magazine* 28: 47-52, March 1953 (bibliography).

Strain, Mrs. Frances B., *New Patterns in Sex Teaching*, rev. ed., New York: Appleton-Century-Crofts, 1951.

Strain, Mrs. Frances B., *The Normal Sex Interests of Children from Infancy to Childhood*, New York: Appleton-Century-Crofts, 1949.

5.19. UN: The Fear of a Supra-National State

Discuss the following headlines:

"UN—DEN OF RED SPIES"

"Testimony Before Senate Committee Brands UN as Hotbed for Traitors"

"Charter for UN Drafted by Zionist"

---

[33] Unpublished Master's theses by O. Siegel and I. Calef, cited in "How Should You Provide for Sex Education?" *National Association of Secondary-School Principals Bulletin* 37: 16-17, May 1953.

"UN A MARXIST SETUP"

"United Nations Enemy of American Republic"

"Purpose of UN Framework for World Government, is to Abolish U.S."

(All the above headlines are taken from page 1 of the October 15, 1952 issue of *Common Sense,* Union, N. J.: Conde McGinley, editor. By permission.)

As these headlines indicate, some conservative elements in the United States oppose the United Nations and other forms of world government because they fear it may develop into a super-state inimical to the interests of our capitalistic society, and a threat to the sovereignty of our nation. **What basis is there for these fears? Is internationalism a danger to our republic?**

* Ballinger, Willis, "The Seven Legends of Internationalism," *Human Events,* Vol. 10, No. 43, Oct. 28, 1953, Washington, D. C., 1953.

Beauford, L. J. C., "The United Nations—A Benefit," *versus* James J. Flynn, "The United Nations—A Liability," *Catholic World* 178: 246-259, January 1954.

Bricker, Senator John W., "Shall the United Nations Make Our Laws?" *American Mercury* 77: 39-45, October 1953.

Hall, Gordon D., "The Hate Campaign Against the U.N." (Pamphlet), Boston: Beacon, 1952.

O'Leary, Ralph, "The Minute Women: Daughters of Vigilantism," *Nation* 178: 26-28, Jan. 9, 1954.

* Uhl, Alexander, "The Assault on the UN," Washington, D. C.: Public Affairs Institute, 1953 (bibliography).

5.20. UN (cont.): The Fear of Continued International Chaos

On the other side of the argument are those who feel that some form of world government is inevitable. It is only a question whether it is to be (a) a world ruled by Russia, (b) a world ruled by America, or (c) some form of international law and order agreeable to the many nations concerned. Those who believe in alternative (c) would develop the present United Nations into a stronger, more permanent form of world government.

Clark, Grenville, and Sohn, Louis B., *Peace Through Disarmament and Charter Revision,* The Authors, Dublin, New Hampshire, 1954.

Conway, Edward A., S.J., and Weigel, Gustave, S.J., eds., *Pope Pius XII and World Community*, New York: America Press, 1954 (bibliography).

Crichton, Andrew, and others, "World Government Highlights: Facts, Opinions and Personalities," rev. ed., New York: United World Federalists, 1953 (Pamphlet).

Feller, Abraham H., *United Nations and World Community*, Boston: Little, 1952.

Goodfriend, Arthur, *The Only War We Seek* (illustrated), New York: Farrar, 1951.

* Guérard, Albert, *The Education of a Humanist*, Cambridge, Mass.: Harvard University Press, 1949 (Part IV).

Joyce, James Avery, *World in the Making: The Story of International Cooperation*, New York: Schuman, 1953.

Renner, George T., ed., *Global Geography*, New York: Crowell, 1947.

* Roosevelt, Eleanor, and DeWitt, William A., *UN: Today and Tomorrow*, New York: Harper, 1953.

5.21. UN (cont.): Teaching About International Relations

Most educators believe that, since the United States is now a member of the United Nations, it is necessary to explain the reasons for the development of contemporary efforts toward world government. This does not mean that school teachers ignore opposition to the United Nations. But it does mean that schools must teach about the world we live in—which now includes a United Nations.

Arndt, Christian O., and Everett, Samuel, eds., *Education for a World Society*, Eleventh Yearbook, John Dewey Society, New York: Harper, 1951.

* Butterweck, Joseph S., "Education for World-Mindedness," *Nation's Schools* 52: 38-40, August 1953.

Cherrington, Ben M., "International Understanding: The United Nations, Nationalism, and the Schools," *Social Education* 17: 247-250, October 1953.

* Deutsch, Karl W., *Political Community at the International Level: Problems of Definition and Measurement*, Doubleday Short Studies in Political Science, New York: Garden City, 1954 (Pamphlet).

* Everett, Samuel, and others, "Teaching and World Affairs," (Pamphlet), Middle States Council for the Social Studies, 1954 (bibliography). (Procurable from John Niemeyer, Oak Lane Country Day School of Temple University, Oak Lane, Philadelphia, Pa.)

Keohane, R. E., "Education in World Affairs," *School Review* 61: 449-452, November 1953 (Annotated bibliography).

* Kenworthy, Leonard S., "Studying the UN: 7 Points to Stress," *Clearing House* 28: 8-9, September 1953.

Kenworthy, Leonard S., "Primer on World Politics," *Progressive* 18: 10-11, August 1953.

Rankin, E. R., ed., "Building World Peace . . . High School World Peace Study and Speaking Program," (Pamphlet), Chapel Hill, N. C.: University of North Carolina Extension Bulletin, Vol. 38, No. 2, November 1953 (bibliography).

* Robinson, J. William, "The 'Realistic' Approach in Teaching International Relations," *School and Society* 75: 209-211, April 5, 1952.

* Scrivner, Katherine, "We Are Teaching About the United Nations," *National Education Association Journal* 40: 601-603, December 1951.

Simonson, Rebecca C., "UNESCO and Patriotism," *American Teacher* 37: 15-16, January 1953.

5.22. Crucial Issues in Education—A Summary Question

Summarize and classify the major recent criticisms of public education.

*Anderson, Archibald A., Burton, William H., McCloskey, Gordon, and others, "Meeting the Attacks on Education," *Progressive Education* 29: 65-122, January 1952.

Association for Supervision and Curriculum Development, 1953 Yearbook: *Forces Affecting American Education,* Washington, D. C.: National Education Association, 1953.

* Bestor, Arthur E., Jr., *Educational Wastelands,* Urbana, Ill.: University of Illinois Press, 1953. (Reviews and criticisms: *Bulletin of the National Association of Secondary-School Principals* 37: 460-504, April 1953; *Progressive Education* 31: 65-84, January 1954; *Educational Theory* 4: 16-48, January 1954; *School and Society* 79: 39-42, Feb. 6, 1954; and in several other magazines.)

Bigelow, Karl W., and Bestor, Arthur E., Jr., "How Should America's Teachers Be Educated?" *Teachers College Record* 56: 16-24, October 1954.

Brameld, Theodore, "Four Point Agenda for Education," *Nation* 173: 525-526, Dec. 15, 1951.

* Brandt, Joseph A., "This, Too, Happened in Pasadena," *Harper's* 205: 76-79, November 1952.

* Brown, Spencer, "The Hot War Over the Schools," *Commentary* 17: 230-241, March 1954.

Buckley, William F., Jr., *God and Man at Yale,* Chicago: Regnery, 1951. Reviewed by McGeorge Bundy, *Atlantic* 188: 50-52, November 1951; discussion, *ibid.* 188: 80-84, December 1951.

Cary, Sturges F., ed., *New Challenges to Our Schools,* New York: Wilson, 1953.

* Caswell, Hollis D., "The Great Reappraisal of Public Education," *National Education Association Journal* 42: 99-103, February 1953.

Chaffee, Zechariah, Jr., "Freedom of Speech and Press" (Pamphlet), New York: Carrie Chapman Catt Memorial Fund, Inc., 1954.

Cross, Ethan A., "Education in Transition," *Educational Forum* 17: 293-304, March 1953.

* Darling, Edward A., *How We Fought for Our Schools: A Documentary Novel,* New York: Norton, 1954.

Elicker, Paul E., "How Good are Our Schools?" *Collier's* 133: 78-83, June 11, 1954.

* Gray, William S., and Iverson, William W., "What Should Be the Profession's Attitude Toward Lay Criticism with Special Reference to Reading," *Elementary School Journal* 53: 1-44, September 1952; condensed, *Educational Digest* 18: 38-40, November 1952.

Hechinger, Fred, and others, "The Public School Crisis," *Saturday Review* 36: 15-23, Sept. 12, 1953.

Hunt, Herold C., "Major Problems of the Schools," *Educational Record* 35: 12-17, January 1954 (bibliography).

Illson, Murray, "Five Cities on the Spot," *Saturday Review* 36: 16 f., March 7, 1953.

Kennan, Richard B., "Freedom of Thought in American Life," *Social Education* 18: 149-154, April 1954.

Kiplinger Report, "How Good *Are* Our Public Schools?" *Reader's Digest* 65: 34-36, September 1954; condensed from *Changing Times,* June 1954.

Kirk, Grayson, "The New Three R's," *School and Society* 40: 145-150, Nov. 13, 1954.

Melby, Ernest O., and Puner, Morton, eds., *Freedom and Public Education,* New York, Praeger, 1953.

Russell, Bertrand, "The Educators Re-examined," *New York Times Magazine,* p. 9 f., Sept. 7, 1952.

*Scott, C. Winfield, and Hill, Clyde M., eds., *Public Education Under Criticism,* New York: Prentice-Hall, 1954.

Slothower, W. R., and McClelland, James, "Two Essays on the Roots of Progressive Educational Thought," *Progressive Education* 29: 166-170, March 1952.

Smith, Mortimer B., "Who Criticizes Public Schools?" *Christian Century* 68: 736-738, June 20, 1951; Smith, M., *Diminished Mind*, Chicago: Regnery, 1954.

Tonsor, Charles A., "Lay Revolt Against Education Procedures," *National Association of Secondary-School Principals Bulletin* 36: 92-94 (see also 95-100), October 1952.

van Til, William, "Great Debates in American Education," *National Education Association Journal* 42: 42-44, January 1953.

Willett, Henry I., "Public Schools Under Pressure," *Atlantic* 194: 57-62, October 1954.

Woodring, Paul, *Let's Talk Sense About Our Schools,* New York: McGraw-Hill, 1953. (Reviewed with other books by James C. Bay, *Nation* 178: 539-541, June 26, 1954.)

6. CONCLUSION

DEMOCRACY AND EDUCATION

Democracy is an educational process, and the most significant thing is not rule by majority, but the method of attaining "majority" through education, information and free communication. Unlike dictatorial forms of government, democracy has everything to gain and nothing to lose from the intelligence of its citizens. In the words of James Madison:

A popular government without popular information or the means of acquiring it, is but a Prologue to a Farce or a Tragedy, or, perhaps both. Knowledge will forever govern ignorance; and a people who mean to be their own Governors must arm themselves with the power which knowledge gives.[1]

Democracy is basically a method of gaining confidence in ourselves, whereby we move from force to persuasion, from blind obedience to creative effort, from restriction to liberty. Progress depends on independent, self-reliant citizens who are free to talk, to meet, to think, to seek truth, to move about, to be different, to try something new, to make the most of their lives according to their own highest ideals.

In any society progress depends on developed leadership. True leadership must be renewed from the ranks of the unknown, not from the small group of families already famous and powerful.[2] If one class possesses all the wealth and education, while the laboring class remains both poor and ignorant, labor will inevitably be ser-

---

[1] James Madison, Letter to W. T. Barry, Aug. 4, 1822, in *The Complete Madison: His Basic Writings,* edited by Saul K. Padover, New York: Harper, 1953, p. 337.

[2] See Henry Stillwell Edwards, "The Tenth Generation," National Education Association *Journal,* 22: 139-144, May 1933. Reprinted as NEA Personal Growth Leaflet No. 11.

vile to capital, and our society will be divided into distinctive, permanent classes. But if education is widely and equally diffused according to ability rather than according to wealth, the poor may become rich, children of untutored parents may rise into the professions, and society as a whole will gain from the fuller use of its human resources.

Democracy holds that there is no safe depository of the ultimate powers of society except in the people themselves. If the people make mistakes, the remedy is not to take the power away from them, but to help them in forming their judgment through better education and more open communication. In his First Inaugural, Abraham Lincoln expressed democracy's faith in the people as follows:

> Why should there not be a patient confidence in the ultimate justice of the people? Is there any better or equal hope in the world? . . . Truth and justice will surely prevail by the judgment of the great tribunal of the American people.

Democratic education should develop citizens who are "easy to lead, but difficult to drive; easy to govern, but impossible to enslave." [3] It should make them easy to lead by bringing out latent talent and leadership, conceived in cooperative terms. It should make them impossible to enslave because their education will have emphasized individual self-reliance, free expression and unthwarted communication.

The democratic citizen may admit that, in specialized areas, there are authorities wiser than himself who may guide his steps as a parent guides a child. But external guidance cannot long satisfy a mature mind, if it means the loss of his own freedom, autonomy, and moral dignity. External guidance may be a means, but self-direction is an end in itself. The mature man wants self-confidence, courage to face all difficulties, and the consciousness of being man in the fullest sense of the word. Furthermore, says Alf Ross:

> Such a man is possessed by the wish to see the same inner strength develop in others. As he himself abhors alien rule, neither does he wish to rule over others. He is pleased to see

---

[3] Lord Henry Peter Broughton, Speech in House of Commons, January 29, 1828.

life unfolding itself free and strong in his fellow humans. He finds himself happiest in a circle of equals, not surrounded by slaves. In education, his aim is not to exact submissive obedience, but to foster young individuals who in due course will themselves be able to form their own lives with freedom and responsibility.[4]

In a totalitarian society, teachers are expected to transmit a fixed set of values; education is indistinguishable from propaganda; all problems are approached from an "official" or "approved" point of view; all opposing viewpoints are presented as mere straw men easily knocked over. Such "education" develops minds undisciplined in resourcefulness and versatility, minds either soft or inflexible. The few adults who outgrow such "education in immaturity" look back on their schooling as a form of prolonged infancy, and upon their teachers as intellectual baby-sitters hired to keep young minds asleep.

In a democratic society, on the other hand, schools also transmit truths and values; but here they are transmitted in a tentative, experimental manner—as the best that human thinking has arrived at thus far. The democratic teacher has a tremendous respect for traditions, but he views them critically—as subject to modification and improvement. Man is a time-binding animal, and tradition is a splendid banquet which our ancestors have provided for us. But in a society which has respect for the new as well as for the old, for the living as well as for the dead, each generation must learn to pick and choose: each generation must learn which of tradition's foods are still edible, which no longer nourishing. This process can occur when all viewpoints are privileged to defend themselves and thereby fairly win or lose a place in the living world. We cannot avoid this confidence in ourselves or in the generations to come.

In summary, democratic education has two major functions: to impart accumulated knowledge and traditions, and to encourage the discovery of new truth. On the one hand schools should train men to shape the society of their generation on the basis of the accumulated wisdom of the past. On the other hand, schools

---

[4] Alf Ross, *Why Democracy?*, Cambridge, Mass.: Harvard University Press, 1952, p. 104. By permission.
Compare Harry A. Overstreet, *The Mature Mind*, New York: Norton, 1949.

should stimulate creative thinking—thinking which continually renders previous knowledge suspect. This dual function of education was expressed by the founder of Christianity who came "not to destroy but to fulfil the law" and "not to send peace but a sword." [5]

If these two purposes seem contradictory, it is only because the nature of our dynamic society is not understood. In a democracy, liberty depends on liberalism—defined as faith in change by reason and persuasion rather than by force or violence. By placing its primary emphasis on the individual, democracy becomes an open society, in which individuals can challenge any and all traditions and can insist on private experience as the ultimate criterion of truth and value.

"The case for democracy," wrote Carl Becker, "is that it accepts the rational and humane values as ends, and proposes as the means of realizing them the minimum of coercion and the maximum of voluntary assent." [6] In democratic schools, the rational side of human nature should be disciplined to think independently, the humane side to think cooperatively. If education is properly balanced, democratic citizens learn to "think independently together." [7] When reason and humanity are properly balanced, men learn to think for themselves, but they also learn to modify their thinking (or rationalization) in terms of opposing opinions of other men— men for whom they have respect and affection, but who happen to think differently from them.

In a dynamic society, debate and controversy are signs of health, not of sickness. Varied and conflicting ideas and interests are the

---

[5] *Matthew* 5: 17; 10: 34.

[6] Carl Becker, *New Liberties for Old,* New Haven, Conn.: Yale University Press, 1941, p. 151.

[7] Alexander Meiklejohn, "Teachers and Controversial Issues," *Harper's* 177: 15-22, June 1938. Compare: Committee on Freedom of Inquiry, Philosophy of Education Society, A. S. Clayton, chairman, "The Right to Intellectual Freedom," *Phi Delta Kappan* 34: 433 (back inside cover), June 1953; Solomon Lipp, "A 'Categorical Imperative' for Democratic Educators," *Harvard Educational Review* 24: 118-121, Spring 1954.

Nineteenth-century education may have overemphasized the rational. But modern education has tended to overemphasize the humane and social. One extreme is as bad as the other. Read David Reisman, *The Lonely Crowd,* New Haven, Conn.: Yale University Press, 1950 (pages 55-64, "Changes in the Role of the Teacher").

very lifeblood of a free society—provided that citizens are willing to compromise and to pool their many diverse ideas through joint, cooperative thinking. Schools do not fulfill their major function unless scholars become social catalysts, forcing men to reconsider their opinions, and helping them to formulate reconstructed viewpoints appropriate to the new generation. In this manner, education helps to break the "crust of custom" that tends to form over inherited beliefs and prejudices, there is an ever-evolving synthesis of old and new, and progress is both possible and peaceable.

Viewed in this manner, the so-called "crisis" in contemporary education, with its many "crucial issues," is not a cause for alarm, but for rejoicing.

INDEX

This index includes all authors quoted, but not those referred to in footnotes or bibliography.

Page numbers in parentheses refer to bibliographical references in the "Questions and Readings" at the ends of Chapters 1-5.

let schools to Cleaning instead of politicians